A Genealogy of th
American Presidents and Their First
Two Generations of Descent

A Genealogy of the Wives of the American Presidents and Their First Two Generations of Descent

CRAIG HART

McFarland & Company, Inc., Publishers
Jefferson, North Carolina, and London

LIBRARY OF CONGRESS CATALOGUING-IN-PUBLICATION DATA

Hart, Craig.
A genealogy of the wives of the American presidents and their first two generations of descent / Craig Hart.
p. cm.
Includes bibliographical references and index.

ISBN 0-7864-1956-3 (softcover : 50# alkaline paper) ∞

1. Presidents' spouses—United States—Genealogy. I. Title.
E176.2.H37 2004
929'.2'0973—dc22 2004018626

British Library cataloguing data are available

On the cover: Dolley Payne Todd Madison, 1804 (©2004 Pictures Now); background ©2004 PhotoSpin

Manufactured in the United States of America

McFarland & Company, Inc., Publishers
Box 611, Jefferson, North Carolina 28640
www.mcfarlandpub.com

CONTENTS

Preface

In 1789, Martha Washington became our first First Lady. As of 2004, 38 other women have reached this lofty position. It is unfortunate that five wives of future presidents died before their husbands took office. They are Martha Jefferson, wife of Thomas Jefferson; Hannah Van Buren, wife of Martin Van Buren; Rachel Jackson, wife of Andrew Jackson; Ellen Arthur, wife of Chester Arthur; and Alice Roosevelt, first wife of Theodore Roosevelt. For the genealogical purposes of this book they are included, as is Jane Wyman, first wife (divorced in 1949) of Ronald Reagan. Also included are Mary Harrison, second wife of Benjamin Harrison, and Caroline Fillmore, second wife of Millard Fillmore; both these women married presidents whose term had ended.

People have been fascinated with the First Ladies since the beginning. Many were trendsetters; Jacqueline Kennedy was a good example. First Lady Caroline Harrison, wife of President Benjamin Harrison, was the first president of the Daughters of the American Revolution (DAR).

One aspect of the presidents' wives that has been somewhat overlooked is their genealogy. In order to rectify that, I have written this book. I have found that many of the women are related to each other, and often through royal ancestry. Some of their common royal ancestors are King John, who signed the Magna Carta, William the Conqueror, Charlemagne, and Lady Godiva.

How the Book Works

Each chapter begins with the president's wife's grandchildren, designated as G+2. Next are listed her children, designated as G+1. The president's wife herself is listed next, followed by her parents (G-1), grandparents (G-2), and so on, as far back as her lineage can be traced. Note that not all ancestors proved traceable. In some cases only a grandfather or grandfather's name might be noted, for example, without any information on a spouse.

Abbreviations:

b. = birth	m(1) = first marriage
d. = death	m(2) = second marriage
m. = marriage	

Superscript numbers refer to the contributors of the information. A list of contributors can be found in the "Sources: Individuals" section in the back of the book.

An asterisk (*) indicates that I have gone as far as I can go on that particular line.

Abigail Adams

G+2

Children of Abigail and William Stephens Smith:

Caroline **Smith**, b. London, England[1]

John Adams **Smith**, b. London, England; d. 1825[1]

Thomas **Smith**, b. London, England[1]

William Steuben **Smith**, b. April 2, 1787, London, England; d. 1853, Philadelphia, Pa.[1]

Thomas Hollis **Smith**, b. 1790, New York, New York; d. 1790, New York, New York[1]

Caroline Amelia **Smith**, b. 1795, New York, New York; d. 1852[1]

Children of John Quincy and Louisa Catherine (Johnson) Adams:

George Washington **Adams**, b. April 13, 1801, Berlin, Germany; d. June 17, 1829, Long Island, New York[1]

John **Adams**, b. July 4, 1803, Washington, D.C.; d. October 23, 1834, Washington, D.C., m. February 25, 1828, in the White House to Mary Catherine **Heller** 1806–1880[1]

Charles Francis **Adams**, b. August 18, 1807, Boston, Mass.; d. November 21, 1886, Quincy, Mass., m. September 3, 1829, Mystic Grove, Mass., to Abigail Brown **Brooks**, b. April 25, 1808, Medford, Mass.; d. June 6, 1889[1]

Louisa Catherine **Adams**, b. August 12, 1811, St. Petersburg, Russia; d. September 15, 1812, St. Petersburg, Russia[1]

Children of Charles Francis and Sarah (Smith) Adams:

F. **Adams**, b. 1796, New York, New York[1]

Abigail Louise **Adams**, b. 1798, New York, New York; d. 1838[1]

Susanna Boylston **Adams**, b. ca. 1800; d. 1838[1]

Children of Thomas Boylston and Ann (Harod) Adams:

Abigail Smith **Adams**, b. July 27, 1806, Braintree, Mass.; d. July 4, 1845[1]

Frances **Adams**, b. 1811, Braintree, Mass.; d. 1812, Braintree, Mass.[1]

John Quincy **Adams**, b. 1811, Braintree, Mass.[1]

Isaac **Adams**, b. 1813, Braintree, Mass.; d. 1900, Braintree, Mass.[1]

Joseph Harod **Adams**, b. 1817, Braintree, Mass.; d. 1853, Braintree, Mass.[1]

Ann **Adams**, b. Braintree, Mass.; d. Braintree, Mass.[1]

G+1

Abigail **Adams**, b. July 14, 1765, Quincy, Mass.; d. August 14, 1813, Lebanon, New York, m(1) William Stephens **Smith**, b. November 3, 1755, Long Island, New York; d. June 10, 1816, Lebanon, New York, m(2) Henry Williams **Smith**, b. 1761, Braintree, Mass.[1]

John Quincy **Adams**, b. July 11, 1767, Boston, Mass.; d. February 21, 1848, Washington, D.C., m. July 26, 1797, in London, England, to Louisa Catherine **Johnson**[1]

Susanna **Adams**, b. December 28, 1768, Boston, Mass.; d. July 4, 1770, Boston, Mass.[1]

Charles Francis **Adams**, b. May 29, 1770, Braintree, Mass.; d. November 30, 1800, New York, New York, m. Sarah **Smith**[1]

Thomas Boylston **Adams**, b. September 15, 1772, Braintree, Mass.; d. March 12, 1832 Quincy, Mass., m. May 16, 1805, to Ann **Harod**, b. 1774, Haverhill, Mass.; d. September 3, 1846, Braintree, Mass.[1]

Abigail Smith, b. November 11, 1744, Weymouth, Mass.; d. October 28, 1818, Quincy, Mass., m. October 25, 1764, to John Adams, b. October 19, 1735, Quincy, Mass.; d. July 4, 1826, Quincy, Mass.[2, 13]

G-1

William **Smith**, b. January 29, 1706/1707, Charlestown, Mass.; d. September 17, 1783, Weymouth, Mass., m. Elizabeth **Quincy**, b. 1722, Braintree, Mass.; d. 1775, Weymouth, Mass.[2]

G-2

William **Smith**, b. March 29, 1667, Charlestown, Mass., m.

Abigail **Fowle**, b. August 7, 1682, Charlestown, Mass.; d. January 3, 1731, Charlestown, Mass.[2]

John **Quincy**, b. July 21, 1689, Boston, Mass.; d. 1767, Boston, Mass., m. September 3, 1715, to Elizabeth **Norton**, b. March 15, 1695, Hingham, Mass.; d. Boston, Mass.[2]

G-3

Thomas **Smith**, b. May 10, 1645, Dartmouth, England; d. February 14, 1690, Watertown, Mass., m. Sarah **Boylston**, b. September 30, 1642, Watertown, Mass.; d. August 18, 1711, Charlestown, Mass.[2]

Isaac **Fowle**, b. 1648, Charlestown, Mass.; d. October 13, 1718, Woburn, Mass., m. Beriah **Bright**, b. September 22, 1651, Watertown, Mass.; d. October 13, 1716, Woburn, Mass.[2]

Daniel **Quincy**, b. February 7, 1651, Braintree, Mass.; d. August 10, 1690, Boston, Mass., m. November 8, 1682, to Anna **Shepard**, b. September 13, 1663, Charlestown, Mass.; d. July 24, 1708, Braintree, Mass.[2]

John **Norton**, b. 1665, Hingham, Mass., m. Mary **Mason**, b. 1665, Watertown, Mass.[2]

G-4

Sir Thomas **Smith**, m. Johanna **Altham**[2]

Thomas **Boylston**, b. 1615, m. Sarah* (Last Name Unknown)

George **Fowle**, b. 1610; d. September 19, 1682, m. Mary **Tufts**[2, 3]

Henry **Bright**, b. 1602; d. October 9, 1686, m. Ann **Goldstone**, b. May 16, 1615, D. Woburn, Mass.[2]

Edmund **Quincy**, b. 1627; d. January 7, 1698, m. July 26, 1648, Joanna **Hoare**, June 28, 1624; d. May 16, 1680[2]

Rev. Thomas **Shepard**, b. April 5, 1635; d. December 22, 1677, m. November 3, 1656, Anna **Tyng**, b. January 6, 1638; d. August 5, 1709[2]

William **Norton**, b. 1610, Ipswich, England; d. April 3, 1694, m. Lucy **Downing**, b. 1633, Ipswich, England; d. February 5, 1698[2]

Arthur **Mason**,* b. 1635, m. Joanna **Parker**, b. 1635[2]

G-5

Sir William **Smith**, b. Bucks, England; d. December 12, 1626, England, m. Bridget **Fleetwood**,* b. England; d. England[2]

Edward **Altham**,* b. England; d. England[2]

Thomas **Boylston**, b. 1587, London, England; d. 1648, England[2]

Myles **Fowle**,* b. 1575, England, m. Iden **Thorlton**,*b. 1582, England; d. April 23, 1611, England[2]

Peter **Tufts**,* b. England; d. England, m. Frances (Last Name Unknown)*[3]

Henry **Bright**, b. 1560, Edmunds, England; d. 1609, England, m. Marie **Woodgate**,* b. 1572, Edmunds, England[2]

Henry **Goldstone**, b. July 17, 1591, Wickham, England; d. July 25, 1638, Beddingfield, England, m. Anne (Last Name Unknown),* b. 1591, England; d. April 26, 1670, Watertown, Mass.[2]

Edmund **Quincy**, b. 1602, Achurch, England; d. July 17, 1673, Quincy, Mass., m. Judith **Pares**,* b. 1606, Bythome, England; d. November 29, 1654, Quincy, Mass.[2, 4]

Charles **Hoare**, b. 1586, Gloucester, England; d. September 25, 1638, England, m. Joanna **Hinkeman**, b. 1590, Gloucester, England; d. December 20, 1661, Braintree, Mass.[2]

Thomas **Shepard**, b. November 3, 1605, Towcester, England; d. August 25, 1649, Cambridge, Mass., m. 1632, Margaret **Touteville**,* b. 1609, Towcester, England; d. February 1, 1636, Cambridge, Mass.[2]

William **Tyng**,* b. 1605, England; d. January 18, 1652 or 1653, Braintree, Mass., m. Elizabeth **Coytmore**, b. ca. 1590, Wapping, England; d. 1626, Wapping, England[2, 4]

William **Norton**, b. 1573, Sharpenhoe, England, m. Alice **Bownset**, b. England[2]

Emanuel **Downing**, b. 1585, Ipswich, England; d. 1656, Salem, Mass., m. April 10, 1622, Lucy **Winthrop**, b. January 9, 1600 or 1601, London, England[2]

Nicholas **Parker**,* b. England; d. England, m. Anne (Last Name Unknown),* b. England; d. England[2]

G-6

George **Smith**,* b. England; d. England[2]

Henry **Boylston**,* b. 1561, Litchfield, England[2]

Thomas **Bright**,* b. 1529, Edmunds, England; d. September 1, 1587, England, m. July 27, 1554, Margaret **Payton**,* b. 1533, Edmund, England; d. 1600, England[2]

William **Goldstone**, b. 1560, Bedingfield, England; d. February 28, 1609, England, m. Margaret (Last Name Unknown),* b. 1560, Bedingfield, England; d. 1620, England[2]

Edmund **Quincy**, b. 1559, Achurch, England; d. 1628, England, m. Ann **Palmer**,* b. 1572, England; d. ca. 1630, Wisthorpe, England[5]

Charles **Hoare**, b. 1554, Gloucester, England; d. May 29, 1632,

Gloucester, England, m. Margery (Last Name Unknown),* b. England; d. England[2, 5]

Thomas **Hinkeman**, b. 1563, Wellingsborough, England; d. England, m. Anne **Griffith**,* b. 1568, Wales[5]

William **Shepard**, b. 1570, Somersetshire, England; d. 1615, Banbury, England, m. Miss **Bland**,* b. England; d. England[5]

Rowland **Coytmore**, b. Wapping, England; d. 1626, Wapping, England, m. Katherine **Miles**[2]

William **Norton**, b. England; d. England, m. Margarey **Hawes**, b. England; d. England[2]

John **Bownset**,* b. England; d. England, m. Mercy (Last Name Unknown),* b. England; d. England[2]

George **Downing**, b. 1560, Ipswich, England; d. October 3, 1610, England[2]

Adam **Winthrop**, b. August 10, 1548, London, England; d. March 28, 1623, England, m. February 20, 1579/1580, Anne **Browne**,* b. England; d. England[2]

G-7

Walter **Bright**, b. 1495, Edmunds, England; d. January 25, 1551, Edmunds, England[2]

Roman **Goldstone**,* b. 1524, Bedingfield, England; d. November 22, 1575, England[2]

John **Quincy**,* b. 1535, Northampton, England; d. 1587, Northampton, England[2]

Thomas **Hoare**, b. 1534, Leckhampton, England; d. July 31, 1590, Gloucester, England, m. 1558, Margaret (Last Name Unknown),* b. 1537, Gloucester, England[2]

Thomas **Hinkeman**, b. 1532, Wellingsborough, England; d. England, m. Mary **Freeman**,* b. 1541, England[5]

John **Shepard**,* b. 1544, Northamptonshire, England; d. England[5]

William **Coytmore**, b. England; d. England, m. Jane **Williams**, b. Wales[2, 4]

Robert **Miles** or **Myles**, b. 1554, Sutton, England; d. 1646, Sutton, England[5]

Richard **Norton**, b. 1505, Sharpenhoe, England; d. 1571, England, m. Margery **Wingar** or **Wingate**, b. England; d. England[2]

William **Hawes**,* b. England; d. England[2]

George **Downing**, b. Ipswich, England; d. June 26, 1564, England[2]

Adam **Winthrop**, b. October 9, 1498, Lavenhem, England; d.

November 9, 1562, Graton, England, m. 1534, Agnes **Sharpe**, b. August 10, 1513, London, England; d. May 13, 1565, England[2]

G-8

John **Bright**,* b. 1469, Suffolk, England; d. 1545, England, m. Joane **Raleigh**, b. England; d. England[2, 5]

Richard **Hoare**,* b. 1514, England; d. 1541, England, m. Ellen (Last Name Unknown),* b. England; d. England[2]

Richard **Hinkeman**,* b. England; d. England, m. Alice **Pinden**,* b. England; d. England[5]

William **Coytmore**,* b. England; d. England, m. Ellen **Puleston**,* b. England; d. England[4]

William **Williams**,* b. 1506, Wales, m. Dorothy **Griffith**, b. Wales[2]

Jeffrey **Miles** or **Myles**,* b. 1520, Sutton, England; d. 1557, Sutton, England, m. Alice (Last Name Unknown),* b. England; d. England[5]

John **Norton**,* b. England; d. England, m. Joan **Cowper***[2]

Robert **Wingar** or **Wingate**,* b. England; d. England, m. Joane **Porter**,* b. England; d. England[2]

Jeffrey **Downing**,* b. Essex, England; d. England, m. Elizabeth **Wingfield**, b. England; d. England[2]

Adam **Winthrop**,* b. 1466, England; d. Lavenhem, England, m. Jane **Burton**,* b. 1470, England; d. England[2]

Robert **Sharpe**,* b. England; d. England, m. Elizabeth (Last Name Unknown),* b. England; d. England[2]

G-9

Walter **Raleigh**, b. England; d. England, m. Joan **Drake**, b. England; d. England[2]

Sir William **Griffith**, b. Wales, m. Jane **Stradling**, b. England; d. England[2, 4]

Sir Thomas **Wingfield**, b. England; d. England, m. Elizabeth **Woodhouse**, b. England[2]

G-10

Winmond **Raleigh**,* b. England; d. England, m. Miss **Grenville**, b. England; d. England[2]

John **Drake**, b. England; d. England, m. Agnes **Kailway**,* b. England; d. England[2]

Sir William **Griffith**, b. Wales, m. Joan **Troutbeck**, b. Wales[2]

Thomas **Stradling**, b. 1454, England; d. September 8, 1480, England, m. Jane **Mathew**, b. England; d. England[2]

Sir John **Wingfield**, b. England; d. England, m. Margaret **Dorward**,* b. England; d. England[2]

Sir Thomas **Woodhouse**,* b. England; d. England[2]

G-11

Sir Thomas **Grenville**,* b. England; d. England[2]

John **Drake**,* b. England; d. England[2]

Sir William **Troutbeck**,* b. England; d. England, m. Lady Margaret **Stanley**, b. England D. England[2]

Sir Henry **Stradling**, b. 1423, England; d. 1477, Famagusta, Cyprus, m. Elizabeth **Herbert**,* b. England; d. England[2, 4]

Thomas **Mathew**, b. England; d. England, m. Catrin verch Morgan,* b. Wales[2, 4]

Sir John **Wingfield**, b. England; d. England, m. Elizabeth **Fitz Lewis**, b. England; d. England[2]

G-12

Thomas **Stanley**, b. ca. 1406, Lathom, England; d. 1459, Knowsley, England, m. Joan **Goushill**, b. England; d. England[2, 6]

Sir Edward **Stradling**, b. 1389, England; d. 1453, England, m. Joan **Beaufort**, b. 1402, Westminster, England; d. England[2, 4]

Dafydd **Mathew**,* b. Wales, m. Gwenllian verch Dafydd*[4]

Sir Robert **Wingfield**,* b. England; d. England, m. Elizabeth **Goushill**, b. England; d. England[2]

Sir John **Fitz Lewis**,* b. England; d. England, m. Ann **Montacute**, b. England; d. England[2]

G-13

John **Stanley**, b. Lathom, England; d. November 27, 1437, Anslesey, Wales, m. Isabel **Harrington**,* b. England; d. England[6]

Sir Robert **Goushill**,* b. England; d. England, m. Lady Elizabeth **Fitz Alan**, b. England; d. England[7]

William **Stradling**,* b. England; d. England, m. Isabel **St. Barbe**[*2]

Henry **Beaufort**, b. 1357, England; d. 1447, England, m. Lady Alice **Fitz Alan**, b. England; d. England[2, 4, 7]

Sir John **Goushill**,* b. England; d. England, m. Eleanor **Fitz Alan**, b. England; d. England[2, 7]

John **Montacute**, Earl of Salisbury, b. England; d. England, m. Maud **Francis**,* b. England; d. England[2]

G-14

Sir John **Stanley**, b. England; d. England, m. Isabel **Lathom**, b. 1364, Knowsley, England; d. October 26, 1414, England[6]

Richard **Fitz Alan**, b. 1346, Arundel, England; d. September 21, 1397, London, England, m. Elizabeth **De Bohun**, b. England; d. England[2, 7]

John of Gaunt (**Beaufort**), b. 1340, Flandre, Belgium; d. February 3, 1398 or 1399, England, m. Katherine **Roet**, b. 1350, Hainault, Belgium; d. May 10, 1403, Lincoln, England[2, 4, 7]

Richard **Fitz Alan**,* m. Elizabeth **De Bohun*** (Refer to Richard **Fitz Alan** earlier in G-14 to continue their lines.)[2, 7]

Sir John **Fitz Alan**, b. England; d. England, m. Eleanor **Maltovers**, b. England; d. England[2, 7]

Sir John **Montacute**, b. England; d. England, m. Margaret **Montherimer**, b. England; d. England[2]

G-15

William **Stanley**,* b. England; d. England, m. Alice **Massey**, b. England; d. England[6]

Sir Thomas **Lathom**, b. England; d. England, m. Isabella **Pilkington**, b. England; d. England[2]

Sir Richard "Copped Hat" **Fitz Alan**, b. 1306, Arundel, England; d. January 24, 1376, England, m. Lady Eleanor **Plantagenet**, b. 1316, Grismond Castle, England; d. January 11, 1372, England[2, 7]

William **De Bohun**, b. England; d. England, m. Elizabeth **Badlesmere**, b. England; d. England[2, 7]

King Edward III, b. November 13, 1312; d. June 21, 1377, England, m. Philippa **De Hainault**, b. 1312, Hainault, Belgium; d. August 15, 1369, Windsor, England[2, 4]

Sir Paen **Roet**,* b. England; d. England, m. Catherine **Swynford**,* b. England; d. England[2]

Sir Richard "Copped Hat" **Fitz Alan**,* m. Lady Eleanor **Plantagenet*** (Refer to Sir Richard "Copped Hat" **Fitz Alan** earlier in G-15 to continue their lines.)[2, 7]

William **De Bohun**,* m. Elizabeth **Badlesmere*** (Refer to William **De Bohun** earlier in G-15 to continue their lines.)[2, 7]

Sir Richard "Copped Hat" **Fitz Alan**,* m. Lady Eleanor **Planta-**

genet* (Refer to Sir Richard "Copped Hat" **Fitz Alan** earlier in G-15 to continue their lines.[2, 7])

Sir John **Maltovers,*** b. England; d. England[2, 7]

Sir William **Montacute,*** b. England; d. England[2]

Thomas **Montherimer**, b. England; d. England[2]

G-16

Hamon **Massey,*** b. England; d. England, m. Mathilda **Timperley,*** b. England; d. England[6]

Thomas **Lathom,*** b. England; d. England, m. Eleanor **Ferrers,*** b. England; d. England[6]

Edmund **Fitz Alan**, b. May 1, 1285, England; d. November 17, 1326, England, m. Alice **De Warren**, b. 1286, England; d. 1338, England[2,7]

Henry **Plantagenet**, b. 1281, England; d. England, m. Maud **De Chaworth**, b. 1282, England; d. England[2, 7]

Humphrey **De Bohun**, b. England; d. England, m. Elizabeth **Plantagenet**, b. England; d. England[2, 7, 8]

Bartholomew **Badlesmere**, b. England; d. England, m. Margaret **De Clare**, b. England; d. England[2, 7, 8]

King Edward II, b. April 25, 1284, England; d. January 25, 1308, England, m. Isabelle of France, b. 1295, France; d. 1327, England[2, 4]

William III, Count **De Hainault**, b. 1280, Hainault, Belgium; d. June 7, 1337, Hainault, Belgium, m. Jeanne, Countess **De Hainault**, b. Naples, Italy; d. October 31, 1290, Hainault, Belgium[2, 4]

Sir Ralph **Montherimer**, b. England; d. England, m. Joan of Acres (**Plantagenet**), b. England; d. England[2]

G-17

Richard **Fitz Alan**, b. February 3, 1267, Essex, England; d. March 9, 1302, England, m. Alisona, Countess **De Saluzza**, b. 1271, Essex, England; d. September 25, 1292, England[2, 7]

William **De Warren,*** b. 1260, England; d. England, m. Joan **De Ware,*** b. England; d. England[2]

Edmund, Prince of England, b. January 16, 1244, England; d. England, m. Blanche, Queen of Navarre, b. 1248, Arras, France; d. May 2, 1302, Paris, France[2, 7]

Patrick **De Chaworth**, b. 1250, Stokes, England; d. England, m. Isabel **De Beauchamp**, b. England; d. May 30, 1306, England[2, 7]

Humphrey **De Bohun**, b. England; d. England, m. Maud **Fiennes**, b. England; d. England[7, 8]

Bartholomew **Badlesmere**, b. England; d. England[2]

King Edward I, b. 1239, England; d. 1272, England, m. Eleanor **De Castille**, b. 1244, Castille, Spain; d. November 29, 1290, England[2]

John II **De Holland**,* b. Holland; d. Holland, m. Philippa **De Luxembourg**, b. Luxembourg[2]

Charles **De Valois**, b. Valois, France; d. France, m. Marguerite De Sicily, b. Naples, Sicily; d. France[2]

Thomas **De Clare**, b. England; d. England, m. Julian A. **Fitz Mauris**,* b. England; d. England[9]

King Edward I,* m. Eleanor **De Castille*** (Refer to King Edward I earlier in G-17 to continue their lines.)[2]

G-18

John **Fitz Alan**, b. September 14, 1246, Essex, England, m. Isabella **De Mortimer**, b. 1259, Wigmore, England; d. England[7, 9]

Thomas **De Saluzza**,* m. Leugia **De Eva***[2]

King Henry III, b. October 1, 1207, Winchester Castle, England; d. November 11, 1272, Winchester, England, m. Eleanor, De Provence, b. 1217, Provence, France; d. June 24, 1291, London, England[2, 7]

Robert I, Count **De Artois**, b. France; d. France, m. Duchess Mathilda **De Artois**, b. France; d. France[2, 7]

Patrick **De Chaworth**, b. 1250, Stokes, England; d. England, m. Hawise **De Londree**

Gunncelin **Badlesmere**,* b. England; d. England[2]

William **De Beauchamp**, m. Maud **Fitz John**[2, 7]

Humphrey **De Bohun**, b. England; d. England, m. Eleanor **De Broose**, b. England; d. England[7, 8]

William **De Beauchamp**,* b. 1215, Elmley Castle, England; d. January 7, 1268, m. Isabel **De Mauduit**,* b. England; d. England[2]

Ferdinand Alphonsez III, b. 1198, Castille, Spain; d. May 30, 1252, Spain, m. 1237, Joana, Countess **De Ponth** [2]

King Henry III,* b. 1207, England; d. 1272, England, m. Eleanor, Queen of England* (Refer to King Henry III earlier in G-18 to continue their lines.)[2, 7]

John I **De Hainault**,* b. Hainault, Belgium, m. Adelaide De Holland[2]

Henri III, Count of Luxembourg,* m. Marguerite of Bar Mousson*[2]

Philippe III, King of France,* b. France; d. France, m. Isabella **De Aragon***[2]

Charles II, Prince of Slerne,* m. Marie of Hungary*[2]

Richard **De Clare**, b. England; d. England, m. Maud **De Lacy**, b. England; d. England[9]

G-19

John **Fitz Alan**, b. 1223, Essex, England; d. 1267, England, m. Mathilda **De Verdon**,* b. England; d. England[7, 8]

Roger **De Mortimer**, b. 1231, Wales; d. October 27, 1282, Essex, England, m. Maude **De Broose**, b. England; d. England[10]

King John, b. 1166, England; d. 1216, England, m. Isabella, Queen of England, b. 1180, Angouleme, France; d. May 31, 1246, Fontervault, France[2,7]

Raimond IV **De Provence**, b. 1196, Provence, France; d. August 19, 1245, France, m. Beatrix, Countess **De Provence**, b. 1198, Savoy, France; d. France[2, 7]

King Louis VIII, "Le Lion," b. France. D. France, m. Blanca Alphonsa **De Castille**, b Castille, Spain[2, 7]

Henri II,* b. France; d. France, m. Maria **Von Schwaben**, b. 1201, Germany[2]

Payne II **De Chaworth**, b. 1183, Kemsford, England; d. 1237, England, m. Gunrede **De La Forte** [2]

Thomas **De Londree**,* b. England; d. England, m. Eva **De Tracy**,* b. England; d. England[2]

William **De Beauchamp**,* b. England; d. England, m. Joan **De Mortimer**,* b. England; d. England[2]

John **Fitz Geoffrey**,* b. England; d. England, m. Isabelle **Bigod**, b. England; d. England[2, 12]

Humphrey **De Bohun**, b. 1208, Hungerford, England; d. September 14, 1275, England, m. Mary **De Lusignan**[8]

William **De Broose**, b. England; d. England, m. Eva **Marshall**, b. England; d. England[6]

Alphonso Ferdinandez, King of Castille and Leon,* b. 1168, Zamora, Spain; d. September 24, 1230, Castille, Spain, m. 1197, Berengaria Alphonsa **De Castille***

Simon **De Martin**,* b. 1180; d. 1239, m. 1208, Maria, Countess **De Ponthieu**,* b. 1196, Ponthieu, France[2]

Florence IV*[2]

Gilbert **De Clare**, b. 1182, England; d. October 25, 1230, England, m. Isabel **Marshall**, b. October 9, 1200, England; d. September 17, 1240, England[9]

John **De Lacy**, b. England; d. England, m. Margaret **De Quincy**, b. England; d. England[9]

G-20

John **Fitz Alan,*** b. 1164, Essex, England; d. 1240, England, m. Isabelle **De Albini,*** b. 1165, Essex, England; d. England[7, 8]

Ralph **De Mortimer**, b. England; d. England, m. Gwladys verch Llewelyn,* b. Wales[10]

William **De Broose,*** m. Eve **Marshall*** (Refer to William **De Broose** in G-19 to continue their lines.)[7, 8]

King Henry II, b. 1133, England; d. 1189, England, m. Eleanor **De Aquitaine**, b. 1122, Aquitaine, France; d. 1204, France[2, 4]

Aymer **Taillefer,*** b. 1174; d. 1218, m. 1193, Alice **De Courtenay,*** b. Courtenay, France; d. 1218[2, 4]

Alphonso II, Count **De Provence,*** 1174, Barcelona, Spain; d. 1209, Perpinan, France, m. 1193, Gersinde **De Sabran,*** b. 1175, Sabran, Spain; d. France[2, 4]

Thomas 1, Count **De Savoy**, b. March 20, 1177, Carbonnierres, France; d. January 20, 1233, Savoy, France, m. Marguerita **De Faucigny**, b. Faucigny, France[2, 4]

Philippe Augusta II,* m. Isabella **De Hainault,*** b. Hainault, Belgium[2, 4]

Alphonso Sanchez VIII,* b. November 11, 1155, Spain; d. October 6, 1214, Palencia, Spain, m. September 21, 1177, Eleanor, Princess of England, b. October 13, 1152, Falais, France; d. October 31, 1214, Burgas, Spain[2, 4]

Philip **Von Schwaben,*** b. Germany; d. Irene **Angelos***[2, 4]

Patrick **De Chaworth,*** b. England; d. England[2]

William **De La Forte,*** m. Margaret **De Briwere***[2]

Hugh **Bigod**, b. England; d. England, m. Maud **Marshall***[12]

Henry **De Bohun**, b. England; d. England, m. Maud **Fitz Geoffrey***[6, 7, 8]

Raoul **De Lusignan,*** m. Alice **De Eu***[8]

Reginald **De Broose**, b. 1182, Bramber, England; d. 1228, Breconshire, Wales, m. Grace **De Briwere,*** b. 1186, England[2, 6, 8]

William **Marshall**, b. 1170, Pembroke, Wales; d. May 14, 1219, London, England, m. 1189, Isabel **De Clare**, b. 1171; d. 1220[2, 8, 9]

Richard **De Clare,*** b. England; d. England, m. Amicia **De Bellomes***[9]

William **Marshall,*** m. Isabel **De Clare*** (Refer to William **Marshall** earlier in G-20 to continue their lines.)[2, 8, 9]

Roger **De Lacey,*** b. England; d. England, m. Maude **De Clare,*** b. England; d. England[9]

Robert **De Quincy,*** b. England; d. England, m. Hawise **De Meschines,*** b. England; d. England[9]

G-21

Roger **De Mortimer,*** b. 1156, Herefordshire, England; d. June 24, 1214, Herefordshire, England, m. Isabel **De Ferriers**, b. 1172, England; d. England[9]

Geoffrey **Plantagenet**, b. August 24, 1113 Anjou, France; d. September 7, 1151, Chateau Eure, France, m. 1127, Mathilda, Princess of England, b. England; d. England[2]

William X, Count **De Poitou**, b.1099, Poitou, France; d. April 9, 1137, France, m. Eleanor **De Chatellerault**, b. 1100, Chatellerault, France; d. 1130, France[2]

Humbert III, Count **De Savoy,*** b. August 1, 1136, Savoy, France; d. France, m. Beatrix **De Vienne***[2]

William I, Lord **De Faucigny,*** b. 1130, Geneva, Switzerland; d. July 25, 1195, m. 1165, Beatrix **De Raucigny***[2]

King Henry II,* m. Eleanor, Countess **De Aquitaine*** (Refer to King Henry II in G-20 to continue their lines.)[2]

Roger **Bigod,*** b. England; d. England, m. Isabelle **Plantagenet**[12]

Humphrey **De Bohun**, b. 1142, Gloucestershire, England; d. 1182, England, m. Margaret of Huntingdon, b. 1154, England; d. England[7, 8]

William **De Brosse**, b. 1153 Bramber, England; d. August 9, 1211, Corbeil, France, m. Mathilda **De St. Valery,*** b. 1155[2]

John **Marshall**, b. 1126, Pembroke, Wales; d. 1164, Wales, m. Sybille **De Salisbury,*** b. Salisbury, England[2]

Richard **De Clare**, b. 1130, Tunbridge, England; d. April 9, 1176, England, m. Eva **MacMurrough**, b. Leinster, Ireland; d. 1177[2]

G-22

William **De Ferriers**, b. 1136, Derbyshire, England; d. 1190, England, m. Sybil **De Broose**, b. 1145, Bramber, England; d. England[6, 10]

Foulges V, King of Jerusalem , 1092 Anjou, France. D. November 12, 1142, Eremurge, Countess **Du Maines**[2]

King Henry I, m. Mathilda, Princess of Scotland, b. 1082, Dunferline, Scotland; d. May 1, 1118, England[2, 4]

William (Guillaume) IX,* b. 1061, Aquitaine, France; d. February 19, 1126, France, m. Mahaut **de Toulouse,*** b. 1073, Toulouse, France[2, 4]

Aimeri I,* b. 1075, Chatellerault, France; d. 1130, France, m. Dangereuse*[2]

Hamline **Plantagenet,*** b. 1130, Normandy, France; d. May 7, 1202, Lowes, England, m. Isabelle **De Warren**, b. 1137, Surrey, England; d. July 13, 1159, Lewes, England[12]

Humphrey **De Bohun**, b. England; d. England, m. Margaret **De Petries**, b. England; d. England[6, 7, 8]

Henry, Prince of England, b. England; d. England, m. Ada **De Warren**[6, 7, 8]

William **De Broose,*** b. England; d. England, m. Bertha **De Petries**[6]

Gilbert **Marshall*** b. Wales[2, 6, 8]

Walter **De Salisbury,*** b. 1075, Salisbury, England; d. 1147, England, m. Sybil **De Chaworth,*** b. England; d. England[2, 8, 9]

Gilbert **De Clare**, b. 1086, England; d. England, m. Elizabeth **De Beaumont**, b. England; d. England[2, 6, 8]

Dermont **MacMurrough,*** b. 1110, Leinster, Ireland; d. May 1, 1171, Ireland, m. Cacht **Mor,*** b. 1114, Ireland; d. 1191, Ireland[2, 6, 8]

G-23

William **De Ferriers,*** b. 1118, Derbyshire, England; d. England, m. Margaret **Peverill**, b. England; d. England[6, 10]

William **De Broose,*** m. Bertha **De Petries*** (Refer to William **De Broose** later in G-23 to continue their lines.)[2, 6, 8]

Foulges IV, b. 1033, Anjou, France; d. April 14, 1109, France, m. Bertrade **De Montfort**, b. France; d. February 11, 1118, Fontervault, Belgium[2]

Helias, Count **Du Maines**, m. Mathilda **De Chateau-Des***[2]

William The Conqueror, b. October 14, 1024, Falaise, France; d. September 9, 1087, Hermenbraville, France, m. Mathilda **De Flandre**, b. Flandre, Belgium; d. November 2, 1083, Cain, France[2]

Malcolm III, b. 1030, Scotland; d. November 13, 1093, Northumberland, England, m. Margaret, Queen of Scotland, b. 1046, England; d. November 16, 1093, Scotland[2]

William **De Warren,*** m. Adela **De Telvas***[12]

Humphrey **De Bohun,*** b. England; d. England, m. Maud **Devereaux***[6, 7, 8]

Miles **De Petries**, b. Gloucestershire, England; d. Loucestershire, England, m. Sybil **De Neufmarche**, b. 1096, Wales; d. England[7, 8]

David I "The Saint," b. 1080, Scotland; d. May 24, 1153, Carlisle, England, m. Mathilda **Huntingdon**[7, 8]

William **De Warren**, b. 1065, Sussex, Eng,; d. May 11, 1138, England, m. Isabel **De Vermandois**[7, 8]

Philip **De Broose,*** m. Alnorde **De Totnois***[6, 7, 8]

Miles **De Petries**, m. Sybil **De Neufmarche** (Refer to Miles **De Neufmarche** earlier in G-23 to continue their lines.)[7, 8]

Richard **De Clare,*** b. 1035, England; d. 1909, England, m. Rohese **Giffard***[9]

Robert **De Beaumont**, m. Isabel **De Vermandois***[6, 8]

G-24

Geoffrey, Count **De Ferreol,*** b. 1004; d. April 1, 1046, m. Hermengarde **De Anjou**[2]

Simon I,* m. Agnes **De Evereaux***[2]

Jean I **De Beaugenci,*** m. Paula **Du Maines***[2]

Robert, Duke of Normandy, b. 995, Normandy, France; d. July 2, 1035, France, m. Narlette of Falaise*[2]

Baldwin V, Count **De Flandre**, b. Flandre, Belgium, m. Adela, Princess of France[2]

Duncan I "The Gracious," King of Scotland, b. 1001, Scotland; d. November 13, 1093, Northumberland, England, m. Sibylla of Northumberland, b. Northumberland, England; d. England[2]

Edward "The Exile," b. 1016, Wessex, England; d. 1057, London, England, m. 1044, Agatha **Von Braunschweig**, b. 1025, Braunschweig, Germany; d. London, England[2]

Walter **De Petries,*** b. England; d. England, m. Emma **De Ballons***[7, 8]

Bernard **De Neufmarche,*** b. 1075, Herefordshire, England; d. 1125, England, m. Nesta **Fitz Richard**, b. 1079, Herefordshire, England; d. England[7, 8]

Malcolm III, King of Scotland, b. Scotland; d. November 13, 1030, Northumberland, England, m. Margaret **Atherling**, b. 1046, England; d. November 16, 1093, Scotland[7, 8]

William **De Warren,*** b. England; d. England, m. Gundred, Princess of England[7, 8]

Hugh "The Great," b. 1057, France; d. October 18, 1101, France, m. Isabelle **De Vermandois**[8, 12, 15]

Roger **De Beaumont,*** b. Normandy, France; d. Normandy, France, m. Adeline **De Meulan**, b. Normandy, France; d. Normandy, France[8, 9, 12]

G-25

Geoffrey I **De Anjou**, b. November 11, 958, Anjou, France; d. July 27, 987, France, m. Adelaide **De Troyes**, b. France; d. France[2]

Richard II, Duke of Normandy, b. 958, Normandy, France; d. August 28, 1027, Fecamp, France, m. Judith **De Bretagne**, b. Bretagne, France; d. 1017, France[2, 9]

Baldwin IV, Count **De Flandre**, m. Oglive **Von Luxembourg***[2, 9]

Thane, King of the Isles* b. 978, Dunkeld, Scotland; d. 1045, Scotland, m. Bethoc Princess of Scotland, b. Scotland; d. Scotland[2]

Siward **Digera** "The Strong," m. Aelfflaed of Northumberland, b. England; d. England[2]

Edmund II "Ironside," b. 989, Wessex, England; d. November 30, 1016, Oxford, England, m. Eldgyth, Queen of England, b. England; d. England[2]

Ludolph **Von Braunschweig**, b. 1008, Braunschweig, Germany; d. April 23, 1038, Germany, m. Gertrude **Von Egisheim**,* b. Germany; d. Germany[2]

Osbern **Fitz Richard**, b. 1055, England; d. England, m. Nesta verch Gruffydd, b. 1059, Wales[7, 8]

Duncan I "The Gracious," King of Scotland, m. Sibylla of Northumberland (Refer to Duncan I G-24 to continue their lineages.)[2]

Edward "The Exile,"* m. Agatha **Von Braunschweig*** (Refer to Edward "The Exile" G-24 to continue their lines.)[2]

William The Conqueror,* m. Mathilda **De Flandre*** (Refer to William The Conqueror G-23 to continue their lines.)[2]

King Henry I of France, b. Paris, France; d. August 4, 1060, Paris, France, m. Anne of Russia, b. Russia; d. France[8, 12]

Waleran **De Meulan**,* m. Oda **De Conteville**, b. France; d. France[8,9, 12]

G-26

Foulgues II, b. 910, France; d. November 11, 958, France, m. Gerberge **De Gatinais**, b. Gatainais, France; d. France[2]

Robert **De Troyes**, m. Wera **De Vergy**[2]

Richard I, Duke **De Normandy**, b. 933, Fecamp, France; d. November 20, 978, Fecamp, France, m. 962 Gonnor, Duchess **De Normandy**, b. 936, Normandy, France; d. 1031, France[2]

Gonan **Le Torte**,* m. Hermengarde **De Anjou**[2]

Arnoul II, m. Rosalie **De Ivrea***[9]

Malcolm II, King of Scotland, b. 958, Scotland; d. November 25, 1034, Scotland[2]

Beorn, Earl of the Midlands[2]

Ealred, Count of Northumberland, b. Northumberland, England, m. Edgina[2]

King Ethelred II "The Uneasy," b. 966, Wessex, England; d. April 23, 1016, London, England, m. Alfgifu of Deira[2]

Bruno **Von Braunschweig**, b. 960, Germany; d. 1003, Germany, m. Gisela **Von Swaben**, b. 985, Germany; d. February 14, 1043, Germany[2]

Richard **Fitz Scrub***[7, 8]

Gruffud I, b. 1004, Wales; d. Wales m.Edith, Duchess of Mercia, b. Mercia, England; d. England[7, 8]

Robert II, b. 970, France; d. July 20, 1031, France, m. 998, Constance **De Toulouse**, b. 977, Toulouse, France; d. July 25, 1031, France[8, 12]

Yaroslav I, b. Russia; d. Russia, m. Ingegard of Sweden, b. Sweden; d. Russia[8, 12]

Jean **De Conteville**[2]

G-27

Foulgues I, m. **Roscille De Loch**[2]

Herbert II, b. 885; d. 943, m. 921, Hildebrand **De France**, b. France[2]

Guillaume I **Longespee**, m. Sprota **De Bretagne**[2]

Herbastus **De Crepon**[2]

Juhel **Bereguer**, m. Gerberge[2]

Geoffrey I,* m. Adelaide **De Troyes*** (Refer to Geoffrey I G-25 to continue their lines.)[2]

Arnoul I, b. 885; d. 969, m. Adela **De Vermandois**, b. Vermandois, France[9]

Kenneth III, King of Scotland, b. Scotland; d. Scotland[2]

Ulf, Regent of Denmark, b. Denmark, m. Astrid, Svend **Tveskjaegsdatter**[2]

Tchtad of Northumberland, b. Northumberland, England; d. England, m. Elfrida Of Durham[2]

Edgar "The Peaceful" King of England, m. Elfthryth of Devon[2]

Ekbert "One Eye," m. Frederuna[2]

Herman **Von Schwaben**, b. Germany; d. Germany, m. Gerberge **De Bourgoyne**[2]

Llewelyn ap Seisyll, b. 980, Wales; d. 1043, Wales, m. Angard verch Maredudd, b. Wales. D. Wales[7, 8]

Alfgar III, Earl of Mercia, b. Mercia, England; d. Mercia, England, m. Elfgifu*[7, 8]

Hugues **Capet**, b. 938, France; d. October 24, 996, France, m. Adelaide **De Poitiers**, b. Poitiers, France; d. France[8, 12]

William I (Guillaume) **De Arles**, b. 947, Toulouse, France; d. 994, France, m. 982, Adlis-Blanche **De Anjou**, b. France; d. France[2]

Vladimir I, b. Russia; d. Russia, m. Rogneda **De Pololzk**[8, 12]

King Olaf III, b. Sweden; d. Sweden[8, 12]

Baldwin II **De Blois**, b. Blois, France; d. France[8, 9, 12]

G-28

Herbert I, m. Beatrice **De Morvois***[2]

Rollon **Rou**,* b. 870, Norway, m. Poppa **De Valois**,* b. Valois, France[2]

Baldwin II, m. Ethelswida, b. England; d. England[9]

Seisyll ap Endowan,* b. Wales; d. Wales, m. Prawst verch Elise*[2]

Leofric III,* b. May 14, 968, England; d. August 31, 1057, Bromley, England, m. Lady Godiva,* b. 980, England; d. September 10, 1067, England[7, 8]

Morcar of Wessex,* b. Wessex, England; d. England, m. Eadgyth,* b. England; d. England[7, 8]

Hugues "Le Grand," b. 900; d. June 16, 956, m.Avoi-Hatbruide **De Saxe***[2]

Boso III **De Arles**,* m. Constance*[2]

Sviatoslav I, b. Russia; d. Russia, m. Malfredd **Von Lubeck***[8, 12]

Baldwin I **De Blois**, b. Blois, France[2]

G-29

Pepin **De Senlis**, m. Ermgarde*[2]

Baldwin I, m. Judith **De France*** b. France[9]

King Alfred The Great, b. England; d. England, m. Ethelswida,* b. England; d. England[9]

Igor,* b. Russia; d. Russia, m. Olga*[8, 12]

Godfrey **De Neustria**[2]

G-30

King Bernhard of Italy, b. 797, Lombardy, Italy; d. April 17, 818, Italy, m. Cunigunde of Italy*[2]

King Charles "The Bald" of France, b. France; d. France, m. Ermentrude*[9]

King Ethelwulf, b. England; d. England, m. Osburgis* b. England; d. England[9]

Rowland **De Neustria**[2]

G-31

Pepin, b. Germany; d. July 8, 810, Milan, Italy, m. Bertha **De Toulouse***[2]

King Louis I "The Pious," b. France; d. France, m. Ermengarde*[9]

Bosco, King of Burgundy*[9]

King Egbert,* b. England; d. England, m. Redburgo*[9]

Charles "The Younger"[2]

G-32

Charlemagne, b. April 2, 742, France, m. Hildegarde **De Vinzzau***[2]

(Charlemagne is the father of Pepin, King Louis I, and Charles "The Younger.")

G-33

King Pepin* "The Short," b. 714, France; d. France, m. Bertha, Countess De Laon, b. France; d. France[2]

Louisa Adams

G+2

Children of John and Mary Catherine (Heller) Adams:

Mary Louisa **Adams**, b. December 2, 1828, in the White House; d. July 16, 1859, Long Island, New York, m. William Clarkson **Johnson**[1]

Georgeanna Francis **Adams**, b. 1830, Quincy, Mass.; d. 1839, Quincy, Mass.[1]

Children of Charles Francis and Abigail (Brooks) Adams:

Louisa Catherine **Adams**, b. 1831, Washington, D.C.; d. 1870[1]

John Quincy **Adams**, b. September 27, 1833, Washington, D.C.; d. August 14, 1894, Quincy, Mass.[1]

Charles Francis **Adams**, b. May 27, 1835, Boston, Mass.; d. March 20, 1915[1]

Henry Brooks **Adams**, b. February 16, 1838, Boston, Mass.; d. March 27, 1918[1]

Arthur Adams, b. 1841, Quincy, Mass.; d. 1838, Quincy, Mass.[1]

Mary **Adams**, b. 1846, Quincy, Mass.; d. 1928[1]

Brooks **Adams**, b. June 24, 1848, Quincy, Mass.; d. February 12, 1927, Quincy, Mass.[1]

G+1

George Washington **Adams**, b. April 13, 1801, Berlin, Germany; d. June 17, 1829, Long Island, New York[1]

John **Adams**, b. July 4, 1803, Washington, D.C.; d. October 23, 1834, Washington, D.C., m. February 25, 1828, at the White House to Mary Catherine **Heller** 1806–1880[1]

Charles Francis **Adams**, b. August 18, 1807, Boston, Mass.; d. November 21, 1886, Quincy, Mass., m. September 3, 1829, Mystic Grove, Mass. to Abigail Brown **Brooks**, b. April 25, 1808, Medford, Mass.; d. June 6, 1889[1]

Louisa Catherine **Adams**, b. August 12, 1811, St. Petersburg, Russia; d. September 15, 1812, St. Petersburg, Russia[1]

Louisa Catherine Johnson, b. February 12, 1775, London, England; d. May 14, 1852, m. July 26, 1797, John Quincy Adams, b. July 7, 1767, Braintree, Mass.; d. February 23, 1848, Washington, D.C.[2,3]

G-1

Joshua **Johnson**, b. June 25, 1744, Maryland; d. 1802, m. 1802, Catherine **Nuth**,* b. 1757, London, England; d. 1811(2)

G-2

Thomas **Johnson**, b. February 19, 1701, or 1702, Calvert Co., Maryland; d. April 12, 1779, Maryland, m. Dorcas **Sedgewick**, b. November 2, 1705, Connecticut; d. December 11, 1770[2]

G-3

Thomas **Johnson**, b. 1656, England; d. 1714, Maryland, m. Mary **Baker**, b. Liverpool, England[2]

Joshua **Sedgewick**, b. 1673; d. 1733, m. Elizabeth **Fisher**[2]

G-4

Joshua **Johnson**, b. England, m. Dorothy **Scottaw***[2]

Roger **Baker**,*b. England[2]

Thomas **Sedgewick**,* b. England; d. 1698, Maryland[2]

Henry **Fisher**,* b. England[2]

G-5

Thomas **Johnson**,* b. England; d. England[2]

Ellen Arthur

G+2

Children of Chester Alan and Myra Townsend (Fithian) Arthur:

Chester Alan **Arthur**, b. March 21, 1901, Colorado Springs, Colorado; d. April 28, 1972, San Francisco, Calif., m(1) Charlotte **Wilson**, m(2) April 20, 1935, Esther Knesborough **Murphy**, m(3) 1965, Ellen[1]

Ellen **Arthur**, b. 1903[1]

G+1

William Lewis **Arthur**, b. December 10, 1860, New York, New York; d. July 7, 1863, Englewood, New Jersey[1]

Chester Alan **Arthur**, b. July 25, 1864, New York, New York; d. 1937, Colorado Springs, Colorado, m(1) Myra Townsend **Fithian**, m(2) Rowena **Dashwood**[1] Ellen **Arthur**, b. November 21, 1871, New York City; d. September 6, 1915, Mt. Kisco, New York, m. 1907, Charles **Pinkerton**[1]

Ellen Herndon, b. August 30, 1837, Fredericksburg, Virginia; d. January 12, 1880, New York, New York, m. October 25, 1859, Chester Alan Arthur, b. October 5, 1830, Fairfield, Vermont; d. November 18, 1886, New York, New York[2,13]

G-1

William Lewis **Herndon**, October 25, 1813, Culpeper Co., Va.; d. September 12, 1859, m. March 9, 1836, Frances Elizabeth **Hansborough**, b. October 10, 1817, Culpeper Co., Virginia; d. April 5, 1878[2]

G-2

Dabney **Herndon**, b. April 14, 1783, Virginia; d. December 20, 1824, m. November 17, 1806, Elizabeth **Hull**, b. January 12, 1789, Culpeper Co., Va. d. April 20, 1825, Fredericksburg, Virginia[2]

Joseph **Hansborough**, b. September 28, 1790, Virginia; d. August 13, 1864, m. March 12, 1813, Sarah **Myers**,* b. 1792; d. January 3, 1827[2]

G-3

Joseph **Herndon**, b. May 1, 1737, Virginia; d. October 28, 1810, m. August 15, 1765, Mary **Minor**, b. March 7, 1741; d. 1818[2]

John **Hull**, m. Ann **Strachen***[2]

James **Hansborough**, b. January 17, 1768, Virginia; d. May 14, 1853, Virginia, m. Fannie Montieth **Finnell**[2]

Benjamin **Myers***[2]

G-4

Edward **Herndon**, b. 1702, King and Queen Co., Virginia; d. October 4, 1743, Spotsylvania Co., Virginia, m. Elizabeth **Stubblefield**, b. 1700, King and Queen Co., Virginia[2, 3]

John **Minor**, b. 1707; d. 1755, m. 1732, Sarah **Carr**, b. 1719; d. 1774[2]

Edwin **Hull**,* m. Ann **Eustaces***[2]

Peter **Hansborough**, b. June 12, 1744, m. Eleanor **Minor**, b. January 15, 1742; d. 1812[2]

Jonathan **Finnell**,* m. Margaret **Montieth***[2]

G-5

Edward **Herndon**, b. 1678; d. 1758, Caroline Co., Virginia, m. Mary **Waller**, b. May 23, 1674, Newport, England; d. 1727, Caswell City, Virginia[2]

Robert **Stubblefield**,* b. 1680, Spotsylvania, Virginia; d. 1775[4]

Garret **Minor**, b. 1679, Middlesex Co., Virginia; d. 1720, Virginia, m. 1706, Diane **Vivian**, b. 1680, Middlesex Co., Virginia; d. 1718, Middlesex Co., Virginia[2]

Thomas **Carr**, b. 1678, Spotsylvania Co., Virginia; d. May 29, 1737, Albemarle Co., Virginia, m. Mary **Dabney**[5]

James **Hansborough**, b. 1719, Stafford Co., Virginia; d. 1781, Stafford Co., Virginia., m. Lettice **Sumner**,* b. 1728, King George Co., Virginia[2]

G-6

William **Herndon**, b. 1649, England; d. 1722, Va., m. 1698, Catherine **Digges**, b. 1654, England; d. 1727, Virginia[2]

John **Waller**, b. 1645, m. Mary **Pomfrett***[2, 6]

George **Stubblefield**, b. 1680, Spotsylvania Co., Va.; d. 1775[4]

Doodes **Minor**, b. 1640, Nansemond Co., Va.; d. November 13, 1694, Middlesex Co., Virginia, m. Elizabeth **Cocke**[2]

John **Vivian**,* m. Diana **Cummings***[2]

Thomas **Carr**, b. 1640, England; d. 1732, Virginia, m. Mary Lucy*[5]

Cornelius **Dabney**, m. Sarah **Jennings**, b. 1702, England; d. 1791, Madison Co., Ky.[2, 7]

Peter **Hansborough**[2]

G-7

Thomas **Herndon**,* b. England[2]

Edward **Digges**, b. 1621, England; d. 1675, Virginia, m. Mary Elizabeth **Page***[2, 8]

John **Waller**, b. 1610[6]

Simon **Stubblefield**,* b. 1629, England; d. 1688[4]

Doodes **Minor**,* b. 1610, Holland; d. 1687 Virginia[2]

Maurice **Cocke**,* m. Margaret **Unk***[2]

Thomas **Vivian**,* b. England

Sir Robert **Carr**,* b. Scotland[2]

Thomas **Dabney***[2]

Charles **Jennings**, b. July 28, 1665, England, m. Mary **Cary***[7, 9]

Morris **Hansborough (Hanbury)**[2]

G-8

Sir Dudley **Digges**, b. England; d. 1638, England, m. Mary **Kempe***[2, 8]

Edmund **Waller**, b. 1580, England; d. September 21, 1667, m. Mary **Smith***[6]

Jeffrey **Stubblefield**,* b. 1596, England[4]

James **Carr**, b. Scotland[5]

Humphrey **Jennings**, b. August 23, 1629, Birmingham, England; d. July 6, 1689, England, m. Mary **Millward**, b. 1636, England; d. 1708[7, 9]

Nicholas **Hansborough (Hanbury)**, b. England[2]

G-9

Thomas **Digges**, b. 1549, England; d. 1595, England, m. Anne **St. Leger**, b. 1556, England; d. 1637, England[2, 8]

Thomas **Waller**, b. 1546, England; d. 1627, England, m. Dorothy **Gerard**, b. England; d. England[6]

Thomas **Carr**,* b. Scotland; d. Scotland, m. Janet **Kishaldy**,* b. Scotland; d. Scotland[5]

John **Jennings**, b. 1575, England; d. 1653, England, m. Joyce **Weeman**,* b. England; d. England[9]

John **Millward*** b. February 10, 1603, England, m. Ann **Whitchalgh**,* b. 1616, England[9]

John **Hansborough (Hanbury)**, b. England; d. England[2]

G-10

Leonard **Digges**, b. 1520, England; d. 1559, England, m. Bridget or Sarah **Wilsford**, b. England; d. England[2, 8]

Sir Warham **St. Leger**, b. 1525, England; d. 1597, England, m. Ursula **De Neville**, b. England; d. England[2, 8]

William **Waller**, b. England; d. England, m. Jane **Bowland**, b. England; d. England[6]

William **Gerard**, b. England; d. England[3]

William **Jennings**,* b. 1525, England; d. 1602, England, m. Joanna **Elliott**,*b. England; d. England[7, 9]

Jonas **Hansborough (Hanbury)**, b. England; d. England, m. Adrian **Cash**[2]

G-11

James **Digges**,* b. 1470, England; d. 1540, England, m. Philippa **Engham**,* b. 1470, England; d. England[2, 8]

Thomas **Wilsford**,* b. England; d. England, m. Elizabeth **Culpeper**, b. England; d. England[8]

Anthony **St. Leger**, b. 1496, England; d. 1559, England, m. Agnes **Warham**, b. 1500, England; d. 1559, England[8]

George **De Neville**, b. England; d. England, m. Mary **Stafford**, b. England; d. England[2, 8]

Robert **Waller**, b. England; d. England, m. Elizabeth **Fryer**,* b. England; d. England[6]

Thomas **Bowland**,* b. England; d. England[6]

James **Gerard**,* b. England; d. England, m. Margaret **Holcroft**, b. England; d. England[3]

Walter **Hansborough (Hanbury)**,* b. England; d. England, m. Cicely **Rous**,* b. England; d. England[2]

G-12

Walter **Culpeper**,* b. England; d. England, m. Anna **Aucher**,* b. England; d. England[8]

Ralph **St. Leger**,* b. England; d. England, m. Elizabeth **Haut**, b. England; d. England[2, 8]

Hugh **Warham**,* b. England; d. England[2, 8]

George **De Neville**, b. England; d. England, m. Margaret **Fenn**,* b. England; d. England[2, 8, 10]

Edward **Stafford**,* b. England; d. England, m. Eleanor **Percy**, b. England; d. England[2, 8, 10]

John **Holcroft**,* b. 1503, England; d. 1557, England, m. Margaret **Mescy**, b. England; d. England[3]

G-13

Richard **Haut**, b. England; d. England, m. Elizabeth **Tyrell**,* b. England; d. England[11]

Edward **De Neville**, b. 1407, Raby Castle, England; d. October 18, 1476, England, m. Elizabeth **De Beauchamp**, b. September 16, 1415, England; d. June 18, 1448, England[11]

Henry **Percy**, b. England; d. England, m. Maud **Herbert**,* b. England; d. England[2]

Hamon **Mescy**,* b. England; d. England, m. Elizabeth **Botelier**, b. England; d. England[3]

G-14

William **Haut or Haute**, b. 1390, England; d. 1462, England, m. Joan **Wydeville**, b. England; d. England[11]

Ralph **De Neville**, b. England; d. England, m. Joan **Beaufort**, b. England; d. England[11]

Richard **De Beauchamp**, b. England; d. March 18, 1421, England, m. Isabel **Le De Spencer**, b. July 26, 1400, England; d. December 27, 1439, England[11]

Henry **Percy**, b. England; d. England, m. Eleanor **Poynings**,* b. England; d. England[2]

Sir John **Botelier**, b. 1402, England; d. 1430, England, m. Isabel **Harrington**, b. England; d. England[3]

G-15

Nicholas **Haut or Haute**, b. England; d. England, m. Alice **De Croven**,* b. England; d. England[11]

Richard **Wydeville**, b. England; d. England, m. Joan **Bedelgate**, b. England; d. England[11]

John **De Neville**, b. England; d. England, m. Maude **De Percy**, b. England; d. England[10]

John of Gaunt **Beaufort**,* m. Catherine **Roet*** (Refer to John of Gaunt G-14 of Abigail **Adams** to continue their lines.)[2, 4, 7]

William **De Beauchamp**,* b. England; d. England, m. Joan **Fitz Alan**, b. England; d. England[11]

Thomas **Le De Spencer**, b. September 22, 1373, England; d. England, m. January 13, 1399 or 1400, Constance **Plantagenet**,* b. England; d. November 28, 1416, England[2]

Henry **Percy**, b. England; d. England, m. Eleanor **De Neville**, b. England; d. England[2]

William **Botelier**, b. England; d. England, m. Elizabeth **Standish**,* b. England; d. England[3]

Sir William **Harrington**, b. England; d. England, m. Margaret **De Neville**, b. England; d. England[3]

G-16

Edmund **De Haute**,* b. England; d. England, m. Benedicta **Skelong**,* b. England; d. England[11]

John **Wydeville**,* b. England; d. England, m. Katherine **Fernband**,* b. England; d. England[11]

John **Bedelgate**,* b. England; d. England, m. Mary **De Beauchamp**, b. England; d. England[11]

Ralph **De Neville**,* b. England; d. England, m. Alice **De Audley**,* b. England; d. England[10]

Henry **De Percy**,* b. 1300; d. 1352, m. Idoine **De Clifford**,* b. England; d. England[10]

Richard **Fitz Alan**,* m. Elizabeth **De Bohun*** (Refer to Richard **Fitz Alan** G-14 Abigail **Adams** to continue their lines.)[11]

Edward **Le De Spencer**, b. March 24, 1336, England; d. November 11, 1375, m. Elizabeth **De Burghersh**,* b. England; d. England[2]

Henry **Percy**,* b. England; d. England, m. Elizabeth **De Mortimer**, b. England; d. England[2]

Ralph **De Neville**,* m. Joan **Beaufort*** (Refer to Ralph **De Neville** G-14 Ellen **Arthur** to continue their lines.)[2]

Sir John **Botelier,*** b. England; d. England, m. Alice **Plumpton.**, b. England; d. England[3]

Sir Nicholas **Harrington,*** b. England; d. England, m. Isabel **English,*** b. England; d. England[3]

G-17

Randolph **De Neville**, b. October 18, 1262; d. 1331, England, m. Euphemia **Fitz Rogers,*** b. England; d. England[10]

Edward **Le De Spencer**, b. England; d. England, m. Anne **De Ferriers,*** b. England; d. England[12]

Edmund **De Mortimer**, b. February 1, 1351, Breconshire, Wales; d. December 26, 1381, Ireland, m. Philippa **Plantagenet**, b. 1332, Salisbury, England; d. January 5, 1381, Bisham, England[10]

Sir William **Plumpton**, b. England; d. England[3]

G-18

Hugh **Le De Spencer,*** b. England; d. November 24, 1326, England, m. Eleanor **De Clare**, b. England; d. England[12]

Roger **De Mortimer,*** b. November 11, 1328, Ludlow, England; d. February 26, 1359, Rouvrau, France, m. Philippa **De Montagu or Montacute,*** b. 1332, Salisbury, England; d. January 5, 1381, Bisham, England[10]

Lionel **Plantagenet**, b. November 29, 1338, Antwerp, Belgium; d. December 10, 1313, Dublin, Ireland, m. Elizabeth **De Burgh,*** b. England; d. England[10]

Sir Robert **Plumpton,*** b. England; d. England, m. Lucy **De Ros**, b. England; d. England[3]

G-19

Gilbert **De Clare**, b. September 2, 1243, England; d. December 7, 1295, England, m. 1290, Joan **Plantagenet,*** b. England; d. England[12]

King Edward III,* m. Philippa **De Hainault*** (Refer to King Edward III G-15 Abigail **Adams** to continue their lines.)[10]

Sir William **De Ros**, b. England; d. England, m. Eustache **Fitz Hugh,*** b. England; d. England[3]

G-20

Richard **De Clare**, b. August 4, 1222, England; d. July 15, 1262, England, m. Maud **De Lacy**, b. England; d. England[12]

Sir William **De Ros**, b. England; d. England, m. Lucy **Fitz Piers**,* b. England; d. England[3]

G-21

Gilbert **De Clare**, b. England; d. England, m. Isabelle **Marshall**, b. England or Wales[12]

John **De Lacy**, b. 1192, England; d. 1240, England, m. Margaret **De Quincy**, b. England; d. England[13]

Robert **De Ros**, b. England; d. England, m. Isabel of Scotland, b. Scotland; d. Scotland[3]

G-22

Roger **De Clare**,* b. England; d. England, m. Amicia **Fitz Robert**,* b. England; d. England[12]

William **Marshall**,* m. Isabel **De Clare*** (Refer to William **Marshall** G-20 Abigail **Adams** to continue their lines.)[12]

Roger **De Lacy**,* b. England; d. England, m. Mathilda **De Clare**,* b. England; d. England[12]

Robert **De Quincy**, b. England; d. 1217, England, m. Hawise **De Meschines**, b. England d. England[12]

Edward **De Ros**,* b. England; d. England, m. Roese **Trussaby**,* b. England; d. England[3]

King William I of Scotland, b. 1143, Scotland; d. 1214, Scotland[3]

G-23

Saier **De Quincy**, b. England; d. November 3, 1219, England m. Margaret **De Beaumont**, b. England; d. January 12, 1235, England[12]

Hugh **De Meschines**, b. 1147; d. 1181, m. Bertrade **De Evereaux***[12]

Henry of Huntingdon, b. 1114, Huntingdon, England; d. 1152, England, m. Ada **Surrey**,* b. England; d. England[3]

G-24

Robert **De Quincy**,* b. 1125, England; d. England, m. Orable **De Leuchars***[12]

Robert **De Beaumont**, b. 1130, England; d. England, m. Pernel **De Grandmesnil***[12]

Ranulf IV, b. 1099, England; d. 1153, England, m. Maud **Fitz Robert**,* b. England; d. England[12]

King David I of Scotland,* m. Mathilda Huntingdon* (Refer to King David I G-23 Abigail **Adams** to continue their lines.)[3]

William **De Warren,*** m. Isabelle **De Vermandois*** (Refer to William **De Warren** G-23 Abigail **Adams** to continue their lines.)[3]

G-25

Robert **De Beaumont,** b. 1104, England; d. April 5, 1168, England, m. Amice **De Gael,*** b. England; d. England[12]

Ranulf III,* b. England; d. England, m. Lucy **Taillebois,** b. England; d. England[12]

G-26

Robert **De Beaumont,*** m. Isabelle **De Vermandois*** (Refer to Robert **De Beaumont** G-23 Abigail **Adams** to continue their lines.)[12]

Ivo **De Taillebois,*** m. Lucia of Mercia

G-27

Alfgar III, m. Elfgifu*

G-28

Leofric III,* m. Lady Godiva*

Barbara Bush

G+2

Children of George Walker and Laura (Welch) Bush:

Barbara **Bush**, b. November 25, 1981, Dallas, Texas[1]
Jenna **Bush**, b. November 25, 1981, Dallas, Texas[1]

Children of John Ellis "Jeb" and Columba (Gallo) Bush:

George Prescott **Bush**, b. April 24, 1976, Houston, Texas[1]
Noelle **Bush**, b. July 26, 1977, Houston, Texas[1]
Jeb **Bush**, December 13, 1983.[1]

Children of Neil Mellon and Sharon (Smith) Bush:

Lauren **Bush**, b. June 25, 1984, Denver, Colorado[1]
Pierce **Bush**, b. March 15, 1986, Denver, Colorado[1]
Ashley **Bush**, b. February 7, 1989, Denver, Colorado[1]

Children of Marvin Pierce and Margaret (Molster) Bush:

Marshall Lloyd **Bush**, b. May 14, 1986, Fort Worth, Texas[1]
Charles Walker **Bush**, b. November 9, 1989, Fort Worth, Texas[1]

Children of Dorothy Bush and William Leblond:

Samuel Bush **LeBlond**, b. August 26, 1984, Maine[1]
Nancy **LeBlond**, b. November 19, 1986, Maine[1]

Children of Dorothy Bush and Robert P. Koch:

Robert Patrick **Koch**, b. May 20, 1993, Washington, D.C.[1]
Georgia Grace **Koch**, b. January 1, 1996, Washington, D.C.[1]

G+1

George Walker **Bush**, b. July 6, 1946, New Haven, Conn., m. November 6, 1977, Midland, Texas to Laura **Welch**, b. November 9, 1946, Midland, Texas[1]

Robin **Bush**, b. December 20, 1949, Midland, Texas; d. November 11, 1953, New York, New York[1]

John Ellis "Jeb" **Bush**, b. 1953, Midland, Texas, m. 1974, Columba Garnica **Gallo**[1]

Neil Millon **Bush**, b. January 22, 1955, Midland, Texas, m. 1980, Sharon **Smith**[1]

Marvin Pierce **Bush**, b. October 22, 1956, Midland, Texas, m. Margaret **Molster**[1]

Dorothy **Bush**, b. 1959, Houston, Texas, m(1) 1982, William **Leblond**, m(2) 1992, Robert P. **Koch**[1]

Barbara Pierce, b. June 8, 1925, Westchester, New York, m. January 6, 1945, to George Herbert Walker Bush, b. June 12, 1924, Milton, Mass.[2, 12]

G-1

Marvin **Pierce**, b. June 17, 1893, Sharpsville, Pa.; d. July 17, 1969, Rye, Rye, New York, m. August 6, 1918, Pauline **Robinson**, b. 1896, Richwood, Ohio; d. September 23, 1949, Harrison Co., New York[2, 3]

G-2

Scott **Pierce**, b. June 18, 1866, Sharpsville, Pa., m. November 26, 1891, Mabel **Marvin**, b. June 4, 1869, Cincinnati, Ohio[2, 4, 5]

James Edgar **Robinson**, b. August 15, 1868, Union Co., Ohio; d. 1931, m. 1895, Lula Dell **Flickinger**, b. 1875, Union Co., Ohio; d. Union Co., Ohio[3, 6]

G-3

Jonas James **Pierce**, b. September 23, 1839, Swanzey, New Hampshire; d. March 13, 1913, Sharpsville, Pa., m. April 6, 1865, Kate **Pritzel**, b. December 19, 1841, Sweizel, Germany; d. 1931, Pa.[2, 4]

Dr. Jerome Place **Marvin**, b. February 20, 1846, Ohio, m. April 16, 1868, Martha Ann **Stokes**, b. April 19, 1847, Preston, Ohio[2, 5]

John Welch **Robinson**, b. January 11, 1831, Union Co., Ohio; d. Union Co., Ohio, m. February 8, 1855, Sarah **Coe**, b. May 24, 1831, Washington Co., Pa. May 30, 1901, Union Co., Pa.[6]

Jacob Marion **Flickinger**, b. 1849, Tuscarawas Co., Ohio; d. 1917, m. Sarah **Haines**, b. 1855, Byhalia, Ohio; d. March 25, 1888, Union Co., Ohio[3]

G-4

James **Pierce**, b. September 24, 1810, Swanzey, New Hampshire; d. December 2, 1874, Sharpsville, Pa., m. Chloe **Holbrook**, b. March 20, 1816, Swanzey, New Hampshire; d. October 16, 1886, Swanzey, New Hampshire[2, 4]

Anton **Pritzl**,* b. December 26, 1811; d. 1844, m. Marie **Pasquay**,* b. January 21, 1813; d. November 30, 1867[2]

Samuel Ross **Marvin**, b. January 5, 1804, Dover, New Jersey; d. January 29, 1863, m. Julia Anne **Place**,* b. July 23, 1808, Oxford, Ohio; d. July 4, 1884[5]

Richard, m. **Stokes**,* m. Julia Ann **Myers***[5]

John Welch **Robinson**, b. February 11, 1803, Washington Co., Pa.; d. May 16, 1853, Union Co., Ohio, m. Elizabeth **Mitchell**, b. May 28, 1803, Union Co., Ohio; d. July 18, 1872, Union Co., Ohio[6]

Daniel **Coe**,* b. March 3, 1801, m. Mary **Gladding**,* January 18, 1804, Jefferson, Ohio; d. April 28, 1893, Union Co., Ohio[6]

Stephen **Flickinger**, b. May 4, 1823, Tuscarawas Co., Ohio; d. January 22, 1869, Union Co., Ohio, m. Margaret Ann **Figley***[3]

Jonathan **Haines**, m. Mary Jane **Spriggs***[3]

G-5

James **Pierce**, b. September 1768, Woburn, Mass.; d. February 4, 1849, Swanzey, New Hampshire, m. 1795, Mary **Stacy**, b. December 20, 1774, Woburn, Mass. September 15, 1847, Swanzey, New Hampshire[2, 7]

John **Holbrook**, b. September 12, 1778, Uxbridge, Mass.; d. May 7, 1838, Swanzey, New Hampshire, m. Mary **Hill**, b. 1780, Mendon, Mass.; d. December 2, 1856, Swanzey, New Hampshire[2, 8, 9]

Robert **Marvin**, b. September 12, 1772, Lyme, Conn.; d. January 18, 1842, Harrison, Ohio, m. Phebe **Ford**, b. August 1, 1770, Dover, New Jersey; d. July 19, 1852, Harrison, Ohio[5]

James **Robinson**, m. Mary **Welch**[6]

David **Mitchell**, b. April 30, 1762, Lancaster Co., Pa; d. January 28, 1836, Union Co., Ohio, m. 1782, Martha **Black**, b. August 8, 1764, Lancaster Co., PA; d. September 20, 1823, Union Co., Ohio[6]

John **Flickinger**, m. Margaretha **Demuth**, b. March 10, 1793, Northampton Co., Pa[3]

Allen **Haines**, m. Sarah **Ballinger**[3]

G-6

Joshua **Pierce**, b. April 1, 1722, Woburn, Mass.; d. February 13, 1771, Woburn, Mass., m. 1753, Esther **Richardson**, b. August 6, 1727, Woburn, Mass.; d. June 1, 1819, Swanzey, New Hampshire[2]

Philemon **Stacy**, b. 1741, Mass.; d. December 7, 1784, Vermont, m. Mary **Richardson***[2, 7]

John **Holbrook**, b. 1748, Uxbridge, Mass.; d. July 23, 1817, New Hampshire, m. Rhoda **Thayer**, b. November 11, 1746, Mendon, Mass.[2, 8]

Daniel **Hill**, b. September 27, 1755, Mendon, Mass.; d. May 28, 1814, Mendon, Mass., m. Mercy **Hayward**, b. May 16, 1756, Mendon, Mass.; d. October 21, 1822, Mendon, Mass.[4]

Samuel **Marvin**, b. February 14, 1744, Lyme, Conn.; d. 1773, m. November 18, 1764, Jerusha **Peck**, b. July 29, 1747, Wallingford, Conn.; d. Lyme, Conn.[5]

Samuel **Ford**,* m. Grace **Kitchell**[2]

Samuel **Mitchell**, b. November 18, 1726, Lancaster Co., Pa.; d. January 10, 1814, Madison Co., Ohio, m. Margaret **Alexander**,* b. May 5, 1738, Lancaster Co., Pa.; d. August 1, 1812, Union Co., Ohio[6]

Michael **Flickinger**,* m. Mary (Last Name Unknown)*[3]

Christopher **Demuth**, b. August 22, 1755, Pa.; d. January 27, 1822, Tuscarawas Co., Ohio, m. Susanna Catherine **Klein**, b. January 2, 1758, Northampton Co., Pa.; d. July 15, 1817, Tuscarawas Co., Ohio[3]

Joshua **Ballinger**,* m. Sarah **Jones***[2]

G-7

James **Pierce**, b. 1690; d. 1773[2]

Nathan **Richardson**, b. January 24, 1702, Woburn, Mass.; d. October 21, 1775, m. Esther **Pierce**, b. April 25, 1711, Chelmsford, Mass.; d. November 10, 1727[2]

Samuel **Stacy**, b. 1700, Watertown, Mass.; d. Ipswich, Mass., m. Margaret **Baker**, b. May 29, 1701, Ipswich, Mass.; d. January 1, 1764[7]

John **Holbrook**, b. August 1, 1717, Mendon, Mass.; d. 1774, Mendon, Mass., m. Zilpha **Thayer**, b. September 14, 1722, Mendon, Mass.; d. Mendon, Mass.[2, 8]

Moses **Thayer**, May 10, 1710, Mendon, Mass.; d. May 24, 1764, Mendon, Mass., m. Hannah **Hayward**,* b. 1707, Mendon, Mass.; d. 1772, Mendon, Mass.[2, 8]

Daniel **Hill**,* m. Elizabeth **Pulcepher***[4]

Joseph **Hayward**,* b. March 27, 1721, Uxbridge, Mass., m. Ruth **Jones***[4]

Nathan **Marvin**, b. November 21, 1714, Lyme, Conn.; d. March 15, 1755, Lyme, Conn., m. Lydia **Lewis***[5]

Samuel **Peck**, b. October 19, 1704, New Haven, Conn.; d. May 20, 1755, New Haven, Conn., m. January 18, 1727, Mary **Parmalee**,* b. November 12, 1706, Durham, Conn.; d. October 14, 1781, New Haven, Conn.[5]

Joseph **Kitchell**, b. January 25, 1710, Newark, New Jersey; d. March 22, 1779, Parsippany, New Jersey, m. Rachel **Bates**,* b. 1714, Elizabethtown, New Jersey; d. December 24, 1789, Hanover, New Jersey[10]

David **Mitchell**,* b. 1681, Drumore, Ireland; d. November 7, 1757, Lancaster Co., Pa., m. Jean **McClelland**,* b. 1706, Drumore, Ireland; d. 1746, Lancaster Co., Pa.[6]

Gottlieb **Demuth**,* b. October 10, 1715, Shoenan, Moravia; d. October 5, 1776, Shoeneck, Pa., m. Eva Barbara **Gitsler**,* b. November 11, 1713, Hilsheim, Palastine; d. August 20, 1784, Shoeneck, Pa.[3]

Andreas Henry **Klein**,* b. October 4, 1733; d. January 7, 1786, Northampton Co., Pa., m. Jane Elizabeth **Thomas**,* b. March 5, 1734, Pa.; d. August 20, 1870, Shoeneck, Pa.[3]

Samuel **Ballinger**,* m. Elizabeth **Groff***[2]

G-8

James **Pierce**, b. May 7, 1659, Woburn, Mass.; d. 1742, m. Elizabeth **Kendall**, b. January 15, 1653; d. 1715[2]

John **Richardson**, b. January 16, 1668, Woburn, Mass.; d. October 29, 1749, Woburn, Mass., m. Deborah **Brooks**, b. March 29, 1669, Woburn, Mass.; d. February 12, 1703 or 1704, Woburn, Mass.[2]

Stephen **Pierce**, b. 1679, Chelmsford, Mass.; d. September 9, 1749, m. February 5, 1707, Esther **Fletcher**, b. 1681, Chelmsford, Mass.; d. January 31, 1741 or 1742, Chelmsford, Mass.[2]

John **Stacy**, b. March 16, 1666, Ipswich, Mass.; d. February 22, 1732, Gloucester, Mass., m. Mary **Clarke**[7]

William **Baker**,* m. Sarah **Fitts**[7]

Silvanus **Holbrook**, b. Mendon, Mass., m. Naomi **Cook**, b. Braintree, Mass.[2, 8]

Samuel **Thayer**, b. March 28, 1696; d. June 21, 1764, m. Mary **Sampson**, b. 1695, Mendon, Mass.[2, 8]

Isaac **Thayer**, b. February 14, 1664, Mendon, Mass.; d. 1730, Mendon, Mass., m. Mary (Last Name Unknown),* b. 1670; d. 1730, Mendon, Mass.[2, 8]

Samuel **Marvin**, b. 1670, Lyme, Conn.; d. 1743, Hartford, Conn., m. Susannah **Graham***[5]

John **Peck**, b. August 16, 1671, New Haven, Conn.; d. January 28, 1768, New Haven, Conn., m. Susanna **Street**, b. January 15, 1765, New Haven, Conn.; d. April 21, 1704, New Haven, Conn.[5]

Abraham **Kitchell**, b. 1679, Newark, New Jersey; d. 1741, New Jersey, m. Sarah **Bruen**, b. 1679, New Jersey; d. April 30, 1745, Whippany, New Jersey[10]

G-9

Thomas **Pierce**,* b. 1618, England; d. November 6, 1683, Woburn, Mass., m. Elizabeth **Cole**,* b. 1614, England; d. March 5, 1688, Woburn, Mass.[2]

Francis **Kendall**,* b. 1620, England; d. 1708, Woburn, Mass., m. December 24, 1644, Mary **Tidd**,* b. 1624, England; d. 1705, Woburn, Mass.[2]

Theophilus **Richardson**,* b. 1633, Charlestown, Mass.; d. December 28, 1674, Woburn, Mass., m. Mary **Champney**,* b. 1635, Cambridge, Mass.; d. August 28, 1704, Woburn, Mass.[2]

John **Brooks**,* b. 1623, England; d. September 29, 1691, Woburn, Mass., m. Eunice **Mousall**,* b. 1628, Woburn, Mass.; d. January 1, 1684, Woburn, Mass.[2]

Stephen **Pierce**,* b. July 16, 1651, Charlestown, Mass.; d. June 10, 1733, Chelmsford, Mass., m. Tabitha **Parker**,* b. February 26, 1658, Chelmsford, Mass.; d. January 31, 1741, Chelmsford, Mass.[2]

William **Fletcher**,* b. February 21, 1657, Chelmsford, Mass.; d. May 23, 1712, Chelmsford, Mass., m. Sarah **Richardson**,* March 25, 1660, Chelmsford, Mass.; d. January 30, 1748, Tyngsboro, Mass.[2]

Thomas **Stacy**,* b. 1621, Bocking, England; d. July 23, 1690, m. Susanna **Worcester**, b. 1629, England; d. 1692[7]

Matthew **Clarke**,* m. Abigail **Maverick**, b. August 10, 1637; d. January 1, 1690 Beverly, Mass.[7]

Robert **Fitts**,* b. July 12, 1600, Devonshire, England; d. May 9, 1665, Ipswich, Mass., m. Ann **Baines***[7]

Peter **Holbrook**, b. Mendon, Mass.; d. Mendon, Mass., m. Alice **Godfrey**, b. Weymouth, Mass.; d. Mendon, Mass.[2, 8]

John **Cook**, b. 1653, Braintree, Mass.; d. 1718, Mass., m. January 24, 1684, Naomi **Thayer**, b. November 28, 1662, Braintree, Mass.; d. 1718, Mass.[2]

Thomas **Thayer**, b. February 14, 1664, Mendon, Mass.; d. May 1, 1738, Mendon, Mass., m. Mary **Poole**, b. November 20, 1668, Weymouth, Mass.; d. December 9, 1745, Mendon, Mass.[2, 8, 11, 12]

Stephen **Sampson**, b. 1633, Duxbury, Mass.; d. January 31, 1714 or 1715, m. Elizabeth (Last Name Unknown)*[2, 9]

Fernando **Thayer**, b. 1625, Thornbury, England; d. March 28, 1713, m. Huldah **Hayward**, b. 1634, Braintree, Mass.; d. September 1, 1690, Mendon, Mass.[2, 8, 11]

Reinhold **Marvin**, b. December 20, 1631, Essex, England; d. August 4, 1676, Lyme, Conn., m. November 27, 1663, Sarah **Clark**, b. October 25, 1650, New Haven, Conn.; d. February 1, 1715, New Haven, Conn.[5]

John **Peck**, b. November 17, 1640, New Haven, Conn.; d. October 4, 1694, New Haven, Conn., m. November 3, 1664, Mary **Moss**, b. 1649, New Haven, Conn.; d. November 16, 1725, New Haven, Conn.[5]

John **Bruen**, b. June 2, 1646; d. 1696, Newark, New Jersey, m. Esther **Lawrence**[1]

G-10

William **Worcester**,* b. 1595, Bucks, England; d. October 28, 1662, Salisbury, Mass., m. Sarah **Blake**,* b. England; d. Salisbury, England[7]

Elias **Maverick**, b. 1604, England; d. September 8, 1684, Charlestown, Mass., m. Anne **Harris**, b. 1613, England; d. September 7, 1697, Reading, Mass.[7]

Thomas **Holbrook**,* b. 1624, Glastonbury, England; d. July 22, 1697, Braintree, Mass., m. Joanna **Kingman**,* b. 1624, Somersetshire, England[2, 8]

Richard **Godfrey**,* b. 1631, Lancastershire, England; d. October 16, 1691, Taunton, Mass., m. Jane **Turner**,* b. 1630, Taunton, Mass.; d. November 5, 1732, Taunton, Mass.[2, 8]

Walter **Cook**,* b. 1625, England; d. 1696, Mendon, Mass., m. Katherine (Last Name Unknown)* b. 1628, England; d. January 2, 1696, Mendon, Mass.[2]

Fernando **Thayer**,* m. Huldah **Hayward*** (Refer to G-9 Barbara Bush to continue their lines.)[2, 8, 11]

Thomas **Thayer**,* b. August 16, 1596, Thornbury, England; d. June 2, 1665, Braintree, Mass., m. August 13, 1618, Marjorie **Wheeler**,* b. 1597, Thornbury, England; d. February 11, 1642[2, 8, 11]

Samuel **Poole**, m. Mary **French**

Henry **Sampson*** (Mayflower Pilgrim), b. 1610, England; d. December 24, 1684, Duxbury, England, m. Ann **Plummer**,* b. 1615, England[2, 9]

Thomas **Thayer**,* m. Marjorie **Wheeler*** (Refer to G-10 Barbara Bush to continue their lines.)[2, 8, 11]

William **Hayward**,* b. England, m. Margery **Knight**,* b. England[2, 8, 11]

Reinhold **Marvin**, b. June 7, 1593, Essex, England; d. October 28, 1662, Lyme, Conn., m. Mary (Last Name Unknown)*[5]

James **Clark**,* b. 1608, London, England; d. December 19, 1674, Stratford, Conn., m. April 11, 1652, Sarah **Harvey**,* b. 1622, England; d. July 19, 1689, Conn.[5]

G-11

John **Maverick**, b. 1578, Devonshire, England; d. December 31, 1636, Dorcester, England, m. Mary **Gye**, b. 1580, England[7]

Thomas **Harris**,* b. Gloucester, England, m. Elizabeth **Hilles**,* b. 1577, England[7]

Thomas **Holbrook**,* b. 1599, Somerset, England; d. March 10, 1677, Wetmouth, Mass., m. Jane **Powyes**,* b. 1600, England; d. 1679, Weymouth, Mass.[2, 8]

Edward **Poole***b. 1608, Weymouth, England; d. August 22, 1664, Wemouth, Mass., m. Sarah **Pinney**,* b. Exeter, England[11]

John **French**,* b. May 26, 1612, England; d. August 6, 1692, m. Grace **Kingsley**,* b. 1621, England[11]

Edward **Marvin**,* b. Essex, England; d. November 15, 1615, Essex, England, m. Margaret (Last Name Unknown),* b. Essex, England; d. May 28, 1633, Essex, England[5]

G-12

Peter **Maverick**,* b. 1548, Devonshire, England, m. Dorothy **Tucke**,* b. England[7]

Robert **Gye**, b. 1540, England, m. Grace **Dowrish**,* England[7]

G-13

John **Gye**,* b. England; d. England, m. Mary **Prowse**, b. England; d. England[7]

G-14

Thomas **Prowse**,* b. England; d. England, m. Jane **Baynton**, b. 1478, Poughill, England; d. England[7]

G-15

Henry **Baynton**, b. England; d. England[7]

G-16

John **Baynton,*** b. England; d. England, m. Joan **De Echingham,** b. England; d. England[7]

G-17

William **De Echingham,*** b. 1338, Sussex, England; d. March 2, 1412, Sussex, England, m. Joan **Fitz Alan,** b. Sussex, England; d. Sussex, England[7]

G-18

John **Fitz Alan,** b. Sussex, England; d. Sussex, England, m. Eleanor **Maltovers,** b. 1345, England; d. January 10, 1405, England[7]

G-19

Edmund **Fitz Alan,** b. Sussex, England; d. Sussex, England, m. Alice **De Warren,** b. England; d. England[7]

John **Maltovers,** b. England; d. England, m. Gwenthlin (Last Name Unknown),* b. England; d. England[7]

G-20

Richard **Fitz Alan,** b. Sussex, England; d. Sussex, England, m. Alisona **De Saluzza**[7]

William **De Warren,** b. 1260, Sussex, England; d. December 15, 1286, Surrey, England, m. Joan **De Ware,** b. 1264, Oxford, England; d. November 21, 1293, Sussex, England[7]

John **Maltovers,*** b. England; d. England, m. Millicent **De Berkeley,** b. England[7]

G-21

John **Fitz Alan,** b. England; d. England, m. Isabella **De Mortimer,** b. England; d. England[7]

Thomas **De Saluzza,*** b. 1224, Saluzzo-Cuneo, Italy; d. December 23, 1286, m. Leugia **De Eva***[7]

John **De Warren,** b. England; d. England, m. Alice **De Lusignan***[7]

Robert **De Ware,** b. England; d. England, m. Alice **De Sanford,** b. England; d. England[7]

Maurice **De Berkeley,** b. Staffordshire, England; d. May 31, 1326, England, m. Eva **La Zouche,** b. England; d. England[7]

G-22

John **Fitz Alan**, b. 1223, Essex, England; d. 1267, England; d. Maude **De Verdon**, b. England; d. England[7]

Roger **De Mortimer**,* m. Maude **De Broose*** (Refer to Roger **De Mortimer** G-19 Abigail **Adams** to continue their lines.)[7]

William **De Warren**,* b. England; d. England, m. Maud **Marshall**, b. England; d. England[7]

Hugh IV **De Ware**, m. Hawise **De Quincy**, b. England; d. England[7]

Thomas **De Berkeley**,* b. 1245, Berkeley Castle, England; d. July 23, 1321, Bristol, England, m. Joan **De Ferriers**,* b. England; d. England[7]

Eudes **La Zouche**, b. Devon, England, m. Millicent **De Cantilupe**[7]

G-23

John **Fitz Alan**,* b. England; d. England, m. Isabel **De Albini**, b. England; d. England[7]

William **Marshall**,* m. Isabel **De Clare*** (Refer to William **Marshall** G-20 Abigail **Adams** to continue their lines.)[7]

Robert **De Ware**, m. Isabel **De Boulbec***[7]

Saier **De Quincy**,* b. 1155, Winchester, England; d. November 3, 1219, Palestine, m. Margaret **De Beaumont**,* b. 1156, Hampshire, England; d. January 12, 1236, England[7]

Alan **La Zouche**,* b. 1205, Devon, England; d. England, m. Helen **De Quincy**[7]

G-24

William **De Albini**,* b. England; d. England, m. Mabel **De Meschines**, b. 1123, Cheshire, England; d. England[7]

Aubrey III **De Ware**,* m. Agnes **De Essex***[7]

Roger **De Quincy**,* b. 1174, Winchester, England; d. England, m. Helen of Galloway[7]

G-25

Hugh **De Meschines**, b. England; d. England, m. Bertrade **De Montfort**[7]

Alan, Lord of Galloway, b. 1170, Runnemede, Scotland; d. 1224, Dundrenan, Scotland, m. Helen **De Lisle**[7]

G-26

Ranulph **De Meschines**, b. 1099, Normandy, France; d. December 16, 1153, England, m. Maud **Fitz Robert**, b. England; d. England[7]

Simon II **De Montfort,*** b. France; d. May 13, 1181, France, m. Amice **De Beaumont***[7]

Rolland **McDonald**, Lord of Galloway, m. Helen **De Morville***[7]

G-27

Ranulph **De Meschines*** b. Normandy, France; d. France, m. Lucy **Taillebois**, b. France; d. France[7]

Robert **De Caen**, b. England; d. England, m. Maud **Fitz Hamon,*** b. England; d. England[7]

Uchred, Lord of Galloway,* m. Gunnilda of Dunbar*[7]

G-28

Ivo **Fitz Richard De Taillebois,*** m. Lucia of Mercia, b. England; d. England[7]

King Henry I, b. Selby, England; d. December 1, 1135, England, m. Sybilla **Corbett**[7]

G-29

Alfgar III of Mercia, b. England; d. England, m. Elfgifu*[7]

William, The Conqueror,* m. Mathilda **De Flandre*** (Refer to William the Conqueror G-23 Abigail **Adams** to continue their lines.)[7]

G-30

Leofric III* b. May 14, 968; d. August 31, 1057, Bromley, England, m. Lady Godiva* b. England; d. England[7]

Laura Bush

G+1

Barbara **Bush**, b. November 25, 1981, Dallas, Texas[1]
Jenna **Bush**, b. November 25, 1981, Dallas, Texas[1]

Laura Lane Welch, b. November 4, 1946, Midland, Texas, m. November 5, 1977, Midland, Texas to George Walker Bush, b. July 6, 1946, New Haven, Conn.[1, 2, 9]

G-1

Harold Bruce **Welch**, b. November 21, 1912, Ada, Oklahoma; d. April 23, 1995, Midland, Texas, m. January 29, 1944, El Paso, Texas Jenna Louisa **Hawkins**, b. July 24, 1919, Little Rock, Arkansas[2]

G-2

Mark Anthony **Welch**, b. 1873, Texas, m. 1909, Marie Lula **Lane**, b. 1873, Arkansas[2]

Halsey Sinclair **Hawkins**, b. March 4, 1894, Little Rock, Arkansas; d. August 23, 1982, Midland, Texas, m. April 29, 1918, Little Rock, Arkansas Jessie Laura **Sherrard**, b. March 17, 1898, Robinson, Texas; d. February 17, 1981, El Paso, Texas[2]

G-3

Dr. William Franklin **Welch**, b. 1828, Alabama; d. 1885, m. September 28, 1860, Nancy Jane **Aldridge**, b. 1842; d. 1883, Fannin Co., Texas[2]

Doctor C. **Lane**,* b. 1830, Tennessee, m. Emily (Last Name Unknown)* b. 1836, Tennessee; d. 1910[2]

Charles Wesley **Hawkins**,* b. April 13, 1854, Crawford Co. Indiana; d. 1897, Little Rock, Arkansas, m. Martha Jennie **Allen**, b.

August 8, 1858, Meade Co., Ky.; d. April 26, 1928, Little Rock, Arkansas[2]

Joseph A. **Sherrard**, b. 1862, Mississippi; d. 1920, m. Eva Louise **Le Maire**, b. 1870, New York[2]

G-4

James **Aldridge**, b. September 1, 1813, North Carolina; d. May 8, 1884, m. Mary **Chadwell**, b. July 29, 1813, North Carolina; d. 1888[2, 3]

William Benjamin **Allen**,* b. February 5, 1819, Kentucky; d. January 31, 1902, Meade Co., Kentucky, m. December 30, 1841, Barbara Ann **Chisholm**, b. March 3, 1823, Kentucky; d. February 13, 1902, Meade Co., Kentucky[2]

William F. **Sherrard**,* b. 1828, Mississippi, m. December 13, 1849, Mississippi Martha **Allen**,* b. 1832[2]

Louis **Le Maire**,* b. 1840, France, m. Mary (Last Name Unknown)* b. 1841[2]

G-5

Aaron **Aldridge**, b. 1775, Guilford Co., North Carolina; d. 1821, Maury Co., Tennessee, m. Nancy (Last Name Unknown)*[2, 3]

David **Chadwell**, b. 1790, Rockingham Co., North Carolina; d. 1872, Fannin Co., Texas, m. Jane **Johnson**, b. 1795; d. 1885[2, 3]

John **Chisholm**,* b. 1795; d. 1868, Meade Co., Kentucky, m. May 29, 1816, Harrison Co., Indiana Margaret **Tibbs**, b. March 26, 1791, Kentucky; d. 1870, Meade Co., Kentucky[2]

G-6

William **Aldridge***; d. 1789, Randolph Co., North Carolina, m. Elizabeth (Last Name Unknown)*[2, 3]

John **Chadwell**,* m. Mary **Allen**[2, 3]

Gideon **Johnson**, b. November 1, 1754, Amelia Co., Virginia; d. November 1, 1843, Davidson Co., Tenn., m. November 18, 1779, Mary **De Graffenried**, b. September 3, 1764, Lunenberg Co., Va.; d. January 7, 1823, Williamson Co., Tennessee[2, 3]

Joseph **Tibbs**,* b. January 10, 1765, Cecil Co., Maryland; d. 1854, Meade Co. Kentucky, m. March 31, 1788, Nelson Co., Kentucky Eve **Wiseman**, b. 1770; d. 1830, Sangamon Co., Illinois[2]

G-7

Valentine **Allen**, b. 1726, Henrico Co., Va.; d. 1799, Rockingham

Co., North Carolina, m. Nancy Anne **Arnold**, b. 1733, Goochland Co., Va.; d. 1810, Rockingham Co., North Carolina[2]

Gideon **Johnson**, b. October 11, 1717, New Kent Co., Va.; d. 1807, Rockingham Co., Va., m. Ursula **Allen**, b. Va.; d. Va.[2, 3]

Baker **De Graffenried**, b. August 6, 1744, Lunenberg Co. Va.; d. 1776, Guilford, Va., m. Sarah **Vass**, b. 1744, Richmond Co., Va.; d. Cumberland Co., Kentucky[4, 5]

John **Wiseman**,* b. 1744, Pennsylvania; d. 1802, Nelson Co., Kentucky, m. Rachel (Last Name Unknown),* b. 1745; d. 1808[2]

G-8

William **Allen**, b. 1692, New Kent Co., Va.; d. 1752, Albemarle Co., Va., m. Mary **Hunt**, b. May 15, 1695; d. July 8, 1763[2]

William **Arnold**, b. 1700; d. 1774[2]

Benjamin **Johnson**, b. 1701; d. 1739, m. Marjorie **Massie**[2, 3]

William **Allen**, b. 1714, Hanover Co., Va.; d. 1785, m. Ann **Owen**[2, 3]

Tscharner **De Graffenried**, b. November 28, 1722, Williamsburg,Va.; d. April 10, 1794, Lunenberg Co., Va., m. Mary **Baker**, b. 1722, Chowan Co., North Carolina; d. 1756, Lunenberg Co., Va.[4, 5]

Vincent **Vass**,* m. Ann **Rust**[4, 5]

G-9

William **Allen**, m. Ann **Hudson***[2]

William **Hunt**, m. Tabitha **Endloe or Endlow**[2]

Edward **Johnson**,* m. Elizabeth **Walker**[6]

George **Massie**[8]

Robert **Allen**,* m. Sarah (Last Name Unknown)*[2, 3]

Thomas **Owen**, b. 1671, Va.; d. 1744, Henrico Co., Va., m. Elizabeth **Brooks***[7]

Christopher **De Graffenried**, b. 1691, Bern, Switzerland; d. October 27, 1742, Amelia Co., Va., m. July 12, 1714, Charleston, South Carolina to Barbara **Needham***[4, 5]

Henry **Baker*** b. 1684; d. 1738, Chowan Co., North Carolina[4, 5]

Benjamin **Rust**,* m. Sarah **Metcalfe***[4, 5]

G-10

Valentine **Allen**, b. 1630; d. 1676, m. Mary **Page**, b. 1630[2]

William **Hunt**,* b. 1636; d. November 11, 1676, m. Judith **Burton**[2]

Alexander **Walker***[2, 3]

Peter **Massie**, b. 1640; d. December 25, 1719, m. Penelope **Cooper**,* b. 1646[8]

Bartholomew **Owen**, b. 1619, Steventon, England; d. 1677, Southwarke, Va., m. Joanne **Jennings***[7]

Christopher **De Graffenried**, b. November 15, 1667; d. 1743, m. Regina **Tscharner***[4, 5]

G-11

John **Allen**,* m. Cynthia **Major***[2]

John **Page**,* m. Alice **Luken***[2]

Richard **Burton***[2]

Thomas **Massie**, b. 1610; d. 1688, m. Judith **Brereton***[8]

Robert **Owen**, b. 1583, Steventon, England; d. November 3, 1583, Steventon, England, m. Joanna **White**[7]

Anton **De Graffenried**, b. 1639, m. Catherine **Jenner***[4, 5]

G-12

Hugh **Massie**, b. 1580, England; d. 1639, m. Ann **Dodd**,* b. England; d. England[8]

Richard **Owen**,* b. 1555 Steventon, England; d. England, m. Joanna **Daniel**., b. 1560, Steventon, England; d. England[7]

John **White**,* b. England; d. England, m. Agneta **Pinnock**,* b. England; d. England[7]

Christopher **De Graffenried**, b. 1603, England; d. 1687, m. Anna **Von Muhlman***[4, 5]

G-13

David **Massie**, b. 1566, England; d. October 29, 1623, England, m. Dorothy **Leigh**,* b. 1566, England; d. England[8]

Robert **Daniel**, b. 1538, Tabley, England; d. England[7]

Abraham **De Graffenried**, b. 1580, England; d. 1620, England, m. Ursula **Von Diesbach***[4, 5]

G-14

Thomas **Massie**,* b. 1540, England; d. 1565, m. Elizabeth **Middleton**,* b. England; d. England[8]

Thomas **Daniel**, b. 1508, Tabley, England; d. 1551, England, m. Margaret **Wilbraham**, b. 1510, England; d. England[7]

Anton **De Graffenried**, b. 1545, England; d. 1611, England, m. Sarah **Abbuhl**, b. Bern, Switzerland[4, 5]

G-15

Piers **Daniel**, b. 1484, Tabley, England; d. 1523, England, m. Julianna **Newton**,* b. England; d. England[7]

William **Wilbraham**,* b. England; d. England, m. Helena **Egerton**, b. England; d. England[7]

Peter **De Graffenried**, b. 1507, England; d. 1562, England, m. Elizabeth **Lenker***[4, 5]

G-16

Thomas **Daniel**, b. 1445, Cheshire, England; d. 1484, England, m. Blanche **Warburton**,* b. England; d. England[7]

Philip **Egerton**, b. 1445, England; d. 1474, England, m. Marjorie **Mainwaring**, b. England; d. England[7]

Venner Nicholas **De Graffenried**, m. Barbara **Von Ringenberg*** or Benedetta **Matter***[4, 5]

G-17

Thomas **Daniel**, b. 1415, Cheshire, England; d. 1475, Cheshire, England, m. Maude **Leycester**,* b. England; d. England[7]

John **Egerton**, b. 1404, England; d. 1445, England, m. Margaret **Fitton**,* b. England; d. England[7]

William **Mainwaring**, b. England; d. England, m. Margaret **Warren**, b. 1400, England; d. England[7]

Johannes **De Graffenried**,* m. Anne **Von Ensaye***[4, 5]

G-18

Thomas **Daniel**,* b. 1380, England; d. 1432, England, m. Elizabeth **Aston**,* b. England; d. England[7]

Philip **De Egerton**, b. England; d. England, m. Mathilda **De Malpas***[7]

Randall **Mainwaring**, b. 1375, England; d. 1456, England, m. Marjorie **Venerables**, b. England; d. England[7]

John **Warren**, b. 1365, England; d. England, m. Mathilda **Cheney**, b. England; d. England[7]

G-19

Urian **De Egerton**,* b. 1302, England; d. 1396, England, m. Amelia **Warburton**,* b. Eng; d. England[7]

William **Mainwaring**,* b. 1350, England, m. Elizabeth **Leycester**, b. England; d. England[7]

Hugh **Venerables**, b. 1330, England; d. 1383, England, m. Margery **Cotton**,* b. England; d. England[7]

Griffith **Warren**, b. 1347, England; d. England, m. Margaret **Corbet**,* b. England; d. England[7]

G-20

Nicholas **Leycester**, b. 1330, England; d. England[7]

Hugh **Venerables**, b. 1296, England; d. 1368 England, m. Catherine **De Houghton**,* b. England; d. England[7]

Griffith **Warren**,* b. England; d. England, m. Mathilda **Le Strange**, b. 1337, England; d. England[7]

G-21

Roger **Leycester**, b. 1300, England; d. England[7]

Hugh **Venerables**,* b. 1270, England; d. England, m. Agatha **De Vernon***; d. England[7]

John **Le Strange**,* b. January 25, 1306; d. July 21, 1349, m. Anharad **Butler***[7]

G-22

Nicholas **De Leycester**,* b. 1270, England; d. England, m. Margaret **Dutton**, b. 1275, England; d. England[7]

G-23

Geoffrey **Dutton**,* b. England; d. England, m. Ionia **De Lacey**, b. England; d. England[7]

G-24

John **De Lacey**,* b. England; d. England, m. Margaret **De Quincy**, b. England; d. England[7]

G-25

Robert **De Quincy**, b. England; d. England, m. Ellen verch Llewelyn, b. Wales[7]

G-26

Saier **De Quincy**,* m. Margaret **De Beaumont***[7]

Llewelyn "The Great,"* b. 1173, Dolwyddelan, Wales; d. April 11, 1240, Aberconway, Wales, m. Joan **Fitz John**, b. 1190; d. 1237[7]

G-27

John of Gaunt, m. Agatha **De Ferriers***[7]

G-28

King Henry II,* m. Eleanor **De Aquitaine*** (Refer to King Henry II G-20 Abigail **Adams** to continue their lines.)[7]

Rosalynn Carter

G+2

Children of John William and Judy (Langford) Carter:

Jason **Carter**, b. August 7, 1975[1]
Sarah Rosemary **Carter**, b. December 19, 1978[1]

Children of John William and Elizabeth (Sawyer) Carter:

John **Carter**[1]
Sarah Elizabeth **Carter**[1]

Child of James Earl and Carol (Griffin) Carter:

James Earl **Carter** IV, b. 1977[1]

Child of James Earl and Virginia (Hodges) Carter:

Margaret **Carter**, b. 1988[1]

Children of Donnel Jeffrey and Annette Jene (Davis) Carter:

Joshua Jeffrey **Carter**, b. May 8, 1984[1]
Jeremy Davis **Carter**, b. June 25, 1987[1]
James Carlton **Carter**, b. April 24, 1991[1]

Child of Amy Lynn Carter and James Gregory Wentzel:

Hugo James **Wentzel**, b. July 29, 1999[1]

G+1

Children of James Earl and Rosalynn Eleanor (Smith) Carter:

John William **Carter**, b. July 3, 1947, Portsmouth, Va., m(1) Judy **Langford**, m(2) Elizabeth **Sawyer**[1]

James Earl **Carter** III, b. April 12, 1950, Honolulu, Hawaii, m(1) Carol **Griffin**, m(2) Virginia **Hodges**[1]

Donnel Jeffrey **Carter**, b. August 18, 1952, New London, Conn., m. Annette Jene **Davis**[1]

Amy Lynn **Carter**, b. October 19, 1967, Sumter Co., Georgia, m.

September 1, 1996, in Pond House, Plains, Ga., to James Gregory **Wentzel**[1]

Eleanor Rosalynn Smith, b. August 18, 1927, Plains, Ga., m. July 7, 1946, to James Earl Carter, b. October 1, 1924, Plains, Ga.[2, 7]

G-1

Wilburn Edgar **Smith**, b. November 20, 1896, Marion Co., Georgia; d. October 22, 1940, Plains, Georgia, m. June 20, 1926, Frances Allethea **Murray**, b. December 24, 1905, Plains, Georgia; d. April 1, 2000, Americus, Georgia[2]

G-2

Wilburn Juriston **Smith**, b. 1858, Marion Co., Georgia; d. 1918, Plain, Georgia, m. 1893, Sarah Eleanor **Bell**, b. 1875, Georgia; d. 1951, Plains, Georgia[2]

John William **Murray**, b. June 12, 1871, Plains, Georgia; d. July 15, 1966, Plains, Georgia, m. Rosa Nettie **Wise**, b. October 12, 1880, Plains, Georgia; d. September 30, 1941, Plains, Georgia[2]

G-3

Tenderson **Smith**, b. 1815, Clarke Co., Georgia; d. 1899, Marion Co., Georgia, m. 1838, Frances R. **Thomas**, b. 1821, Georgia; d. 1895, Marion Co., Georgia[2]

William Henry **Bell**, b. 1843, Georgia; d. 1927, Fitzgerald, Georgia, m. Mary Eleanor **Fulford**, b. 1839, Marion Co., Georgia; d. 1890, Sumter Co., Georgia[2]

John William **Murray**, b. 1833, Laurens Co., Georgia; d. 1920, Sumter Co., Georgia, m. Alethea Josephine **Parker**, b. 1842, Lee Co., Georgia; d. 1911, Sumter Co., Georgia[2]

George Calhoun **Wise**, b. 1844, South Carolina; d. 1898, Plains, Georgia, m. 1877, Frances Elizabeth **Coogle**, b. 1857, South Carolina; d. 1942, Georgia[2]

G-4

George Lynch **Smith**, b. March 16, 1779, North Carolina; d. 1867, m. 1812, Delanna **Peddy**, b. September 10, 1794, Wake City, North Carolina; d. 1874[2]

John **Thomas**,* m. Mary (Last Name Unknown)*[2]

Charles Allison **Bell**,* b. 1814, Georgia; d. 1866, Buena Vista, Georgia, m. 1840, Susanna **Singer**, b. 1824; d. 1892[2]

James **Fulford**,* b. 1812, North Carolina; d. Buena Vista, Georgia, m. Martha Ellen **Halley**[2]

Drury **Murray**, b. 1787; d. 1862, m. 1829, Susan **Champion**,* b. 1795, North Carolina; d. 1878, Sumter Co., Georgia[2]

William John **Parker**,* b. 1812, Georgia, m. Alethea **Lawhon**, b. 1814, Georgia[2]

David **Wise**, b. 1809, South Carolina; d. 1882, Georgia, m. Rosa Elizabeth **Etheredge**, b. South Carolina[2]

John Thomas **Coogle**, b. 1817; d. 1891, m. Harrett Rebecca **Kleckley**, b. 1824; d. 1883[2]

G-5

John or James **Smith**,* m. Mary **Lynch***[2]

Andrew **Peddy**, b. 1757, Halifax Co., Virginia; d. 1816, North Carolina, m. Julia **Barker**, b. 1760, Wake City, North Carolina[3]

Johann **Singer**, b. 1784, Stuttgart, Germany; d. 1855, Lumpkin, Georgia, m. 1818, Temperance **Carr**, b. 1791, North Carolina; d. Alabama[4]

Nathaniel **Halley**,* b. February 9, 1776, Prince George Co., Maryland; d. February 15, 1847, Pike Co., Alabama, m. March 19, 1800, Martha **Jacobs**, b. 1780, Prince George Co., Maryland[2]

Nathan **Murray**, b. November 4, 1756, Onslow Co., North Carolina; d. February 6, 1808, Georgia, m. Martha **Albritton**,* b. 1764; d. 1812[2, 5]

Noel **Lawhon**,* b. October 20, 1766, North Carolina; d. September 7, 1849, Lee Co., Georgia, m. July 16, 1796, Sarah **Bethune**,* b. January 20, 1774, North Carolina; d. July 12, 1855, Lee Co., Georgia[2, 5]

John **Wise**,* b. 1779, Lexington Co., South Carolina; d. 1840, m. Anna Mary **Kelly***[2]

John **Coogle**,* m. Betsey (Last Name Unknown)*[2]

Rev. Jacob **Kleckley**, b. November 1, 1791, South Carolina; d. April 23, 1862, Macon Co., Georgia, m. 1822, Frances **Hamiter**, b. June 29, 1798, South Carolina; d. Junly 4, 1883 Macon Co., Georgia[6]

G-6

Andrew **Peddy**,* b. 1730, London, England; d. Wake City, North Carolina, m. Rachel **Jones**, b. 1743, Halifax Co., Virginia; d. Georgia[3]

Johannes **Singer**, b. December 30, 1759, Stuttgart, Germany; d.

December 30, 1828, Stuttgart, Germany, m. Maria Barbara **Zizmann**, b. November 12, 1757, Stuttgart, Germany; d. May 17, 1803, Stuttgart, Germany[4]

Robert **Carr**,* b. June 30, 1760, North Carolina; d. Georgia, m. Obedience (Last Name Unknown),* b. April 4, 1756, North Carolina; d. Georgia[4]

Jonathan **Murray**, b. March 22, 1735, Onslow Co., North Carolina; d. February 14, 1810, Onslow Co, North Carolina, m. Charity **Jenkins**[5]

Johannes **Kleckley**,* b. 1760, Wurttenberg, Germany; d. South Carolina, m. Katerina **Wessinger**,* b. Germany; d. 1820, South Carolina[6]

Jacob **Hamiter**, b. 1764, South Carolina; d. September 21, 1816, m. Anna Barbara **Bickley***[6]

G-7

Philip **Jones**,* m. Rebecca **Wrench***; d. October 21, 1804, Wake City, North Carolina[3]

Vitus **Singer**, b. February 2, 1721, Stuttgart, Germany; d. July 15, 1803, Stuttgart, Germany, m. February 3, 1750, Christina Dorothea **Burkhardt**, b. August 6, 1724 Germany; d. June 1, 1762 Stuttgart, Germany[4]

Jacob **Zizmann**,* b. 1716, Germany; d. May 9, 1787, Stuttgart, Germany, m. Christina (Last Name Unknown)*[4]

James **Murray**,* m. Elizabeth **Edwards***[5]

Johann Sebastian **Hamiter**,* b. 1739, Baden-Wurttenberg, Germany; d. Richland Co., South Carolina[6]

G-8

Elias **Singer**,* b. December 30, 1688, Germany; d. January 10, 1754, Stuttgart, Germany, m. Anna Catherina **Elsasser**, b. December 20, 1687, Stuttgart, Germany; d. April 5, 1740, Stuttgart, Germany[4]

Johan George **Burkhardt**,* b. 1698, Germany, m. Rosina (Last Name Unknown)*[4]

G-9

Vitus **Elsasser**,* b. December 5, 1655, Stuttgart, Germany; d. November 12, 1743 Stuttgart, Germany, m. May 16, 1682, Ursula **Stoll**,* b. June 1, 1659, Stuttgart, Germany; d. November 30, 1695, Stuttgart, Germany[4]

Frances Cleveland

G+2

Children of Esther Cleveland and William Sidney ***Bosanquet:***

Marion Frances **Bosanquet**[1]
Philippa **Bosanquet**[1]

Children of Marion Cleveland and William Stanley ***Dell:***

Frances **Dell**[1]

Children of Marion Cleveland and John Harlan Amen:

Grover Cleveland **Amen**[1]

Children of Richard Folsom and Ellen (Gailor) Cleveland:

Anne Mary **Cleveland**[1]
Thomas Grover **Cleveland**[1]
Charlotte **Cleveland**[1]

Children of Richard Folsom and Jessie (Black) Cleveland:

Frances **Cleveland**[1]
George Maxwell **Cleveland**[1]
Margaret **Cleveland**[1]

Children of Francis Grover and Alice (Erdman):

Marion **Cleveland**[1]

G-1

Ruth **Cleveland**, b. October 3, 1891, New York, New York; d. January 7, 1904, Princeton, New Jersey[1]

Esther **Cleveland**, b. September 9, 1893, White House; d. June 25, 1980, New Hampshire, m. March 14, 1918, William Sidney **Bosanquet**[1]

Marion **Cleveland**, b. July 7, 1895, Buzzard's Bay, Mass.; d. March 1, 1960, New York, New York, m(1) November 25, 1917, William Stanley **Dell**, m(2) John Harlan **Amen**[1]

Richard Folsom **Cleveland**, b. October 28, 1897, Westland, New Jersey; d. January 10, 1974, Baltimore, Maryland, m. June 20, 1923, Memphis, Tenn. to Ellen **Gailor**[1]

Francis Grover **Cleveland**, b. October 28, 1903, Buzzard's Bay, Mass.; d. November 8, 1995, Wolfeboro, New Hampshire, m. June 20, 1925, Alice **Erdman**[1]

Frances Folsom, b. July 21, 1864, Buffalo, New York; d. October 29, 1947, Baltimore, Maryland, m. June 2, 1886, Stephen Grover Cleveland, b. March 18, 1837, Caldwell, New Jersey; d. June 24, 1908, Princeton, New Jersey[2, 21]

G-1

Oscar **Folsom**, b. November 8, 1837, Folsomdale, New York, m. September 2, 1863, Emma Cornelia **Harmon**, b. November 12, 1840, Hornellville, New York[2, 3]

G-2

John, b. **Folsom**, b. January 28, 1811, Warsaw, New York; d. May 19, 1886, m. Clarinda **Charnden**,* b. June 3, 1809; d. January 19, 1873[2]

Elisha **Harmon**, b. Eaton, New York; d. December 27, 1915, Princeton, New Jersey, m. April 27, 1836, Ruth **Rogers**, b. May 12, 1809, Hornellville, New York; d. March 6, 1887, Hornellville, New York[2, 3]

G-3

Asa **Folsom**, b. September 9, 1783, Gilmanton, New Hampshire; d. January 28, 1813, Warsaw, New York, m. Fanny **Bennett***[2]

Rawson **Harmon**, m. Lydia **Murdock**[2, 3]

James **Rogers**, b. 1787, Palmyra, New York, m. Mercy **Champlin**, b. September 19, 1783, Kingston, Rhode Island; d. 1857[2]

G-4

Abraham **Folsom**, b. April 2, 1748, New Hampshire; d. Gilmanton, New Hampshire, m. Elizabeth **Moody**,* b. March 13, 1756; d. July 31, 1838[2]

Anan **Harmon**, b. October 3, 1738, Mass.; d. May 14, 1802, Mass., m. Sarah **Rawson***[2, 3]

Samuel or Amos **Murdock**,* b. March 24, 1697, Roxbury, Mass.;

d. January 17, 1769, Windham, Conn., m. Submit **Throop**, b. December 25, 1706, Bristol, Conn.; d. October 17, 1784, Windham, Conn.[4]

Stephen **Champlin**, b. August 3, 1763, Kingston, Rhode Island; d. December 20, 1848, Conn., m. Elizabeth **Perry**, b. August 20, 1762, Kingston, Rhode Island; d. March 12, 1811[2, 5]

G-5

Daniel **Folsom**, b. 1704, m. Huldah **Eastman**, b. 1714, Salisbury, Mass.[2, 6]

Nathaniel **Harmon**, b. 1713; d. 1792, m. Elizabeth **Bridgeman**[2, 3]

Daniel **Throop**, b. 1669; d. December 9, 1737, m. Deborah **Macey**, b. 1676[4]

Stephen **Champlin**, b. September 29, 1734, Kingston, Rhode Island, m. Dinah **Browning**, b. September 10, 1736, South Kingston, Rhode Island; d. 1799, Rhode Island[2]

James Freeman **Perry**, b. January 23, 1732, South Kingston, Rhode Island; d. October 2, 1813, South Kingston, Rhode Island, m. Mercy **Hazard**, b. January 21, 1740, North Kingston, Rhode Island; d. June 9, 1802, South Kingston, Rhode Island[5, 7]

G-6

Abraham **Folsom**, b. April 4, 1678, Exeter, New Hampshire; d. 1740, Hampton, New Hampshire, m. Anna **Chase**[2]

John **Eastman**, b. August 24, 1675, Salisbury, Mass.; d. 1740, Salisbury, Mass., m. Huldah **Kingsbury**, b. August 16, 1680, Haverhill, Mass.; d. 1740[6]

Nathaniel **Harmon**, b. 1686, Mass.; d. 1763, m. Esther **Austin**, b. January 11, 1686, Mass.[2, 3]

James **Bridgeman**, m. Elizabeth **Allis**

William **Throop**, b. 1637; d. December 4, 1704, m. Mary **Chapman**, b. October 31, 1645[4]

George **Macey**,* b. 1620; d. August 17, 1693, m. Susanna **Street**[4]

Stephen **Champlin**, b. February 16, 1710, Narraganset, Rhode Island; d. July 27, 1771, Rhode Island, m. Mary **Hazard**, b. February 23, 1716; d. March 13, 1773[2, 7]

William **Browning**, b. 1693; d. 1773, m. 1728, Mary **Wilkinson**[2]

Benjamin **Perry**, b. 1677; d. 1748, m. Susanna **Barber**, b. October 23, 1697, Kingston, Rhode Island[5]

Oliver **Hazard**, b. 1710; d. 1772, m. 1736, Elizabeth **Raymond**, b. 1720; d. 1793[7, 8]

G-7

John **Folsom**, b. 1641, Hingham, Mass.; d. 1735, m. November 10, 1675, Abigail **Perkins**, b. April 12, 1655, Hampton, New Hampshire; d. Hampton, New Hampshire[2]

Aquila **Chase**, b. September 26, 1652, Mass., m. Esther **Bond**, b. September 25, 1655 Newbury, Mass.[2]

John **Eastman**, b. March 9, 1640, Salisbury, Mass.; d. March 25, 1770, Salisbury, Mass., m. Mary **Boynton**, b. July 23, 1648, Salisbury, Mass.[6, 14]

Samuel **Kingsbury**, b. 1650, Haverhill, Mass.; d. September 26, 1698, Haverhill, Mass., m. Huldah **Corliss**, b. November 18, 1661, Haverhill, Mass.; d. September 26, 1720, Haverhill, Mass.[6, 14, 15]

Nathaniel **Harmon**, b. 1654; d. 1712, m. Mary **Skinner**[2, 3]

Anthony **Austin**, b. 1636, England; d. 1708, Mass., m. Esther **Huggins**, b. March 17, 1643; d. 1698, Mass.[2, 3, 16, 17]

John **Bridgeman**, b. July 7, 1645, Springfield, Mass; d. April 7, 1712, Northampton, Mass., m. December 11, 1670, Mary **Sheldon**, b. 1654, Windsor, Conn.; d. April 20, 1728, Northampton, Mass.[9]

John **Allis**, b. March 5, 1642; d. 1691, m. Mary **Meekins**[4]

William **Throop**, b. 1613, Nottinghamshire, England; d. December 2, 1669, m. Isabel **Redshaw**,* b. 1617, Nottinghamshire, England; d. June 22, 1658, England[10]

Ralph **Chapman***b. December 9, 1615, Southwark, England; d. June 4, 1672, m. Lydia **Willis**,* b. 1618, England[4]

Nicholas **Street**, b. 1595, England; d. April 22, 1623, m. Ann **Poole**, b. England[4]

Jeffrey **Champlin**,* b. 1676, Kingston, Rhode Island; d. 1718, m. Hannah **Hazard**, b. 1677, Kingston, Rhode Island[2, 7]

Robert **Hazard**, m. Sarah **Borden**[2, 7]

William **Browning**, b. 1650; d. 1730, m. 1687, Rebecca **Wilbur**, b. 1662, Portsmouth, Rhode Island; d. March 18, 1728, Portsmouth, Rhode Island[2, 12]

William **Wilkinson**,* m. Dinah **Knight***[2]

Edward **Perry**,* b. 1630; d. 1695, m. Mary **Freeman***[5]

Moses **Barber**,* m. Susanna **West***[5]

George **Hazard**, b. 1662; d. 1743, m. Penelope **Arnold**, b. 1669; d. 1742[7]

Joshua **Raymond**, b. 1697, England; d. 1763, m. 1719, Elizabeth **Christopher**, b. 1698, England; d. 1730[8]

G-8

John **Folsom,*** b. 1615, England; d. 1681, m. Mary **Gilman**[2,13]

Abraham **Perkins**, b. 1613; d. 1681, m. Mary **Wyeth,*** b. 1618; d. 1706[4]

Aquila **Chase**, b. April 9, 1626, Chesham, England; d. December 27, 1670, Newberry, Mass., m. Ann **Wheeler**, b. 1620, England; d. Newberry, Mass.[2]

John **Bond**,* b. February 5, 1624, England, m. Esther **Blakely**,* b. England[4]

Roger **Eastman**,* b. England, m. Sarah **Smith***[6,14,15]

William **Boynton**,* m. Elizabeth **Jackson***[6,14,15]

Henry **Kingsbury**,* b. 1615, England; d. October 1, 1687, m. Susanna **Gage**,* b. 1617, England; d. February 21, 1678[6,14,15]

George **Corliss**,* b. 1617, England; d. October 19, 1686, m. Joanna **Davis**,* b. 1624, England; d. April 17, 1688[6,14,15]

John **Harmon**,* b. 1617, England; d. 1661, m. Elizabeth **Cummings***[2,7]

Joseph **Skinner**,* b. July 25, 1645; d. September 15, 1690, m. Mary **Filley***[2,7]

Richard **Austin**,* b. 1598, England; d. 1638, Mass., m. Elizabeth (Last Name Unknown)*[2,3,16,17]

John **Huggins**,* b. 1609; d. June 6, 1670, m. Bridget **Green**,* b. April 21, 1611; d. August 26, 1680[2,3,16,17]

James **Bridgeman***m. Sarah **Lyman***[9]

Isaac **Sheldon**, b. 1630; d. July 27, 1708, m. Mary **Woodford***[9]

William **Allis**,* m. Mary **Brownson***[4]

Thomas **Meekins**,* m. Sarah **Bell***[4]

Thomas **Throop**, b. England, m. Elizabeth **Smyth**,* b. England[10]

Nicholas **Street**, b. England, m. Susannah **Gilbert**, b. England[4]

William **Poole**, b. August 27, 1561, England; d. February 9, 1635, m. Marie **Periam**,* b. 1566, England; d. 1605[4]

Robert **Hazard**, b. England, m. Mary **Brownell**, b. England[7]

Thomas **Hazard**,* b. 1660; d. 1746, m. Susannah **Nichols**,* b. England[7]

Richard **Borden**, b. October 25, 1671, Portsmouth, Rhode Island, m. Innocent **Connell***[11]

Nathaniel **Browning**,* b. London, England; d. Portsmouth, Rhode Island, m. Sarah **Freeborn**,* b. 1632, Ipswich, Mass.; d. April 23, 1670, Portsmouth, Rhode Island[12]

Samuel **Wilbur**, m. Hannah **Porter***[12, 19, 20]

Robert **Hazard**, m. Mary **Brownell*** (Refer to Robert Hazard earlier in G-8 Frances **Cleveland** to continue their lines.)[7]

Caleb **Arnold**, b. 1644, England; d. 1729, m. Abigail **Wilbur**[4]

Joshua **Raymond**, b. 1660, England; d. 1704, m. Mercy **Sands**[8]

John **Christopher**, m. Elizabeth **Milford***[8]

G-9 ————————

Edward **Gilman**,* b. 1587, England; d. June 22, 1655, m. Mary **Clark**,* b. England[13]

John **Perkins**, b. 1583, England; d. September 26, 1654, m. Judith **Gater**[4]

Aquila **Chase**, b. August 14, 1580, Henbridge, England; d. July 9, 1643, Newbury, Mass., m. June 22, 1606, Sarah **Jellison**, b. November 10, 1588, London, England; d. August 16, 1643, Newbury, Mass.[2]

John **Wheeler**, b. 1591, Salisbury, England; d. August 29, 1670, Newbury, Mass., m. Ann or Agnes **Yeomans**,* b. 1590, Salisbury, England; d. August 15, 1682, Newbury, Mass.[4]

Ralph **Sheldon**, b. 1605, England; d. 1651, m. Barbara **Stone***[9]

William **Throop**,* b. England; d. England, m. Jennett **Fynningley**,* b. England; d. England[10]

Nicholas **Street**,* b. England; d. England, m. Mary (Last Name Unknown),* b. England; d. England[4]

William **Poole**,* b. England; d. England, m. Katherine **Popham**,* b. England; d. England[4]

Thomas **Hazard**,* b. June 5, 1618, England; d. 1680, m. Martha **Potter**, b. 1612, England; d. 1669, Portsmouth, Rhode Island[7]

Thomas **Brownell**, b. 1608, Yorkshire, England; d. September 24, 1665, Portsmouth, Rhode Island, m. 1638, Anna **Bourne**, b. July 16, 1607, Bobbingsworth, England; d. October 24. 1666, Portsmouth, Rhode Island[18]

John **Borden**,* b. September 5, 1640, Portsmouth, Rhode Island; d. July 4, 1716, Portsmouth, Rhode Island, m. Mary **Earle***[11]

Samuel **Wilbur (Wilbore)**,* b. 1596, Braintree, England; d. 1656, Essex, England, m. Ann **Bradford**,* b. England; d. England[12, 19, 20]

Benedict **Arnold**, b. England; d. 1678, England, m. Demaris **Wescott**, b. England; d. England[4]

Samuel **Wilbur**,* m. Hannah **Porter*** (Refer to Samuel Wilbur G-8 Frances **Cleveland** to continue their lines.)[12, 19, 20]

Joshua **Raymond**,* b. 1639, England; d. England, m. Elizabeth **Smith**,* b. England; d. England[8]

James **Sands**, b. England; d. England, m. Sarah **Walker**, b. England; d. England[8]

Christopher **Christopher**, b. England; d. England, m. Elizabeth **Brewster**, b. England; d. England[8]

G-10

Henry **Perkins**, b. 1536, England; d. April 5, 1609, England, m. Elizabeth **Sawbridge**,* b. 1541, Hillmorton, England; d. 1603, Hillmorton, England[4]

Michael **Gater**,* b. England; d. England, m. Elizabeth **Bailey**,* b. England; d. England[4]

Richard **Chase**, b. July 26, 1562, Henbridge, England; d. Henbridge, England, m. Joan **Bishop**,* b. Henbridge, England; d. May 4, 1597, Henbridge, England[2]

John **Jellison**,* b. England; d. England, m. Martha or Margaret (Last Name Unknown)*[4]

Dominic **Wheeler**,* b. 1565, Salisbury, England; d. January 12, 1616, Salisbury, England, m. Mercy **Jelly**,* b. 1569, Salisbury, England; d. 1615, Salisbury, England[4]

Arthur **Sheldon**,* b. 1575, England; d. 1607, England[9]

Robert **Brownell**, b. 1576, Rawmarsh Parish, England, m. Mary **Wilson**,* b. Ryecroft, England[18]

Richard **Bourne**, b. June 18, 1564, Bobbingsworth, England; d. March 11, 1632, Marshfield, Mass., m. Judith **Cowper**, b. 1578, London, England; d. 1660, Mass.[1]

William **Arnold**,* b. England; d. England, m. Christopher **Peake**,* b. England; d. England[4]

Stukeley **Wescott**,* b. 1592, England; d. 1677, England, m. Julian **Marchantel**,* b. England; d. England[4]

Henry **Sands**,* b. England; d. England, m. Elizabeth **Goffe**,* b. England; d. England[8]

John **Walker**,* b. England; d. England, m. Katherine **Hutchinson**,* b. England; d. England[8]

Jonathan **Brewster**, b. England; d. England, m. Lucretia **Oldham**,* b. England; d. England[8]

G-11

Thomas **Perkins**, b. 1510, England; d. England, m. Alice **Kebble**,* b. 1512, England; d. England[4]

Thomas **Chase**,* b. April 22, 1520, Henbridge, England; d. June

29, 1586, England, m. Elizabeth **Bouchieu,*** b. Henbridge, England; d. October 2, 1569, Chesham, England[2]

Thomas **Brownell,*** b. 1535, Rotherham, England; d. 1602, England, m. October 20, 1560, Margaret **Gilberthorpe,*** b. 1539, Rotherham, England; d. October 15, 1585, York, England[18]

William **Bourne,*** b. 1527, Bobbingsworth, England; d. April 29, 1591, England, m. Margaret **Ryse,*** b. 1531, Potten, England; d. December 29, 1594, Essex, England[18]

John **Cowper,*** b. London, England; d. London, England, m. Elizabeth **Ironsides,*** b. England; d. England[18]

William **Brewster*** (Mayflower Pilgrim), b. England; d. Mass., m. Mary (Last Name Unknown),* b. England; d. Mass.[8]

G-12

Henry **Perkins,*** b. England; d. England, m. Elizabeth (Last Name Unknown),* b. England; d. England[4]

Hillary Clinton

G+1

Chelsea Victoria **Clinton**, b. February 27, 1980, Little Rock, Arkansas[1]

Hillary Diane Rodham, b. October 26, 1947, Chicago, Illinois, m. William Jefferson Clinton, b. August 19, 1946, Hope, Arkansas[1, 3]

G-2

Hugh Ellsworth **Rodham**, b. ca. 1910; d. 1993, Little Rock, Arkansas, m. Dorothy **Howell***[1]

G-3

Hugh **Rodham (Roddam)**, b. August 16, 1879, Durham, England; d. 1965, m. Hannah **Jones***[2]

G-4

Jonathan **Rodham (Roddam)**, b. June 7, 1843, Durham, England, m. Isabella **Bell**,* b. September 24, 1849, Durham, England[2]

G-5

Joseph **Rodham (Roddam)**, b. 1817, Durham, England, m. Elizabeth **Scurfield**, b. 1817, Durham, England[2]

G-6

Jonathan **Rodham (Roddam)**, b. September 26, 1779, Durham, England, m. November 25, 1805, Ann **Parkinson***[2]

Thomas **Scurfield**, b. 1789, Durham, England, m. May 29, 1813, Margaret **Charlton**,* b. 1795, Durham, England[2]

G-7

Joseph **Rodham (Roddam)**,* b. 1755, Durham, England, m. May 21, 1774, Dorothy **Bell**,* b. 1755, Durham, England

John **Scurfield**,* b. 1742, Durham, England; d. May 20, 1800, m. August 19, 1775, Elizabeth **Graham**,* b. 1754, Durham, England

Fenwick **Charlton**,* m. Alice **Stodart***

GRACE COOLIDGE

G+2

Children of John and Florence (Trumbull) Coolidge:

Cynthia **Coolidge**, m. S. Edward **Jeter**[1]

Lydia **Coolidge**, m. Jeremy Whitman **Sayles**[1]

G+1

John **Coolidge**, b. September 7, 1906, Northampton, Mass., m. Florence **Trumbull**[1]

Calvin **Coolidge**, b. April 13, 1908, Northampton, Mass.; d. July 7, 1924, Washington, D.C.[1]

Grace Anna Goodhue, b. January 3, 1879, Burlington, Vermont; d. July 8, 1957, Northampton, Mass., m. October 4, 1905, Calvin Coolidge, b. July 4, 1872, Plymouth, Vermont; d. January 5, 1933, Northampton, Mass.[2, 12]

G-1

Andrew Issacher **Goodhue**, b. January 15, 1848, Hancock, New Hampshire; d. Burlington, Vermont, m. April 7, 1870, Lemira **Barrett**, b. 1848, Nashua, New Hampshire; d. Burlington, Vermont[2]

G-2

Benjamin **Goodhue**, b. July 17, 1818, Hancock, New Hampshire; d. June 21, 1888, Hancock, New Hampshire, m. November 23, 1841, Caroline **Andrews**, b. June 22, 1820, New Boston, New Hampshire; d. April 21, 1888, Hancock, New Hampshire[2, 3]

Townsend **Barrett**, January 15, 1815, Ashburnham, Mass.; d.

Worcester, Mass., m. February 18, 1830, Sarah **Wheeler**,* b. April 11, 1818, Worcester, Mass.[2]

G-3

Ebenezer **Goodhue**, b. May 31, 1778, Ipswich, Mass.; d. August 10, 1869, m. 1802, Mehitable **Knight**, b. September 14, 1782, Antrim, New Hampshire; d. December 25, 1827[2, 3]

Issacher **Andrews**, b. October 16, 1789, New Boston, New Hampshire; d. May 29, 1862, New Boston, New Hampshire, m. October 12, 1811, Abigail **Manning**,* b. May 12, 1785, New Hampshire; d. January 12, 1857, New Boston, New Hampshire[2, 4]

Joel **Barrett**, b. Mass.; d. Mass., m. Mercy (Last Name Unknown)*[2]

G-4

Ebenezer **Goodhue**, b. July 15, 1754, Ipswich, Mass.; d. November 26, 1853 Hancock, New Hampshire, m. Sarah **Potter**,* b. Ipswich, Mass.[2, 3]

Benjamin **Knight**, b. December 25, 1751, Middletown, Mass.; d. July 5, 1827, Mass., m. Lydia **Lake**, b. May 13, 1749, Petersboro, New Hampshire; d. January 2, 1843, Mass.[2]

Joseph **Andrews**, b. April 23, 1757, Essex Co., Mass.; d. October 18, 1834, Mass., m. Margaret **Ober**, b. January 22, 1765, Manchester, Mass.; d. Mass.[2, 4]

Joel **Barrett**, b. November 30, 1737, Chelmsford, Mass.; d. Mass.[2]

G-5

John **Goodhue**, b. January 9, 1721, Ipswich, Mass.; d. January 15, 1815, m. September 20, 1743, Elizabeth **Lamson**, b. 1725, Ipswich, Mass.; d. November 1, 1811, Ipswich, Mass.[2, 3]

Jonathan **Knight**, b. May 4, 1725, Middletown, Mass., m. Phebe **Perkins**, February 3, 1732, Mass.[2, 5]

Eleazer **Lake**, b. September 12, 1724, Mass.; d. March 29, 1796, Mass., m. Sarah **Perkins**[2, 5]

Joseph **Andrews**, b. January 18, 1729, Ipswich, Mass.; d. December 30, 1796, Ipswich, Mass., m. Rachel **Burnham**, b. August 2, 1730, Ipswich, Mass.; d. February 2, 1809[2, 4]

Benjamin **Ober**, b. February 21, 1725, Mass.; d. November 27, 1818, Mass., m. September 20, 1750, Anna **Foster**, b. July 19, 1728, Manchester, Mass.; d. Mass.[2, 4]

Thomas **Barrett**, b. 1687, Mass.; d. July 9, 1761, Mass., m. Rachel

Burge, b. December 21, 1691, Chelmsford, Mass.; d. April 29, 1785, Chelmsford, Mass.[2]

G-6

John **Goodhue**, b. August 12, 1680, Ipswich, Mass.; d. Mass., m. Sarah **Sherwin**, b. October 7, 1683, Ipswich, Mass.; d. Mass.[2, 3]

John **Lamson**, b. November 4, 1698, Ipswich, Mass.; d. Mass., m. Elizabeth **Day**, b. Mass.; d. Mass.[2, 5]

Benjamin **Knight**, b. February 8, 1693, Topsfield, Mass.; d. Mass., m. January 8, 1719, Ruth **Fuller**, b. July 5, 1697, Salem, Mass.; d. April 28, 1774, Mass.[2]

Robert **Perkins**, b. February 28, 1696, Topsfield, Mass.; d. Mass., m. February 24, 1719, Elizabeth **Towne**, b. Mass.; d. Mass.[2, 5]

Eleazer **Lake**, b. 1686, Mass.; d. Mass., m. Lydia **Forde**, b. 1687, Mass.; d. Mass.[2]

Robert **Perkins**,* m. Elizabeth **Towne*** (Refer to Robert **Perkins** earlier in G-6 Grace **Coolidge** to continue their lines.)[2, 5]

Joseph **Andrews**, b. 1682, Ipswich, Mass.; d. Mass., m. November 1, 1704, Hannah **Butler**, b. September 3, 1685, Tisbury, Mass.; d. Mass.[2, 4]

Thomas **Burnham**, b. 1708, Mass.; d. Mass., m. October 3, 1728, Hannah **Cogswell**, b. Mass.; d. Mass.[2]

Richard **Ober**, b. March 1, 1684, Beverly, Mass.; d. February 8, 1724, Canso, Nova Scotia, m. Priscilla **Woodbury**, b. June 23, 1687, Mass.[2, 4]

Israel **Foster**, b. February 27, 1702, Beverly, Mass.; d. 1745, Salem, Mass., m. Anna **Woodbury**, b. September 5, 1703, Manchester, Mass.; d. 1774, Manchester, Mass.[2]

Moses **Barrett**, b. March 25, 1662, Braintree, Mass.; d. November 28, 1743, Chelmsford, Mass., m. Anna or Hannah **Smith**, b. 1664, Dorcester, England; d. April 6, 1745, Chelmsford, Mass.[2, 4]

John **Burge**, m. Tryall **Thayer**[2, 6]

G-7

Joseph **Goodhue**, b. 1639, Ipswich, Mass.; d. September 2, 1697, Ipswich, Mass., m. July 13, 1661, Sarah **Whipple**, b. November 3, 1641, Bocking, England; d. July 23, 1681, Ipswich, Mass.[2, 3]

John **Sherwin**,* b. 1644, Ipswich, Mass.; d. October 15, 1726, Ipswich, Mass., m. November 25, 1667, Frances **Loomis**,* b. 1646, Ipswich, England; d. 1690, Ipswich, Mass.[2, 5]

John **Lamson**, b. November 21, 1669, Ipswich, Mass.; d. September 1, 1760, Mass., m. Abigail **Adams**, b. 1669, Ipswich, Mass.; d. April 3, 1753, Mass[2, 5]

John **Day**,* b. February 17, 1665, Ipswich, Mass.; d. February 28, 1722, Ipswich, Mass., m. Elizabeth **Kimball**[5]

Philip **Knight**, b. December 27, 1669, Topsfield, Mass.; d. August 19, 1696, Mass., m. Rebecca **Towne**, b. February 2, 1668, Topsfield, Mass.; d. Mass.[2, 4]

Thomas **Fuller**, b. May 3, 1671, Salem, Mass.; d. 1753, Middletown, Mass., m. May 3, 1695, Elizabeth **Andrews**,* b. 1675, Salem, Mass.; d. Middletown, Mass.[2]

Thomas **Perkins**, b. November 4, 1667, Ipswich, Mass.; d. 1722, Mass., m. June 6, 1683, Sarah **Wallis**, b. July 24, 1658, Ipswich, Mass.; d. June 1, 1683, Mass.[2, 5]

Samuel **Towne**, b. February 11, 1673, Topsfield, Mass.; d. May 22, 1714, Mass., m. October 20, 1696, Elizabeth **Knight**, b. January 25, 1676, Topsfield, Mass.; d. Mass.[2, 5]

Henry **Lake**,* b. 1650; d. May 22, 1733, m. May 9, 1681, Priscilla **Wilde**, b. April 6, 1658, Topsfield, Mass.; d. March 23, 1688, Topsfield, Mass.[2]

Matthew **Forde**, b. 1661, Boxford, Mass.; d. Mass., m. Lydia **Griffin**, b. June 21, 1664, Haverhill, Mass.; d. Bradford, Mass.[4]

Samuel **Towne**,* m. Elizabeth **Knight** (Refer to Samuel **Towne*** earlier in G-7 Grace **Coolidge** to continue their lines.)[5]

Joseph **Andrews**, b. 1657, Ipswich, Mass.; d. 1724, Mass., m. Sarah **Ring**[2, 4]

Thomas **Butler**, b. 1654, Tisbury, Mass.; d. October 20, 1732, Mass., m. Jemima **Daggett**, b. 1666, Edgartown, Mass.; d. Mass.[2]

John **Burnham**, b. April 8, 1671, Chebacco, Mass.; d. 1746, Mass., m. April 13, 1693, Sarah **Choate**, b. 1672, Ipswich, Mass.; d. Mass.[2]

John **Cogswell**, b. May 12, 1665, Chebacco, Mass.; d. 1710, Mass., m. Hannah **Goodhue**, b. July 4, 1673, Ipswich, Mass.; d. December 25, 1742, Mass.[2]

Richard **Ober**, November 21, 1641, Abbotsbury, England; d. March 4, 1716, Beverly, Mass., m. December 26, 1671, Abigail **Woodbury**, b. August 28, 1655, Beverly, Mass.; d. January 28, 1741, Beverly, Mass.[2, 4]

Peter **Woodbury**, b. March 28, 1653, Salem, Mass.; d. 1695, Mass., m. 1667, Sarah **Dodge**, b. 1641, Beverly, Mass.; d. September 11, 1726, Mass.[2]

John **Foster**, b. September 15, 1680, Salem, Mass.; d. Mass., m. March 7, 1704; Margaret **Ware**, b. June 6, 1683, Wrentham, Mass.; d. Mass.[2]

Joseph **Woodbury**, b. September 20, 1659, Beverly, Mass.; d. 1714, Mass., m. December 19, 1687, Elizabeth **West**, b. September 23, 1666, Beverly, Mass.; d. October 27, 1714, Manchester, Mass.[2]

Thomas **Barrett**, b. 1634, Braintree, Mass.; d. December 8, 1702, Mass., m. Frances **Woolderson**,* b. 1634, Braintree, Mass.; d. July 21, 1694. Chelmsford, Mass.[2, 5, 7]

John **Smith**, b. 1629, Dorcester, Mass.; d. September 17, 1678, Dorcester, Mass., m. 1657, Miriam **Deane**, b. 1633, Dorcester, Mass.; d. October 19, 1706, Dorcester, Mass.[2, 5]

John **Burge**, b. 1601, London, England; d. October 22, 1679, Dorcester, Mass., m. Rebecca **Upham**[2, 6]

Shadrack **Thayer**, b. 1629, Thornbury, Mass.; d. October 19, 1678, Mass., m. Mary **Barrett**, b. 1633, Braintree, Mass.; d. April 2, 1658, Mass.[2, 6]

G-8

William **Goodhue**,* b. 1612 or 1613, England; d. 1700, Ipswich, Mass., m. Margery **Watson**, b. 1617, England; d. August 28, 1668, Ipswich, Mass.[2, 3]

John **Whipple**, b. August 29, 1596, England; d. June 30, 1669, m. Sarah **Hawkins**, b. 1600, England; d. 1658[2, 3]

Edward **Loomis**,* b. 1620, Bocking, England; d. Ipswich, Mass.[5]

John **Lamson**, b. 1642; d. 1717, m. December 17, 1668, Martha **Perkins**, b. 1649; d. 1728[2]

Nathaniel **Adams**,* b. 1641; d. April 11, 1715, m. June 30, 1668, Mercy **Dickinson**,* b. 1646; d. December 12, 1735[2]

Richard **Kimball**,* b. 1622, Rattlesden, England; d. May 20, 1676, Wenham, Mass., m. Mary **Cooley**,* b. 1628, Rattlesden, England; d. September 2, 1672, Springfield, Mass.[5]

Philip **Knight**,* b. 1646, m. Margaret **Wilkins**,* b. 1648[2, 4]

Edmund **Towne**, b. 1628, m. Mary **Browning***[2, 4]

Thomas **Fuller**,* b. April 30, 1644; d. 1721, m. Ruth **Richardson**,* b. April 14, 1647[2]

Thomas **Perkins**, b. April 28, 1622, Hillmorton, England; d. May 7, 1686, m. Phoebe **Gould**, b. 1620, England[2, 5]

Nicholas **Wallis**,* b. 1632, Ipswich, Mass.; d. February 1, 1711, Ipswich, Mass., m. Sarah **Bradstreet**,* b. 1638[2, 5]

Edmund **Towne**,* m. Mary **Browning*** (Refer to Edmund **Towne** earlier in G-8 to continue their lines.)[2, 4]

Philip **Knight**,* m. Margaret **Wilkins***[2, 4]

John **Wilde**,* b. 1620, England; d. May 14, 1705, Topsfield, Mass., m. Priscilla **Gould**, b. 1620, England; d. Topsfield, Mass.[2]

Timothy **Forde**,* b. 1611, England; d. August 28, 1684, m. Eliza (Last Name Unknown),* b. 1615, England; d. July 25, 1681[2]

John **Griffin**,* b. England, m. Lydia **Shatswell**,* b. England[4]

John **Andrews**,* b. 1618, England; d. April 20, 1708, m. Jane **Jordan**,* b. 1618, England[2, 4]

Daniel **Ring**,* b. 1630, m. Mary **Kinsman***[2, 4]

John **Butler**,* m. Mary **Lynde***[2]

Thomas **Daggett**,* b. 1630; d. 1691, m. Hannah **Mayhew**, b. June 15, 1635[2, 8, 11]

John **Burnham**,* b. 1648, Chebacco, Mass.; d. January 12, 1704, Chebacco, Mass., m. Elizabeth **Wells**,* b. 1648[2]

John **Choate**,* b. 1624; d. December 4, 1695, m. Ann (Last Name Unknown),* b. 1637; d. February 6, 1727[2]

William **Cogswell**, b. 1619, England; d. December 15, 1700, m. Susannah **Hawks**,* b. 1633[2]

William **Goodhue**,* b. 1645; d. October 12, 1712, m. Hannah **Dade***[2]

John **Ober**,* b. February 19, 1613, England; d. November 12, 1640, m. Elizabeth **Butcher**,* b. 1618, England[2]

Nicholas **Woodbury**, b. 1617, England; d. May 29, 1686, m. 1651 Anna **Palgrave**, b. October 29, 1626; d. June 10, 1701[2]

Humphrey **Woodbury**, b. England; d. 1686, m. Elizabeth (Last Name Unknown),* b. 1614; d. 1689[2]

Richard **Dodge**,* b. 1602, England; d. June 15, 1671, m. Edith (Last Name Unknown),* b. 1603; d. June 27, 1677 or 1678[2]

John **Foster**,* b. 1647; d. 1714, m. Mary **Stuart**,* b. 1650[2]

Robert **Ware**,* b. August 1, 1653; d. September 16, 1727, m. Sarah **Metcalf**, December 7, 1648; d. April 13, 1718[2]

Nicholas **Woodbury**,* m. Anna **Palgrave*** (Refer to Nicholas **Woodbury** earlier in G-8 Grace **Coolidge** to continue their lines.)[2]

Thomas **West**,* b. 1642; d. March 8, 1723, m. Elizabeth **Jackson**,* b. 1642; d. October 12, 1708[2]

Thomas **Barrett**,* b. 1602, England; d. October 6, 1668, Chelmsford, Mass., m. Margaret **Huntington**,* b. 1606, England; d. July 8, 1681[2, 5]

John **Smith**,* b. 1600, England, m. Dorothy (Last Name Unknown),* b. 1600, England[2]

Stephen **Deane**,* b. 1606, England; d. October 6, 1634, Plymouth, Mass., m. Elizabeth **Ring**,* b. February 23, 1602, England; d. December 28, 1687, Plymouth, Mass.[2, 5]

Robert **Burge**,* b. England, m. Alice (Last Name Unknown),* b. England[6]

George **Upham**,* b. England[6]

Thomas **Thayer**,* b. August 16, 1596, England; d. June 2, 1665, m. Margery **Wheeler**, b. 1597, England; d. February 11, 1642[6]

Thomas **Barrett**,* m. Margaret **Huntington*** (Refer to Thomas **Barrett** earlier in G-8 Grace **Coolidge** to continue their lines.)[2]

G-9

Matthew **Whipple**,* b. 1566, Bocking, England, m. Joanna (Last Name Unknown),* b. Bocking, England[2, 3]

William **Lamson**,* b. 1616, England; d. January 1, 1658, Ipswich, Mass., m. Sarah **Ayers**,* b. 1620, England; d. 1692, Ipswich, Mass.[2, 5]

John **Perkins**, b. December 23, 1583, Hillmorton, England; d. September 29, 1654, Ipswich, Mass., m. Judith **Gater**, b. March 19, 1588, Hillmorton, England[2, 5]

Zaccheus **Gould**, b. 1589, Hemel, England; d. November 13, 1668, Topsfield, Mass., m. Phebe **Deacon**, b. April 3, 1597, Hemel, England; d. September 20, 1663, Topsfield, England[2, 5]

William **Towne**, b. March 18, 1600, England; d. April 30, 1685, Mass., m. Joanna **Blessing**, b. 1600, Norfolk, England; d. June 22, 1675, Topsfield, England[5]

Zaccheus **Gould**,* m. Phebe **Deacon*** (Refer to Zaccheus **Gould** earlier in G-9 to continue their lines.)[2, 5]

Governor Thomas **Mayhew**,* b. 1593, Tisbury, England, m. Jane **Gallion**,* b. 1612, England; d. Medford, Mass.[9, 10, 11]

John **Cosgwell**,* b. 1592, Westbury, England; d. November 29, 1669, m. Elizabeth **Thompson**,* b. 1594, Westbury, England; d. January 2, 1676[2, 4]

William **Woodbury**,* b. 1599, South Petherton, England; d. January 29, 1676, Beverly, Mass., m. Elizabeth **Patch**,* b. April 16, 1593, South Petherton, England; d. November 9, 1676, Beverly, Mass.[2]

Richard **Palgrave**,* b. January 29, 1597, Pulham, England; d. March 30, 1630, Norfolk, England, m. Joan **Harris**,* b. 1601, Norfolk, England; d. 1637[2]

John **Woodbury**,* b. 1579, South Petherton, England; d. 1641, Salem, Mass., m. June 21, 1596, Joan **Humphrey**,* b. 1579, Budleigh, England; d. June 5, 1609, Bulescombe, England[2]

Michael **Metcalf**,* b. August 29, 1620, Norwich, England; d. March 27, 1664, Denham, Mass., m. Mary **Fairbanks**,* b. April 18, 1622, England; d. Dedham, Mass.[2]

Abell **Wheeler**,* b. May 2, 1568, Thornbury, England; d. 1612, Thornbury, England, m. Jane **Shepherd**,* b. 1567, England; d. 1629, England[11]

G-10

Henry **Perkins**, b. 1536, Hillmorton, England; d. 1609, England, m. Elizabeth **Sawbridge**,* b. 1538, Hillmorton, England; d. 1603, Hillmorton, England[2, 5]

Michael **Gater**,* b. 1562, Hillmorton, England, m. Elizabeth **Bailey**,* b. England[2, 5]

Richard **Gould**,* b. 1553, Bovington, England; d. 1604, Chesham, England, m. Elizabeth **Young**,* b. England; d. England[2, 5]

Thomas **Deacon**,* b. 1573, Corner Hall, England, m. Martha **Field**,* b. February 15, 1579, Hemel, England[2, 5]

Richard **Towne**,* b. December 12, 1568, Braceley, England; d. February 9, 1572, Braceley, England, m. Ann **Denton**,* b. 1575, England; d. May 10, 1630, England[2, 4]

William **Blessing**,* b. 1575, Norfolk, England; d. England, m. Joan **Preaste**,* b. England; d. England[4]

G-11

Thomas **Perkins**,* b. 1510, England; d. 1592, England, m. Alice **Kebble**,* b. 1512, England; d. England[2, 5]

MARY GENEVA (MAMIE) EISENHOWER

G+2

Children of John Sheldon and Barbara Jean (Thompson) Eisenhower:

Dwight David **Eisenhower**, b. March 31, 1948, West Point, New York, m. Julie **Nixon**, daughter of President Richard Milhous and Patricia (**Ryan**) **Nixon**.[1]

Barbara Ann **Eisenhower**, b. May 30, 1949, West Point, New York, m(1) Fernando **Echavarria**, m(2) Wolfgang **Flottl**[1]

Susan Elaine **Eisenhower**, b. December 31, 1951, Fort Knox, Kentucky, m(1) Alexander Hugh **Bradshaw**, m(2) John Fraser **Mahon**, m(3) Rvald **Sagdeyev**[1]

Mary Jean **Eisenhower**, b. December 21, 1955, Washington, D.C., m(1) John Brewton **Millard**, m(2) Kenneth **Moore**, m(3) Clifton **Windham**, m(4) Ralph **Atwater**[1]

G+1

Doud Dwight **Eisenhower**, b. September 24, 1917, San Antonio, Texas; d. January 2, 1921, Fort Mead, Maryland[1]

John Sheldon **Eisenhower**, b. 1922, Denver, Colorado, m. July 10, 1947, Barbara Jean **Thompson**[1]

Mamie Doud, b. November 14, 1896, Boone, Iowa; d. November 1, 1979, m. July 1, 1916, Dwight David Eisenhower, b. October 14, 1890, Denison, Texas; d. March 28, 1969, Washington, D.C.[1,2]

G-1

John Sheldon **Doud**, b. November 18, 1870, Rome, New York; d.

June 23, 1951, Denver, Colorado, m. August 10, 1894, Elvera Mathilda **Carlson**, b. May 13, 1878, Boone, Iowa; d. September 28, 1960, Denver, Colorado[2]

G-2

Royal Houghton **Doud**, b. February 6, 1838, Rome, New York; d. November 13, 1901, Chicago, Illinois, m. Mary Cornelia **Sheldon**, b. June 18, 1840, Martinberg, New York; d. January 8, 1908, Boone, Iowa[2]

Carl Severin **Jeremiasson**, b. July 17, 1841, Halland Co., Sweden; d. December 22, 1908, Boone, Iowa, m. March 27, 1868, Johanna Maria **Andersdotter**, b. August 1, 1841, Fjarar, Sweden; d. July 16, 1906, Boone, Iowa[2]

G-3

Eli **Doud**, b. December 15, 1799, Amsterdam, New York; d. 1876, m. 1820, Maria **Riggs**, b. 1807, Oneida Co., New York; d. January 4, 1895[2]

James Henry **Sheldon**, b. January 20, 1816, Martinberg, New York; d. September 4, 1871, Martinberg, New York, m. Susan, m. **Hill***[2]

Jeremias **Petersson**,* b. April 28, 1811, Traslov, Sweden, m. Inger Lena **Jonsdotter**,* b. February 7, 1806, Rolfstor, Sweden; d. November 24, 1859, Dagsas, Sweden[2]

Anders **Andersson**, b. March 28, 1793, Fjarar, Sweden; d. November 2, 1880, m. June 8, 1834, Brita **Larsdotter**, b. June 12, 1812, Forlanda, Sweden[2]

G-4

Benjamin **Doud**, b. May 10, 1761, Middletown, Conn.; d. January 6, 1852, m. Maria **Savage***[2]

George **Riggs**, b. December 4, 1786, Oxford, Conn.; d. July 24, 1857, m. Phoebe **Caniff***[2]

Asa Lord **Sheldon**, b. September 29, 1781, Providence, Rhode Island; d. November 8, 1869, m. November 18, 1807, Harriett **Holmes**,* b. November 2, 1789, Duchess Co., New York; d. January 21, 1869[2]

Andersolo **Fosson**, b. Sweden; d. Sweden, m. Elin **Monsdotter**, b. Sweden; d. Sweden[2]

Lars **Nilsson**, b. Sweden; d. Sweden, m. Gunnhild **Andersdotter**, b. Sweden; d. Sweden[2]

G-5

Richard **Doud**, b. 1724, Conn., m. 1746, Phoebe **Foster**,* b. December 30, 1721, Middletown, Conn.[2]

James **Riggs**, b. November 9, 1758; d. September 22, 1839, m. February 25, 1778, Sarah **Clark**, b. August 7, 1757, Turin, New York[2]

James **Sheldon**, b. April 9, 1757, Rhode Island; d. June 18, 1819, New York, m. Mary **Lord**[2]

G-6

David **Doud**, b. 1685, Conn.; d. 1740, m. September 24, 1718, Mary **Cornwall**, August 25, 1700, Middletown, Conn.[2]

John **Riggs**, b. August 31, 1735; d. 1825, m. Abigail **Peat**, b. 1739[2]

George **Clark**, b. May 4, 1727; d. March 12, 1799, m. Sarah **Outman**[2]

Rev. James **Sheldon**, b. December 19, 1728, Providence, Rhode Island; d. December 5, 1819, New York, m. Diadem **Perry***[2]

Asa **Lord**, b. 1736, m. Abigail **Mumford**, b. August 27, 1726[2]

G-7

John **Doud**, b. May 24, 1650, Guilford, Conn.; d. 1712, Madison, Conn., m. 1688, Mary **Bartlett**,* b. Guilford, Conn.[2]

John **Cornwall**, b. August 13, 1671; d. 1748, m. March 23, 1699, Mary **Hilton**, b. 1673, Middletown, Conn.; d. Middletown, Conn.[2]

John **Riggs**, b. December 17, 1712; d. May 10, 1777, m. October 29, 1734, Hannah **Johnson**[2]

Richard **Peat**, b. August 30, 1696, m. 1724, Sarah **Curtis**, b. July 28, 1705[2]

George **Clark**, b. 1707; d. September 28, 1754, m. Abigail **Law**, b. March 12, 1708[2]

John **Outman**,* m. Elizabeth **Janes**[2]

Timothy **Sheldon**, b. March 1, 1689, m. Rebecca (Last Name Unknown)*

Eleazer **Lord**, b. December 23, 1699, Saybrook, Conn.; d. March 7, 1786, m. Zervia **Leffingwell**[2]

Thomas **Mumford**, b. September 14, 1707, m. Abigail **Chesebrough**[2]

G-8

Henry **Doud**,* b. England; d. 1668, Guilford, Conn., m. Elizabeth (Last Name Unknown)*[2]

John **Cornwall**,* b. 1640; d. November 2, 1707, m. Martha **Peck***[2]

John **Hilton**,* b. 1646, Wethersfield, Conn.; d. 1686, Middletown, Conn.[2]

Ebenezer **Riggs**, b. October 15, 1678 Derby, Conn.; d. May 11, 1712 Derby, Conn., m. Lois **Hawkins***[2]

Ebenezer **Johnson**, b. February 27, 1687; d. 1751, m. Elizabeth **Hines**, b. 1690; d. January 18, 1760[2]

Benjamin **Peat**, b. 1665; d. 1704, m. Priscilla **Fairchild**, b. April 20, 1667[2]

Stephen **Curtis**,* b. August 24, 1673, Woodbury, Conn., m. Sarah **Minor**,* b. June 19, 1628[2]

George **Clark**,* m. Mary **Coley***[2]

Jonathan **Law**, b. 1637; d. January 9, 1711 or 1712, m. 1664, Abigail **Andrews**, September 25, 1724, Milford, Conn.[2]

William **Janes**,* m. Sarah **Clark***[2]

Timothy **Sheldon**,* b. March 29, 1661; d. 1744, m. Sarah **Bascom***[2]

Benjamin **Lord**,* b. March 3, 1666; d. November 29, 1713, m. Elizabeth **Pratt**,* b. April 3, 1673; d. 1714[2]

Thomas **Leffingwell**, b. 1674; d. 1733, m. Lydia **Tracy**[2]

Thomas **Mumford**, b. April 1, 1687, m. June 3, 1705, Hannah **Remington**[2]

Samuel **Chesebrough**,* m. Abigail **Ingraham***[2]

G-9

Samuel **Riggs**, b. 1640, Milford, Conn.; d. 1738, m. Sarah **Baldwin**, b. 1649, England[2]

Ebenezer **Johnson**,* m. Elizabeth **Wooster**[2]

John **Hines**,* m. Mary **Fenn**[2]

Richard **Law**,* b. England; d. 1687, Stamford, Conn., m. Margaret **Kilbourn**, b. 1607, England; d. Stamford, Conn.[2]

Samuel **Andrews**, b. January 29, 1655 or 1656, m. Abigail **Treat**[2]

Thomas **Leffingwell**, b. 1649; d. 1724, m. Mary **Bushnell**[2]

Solomon **Tracy**, m. Sarah **Huntington**, b. 1654, Saybrook, Conn.; d. 1683[2]

Thomas **Mumford**, m. Abigail (Last Name Unknown)*[2]

John **Remington**,* m. Abigail **Richmond***

G-10

Edward **Riggs**,* b. 1614, England; d. 1668, Newark, New Jersey, m. Elizabeth **Roosa***[2]

Richard **Baldwin**, b. 1622, England; d. Conn., m. Elizabeth **Alsop**[2]

Edward **Wooster**,* m. Tabitha **Tomlinson**[2]

Benjamin **Fenn**, b. 1640, Conn.; d. 1689, m. Mehitable **Gunn**[2]

Thomas **Kilbourn**,* b. Cambridgeshire, England, m. Frances **Moody***[2]

Samuel **Andrews**, b. 1621, England; d. June 21, 1701, m. September 22, 1652, Elizabeth **White***[2]

Richard **Treat**, b. England, m. Jane **Tapp**[2]

Thomas **Leffingwell**,* b. 1622, England; d. 1714, m. Mary (Last Name Unknown)*[2]

Richard **Bushnell**,* b. 1620, England; d. 1658, m. October 11, 1648, Mary **Marvin**,* b. 1629, England[2]

Thomas **Tracy**, b. England, m. Mary (Last Name Unknown)*[2]

Simon **Huntington**, b. England, m. Margaret **Baret**,* b. England[2]

Thomas **Mumford**,* b. England, m. Sarah **Sherman**, b. 1636, England[2]

G-11

Sylvester **Baldwin**, b. England, m. Sarah **Bryan**,* b. England[2]

John **Alsop**, b. England, m. Temperance **Gilbert**,* b. England[2]

Henry **Tomlinson**,* b. England D. March 16, 1681, Stratford, Conn., m. Alice **Hyde**,* b. England[2]

Benjamin **Fenn**, b. England, m. Sarah **Baldwin**, b. 1621, England; d. 1663[2]

Jasper **Gunn**,* b. England[2]

William **Andrews**,* b. England; d. 1652, Cambridge, Mass., m. Mary (Last Name Unknown),* b. England[2]

Richard **Treat**, b. 1584, England; d. 1669, Wethersfield, Conn., m. Alice **Gaylord**, b. England[2]

Edmund **Tapp**,* b. England, m. Elizabeth **Powell**,* b. England[2]

William **Tracy**, b. England, m. Mary **Conway**, b. England[2]

George **Huntington**, b. England, m. Anne **Fenwick**,* b. England[2]

Christopher **Baret**,* b. England[2]

Philip **Sherman**, b. February 5, 1610, England; d. 1687, m. Sarah **Odding**,* b. England[2]

G-12

Sylvester **Baldwin**, b. England; d. England, m. Jane **Wells**,* England; d. England[2]

Anthony **Alsop**, b. England; d. England, m. Jane **Smith**,* b. England; d. England[2]

John **Fenn**,* b. England; d. England, m. Joan **Turney**,* b. England; d. England[2]

Sylvester **Baldwin**,* m. Sarah **Bryan*** (Refer to Sylvester **Baldwin** G-11 Mamie **Eisenhower** to continue their lines.)[2]

Robert **Treat**, b. England; d. England, m. Honor (Last Name Unknown),* b. England; d. England[2]

Hugh **Gaylord**,* b. England; d. England[2]

John **Tracy**, b. England; d. England, m. Anne **Throckmorton**, b. England; d. England[2]

John **Conway**,* b. England; d. England, m. Elinor **Greville**, b. England; d. England[2]

Christopher **Huntington**, b. England; d. England, m. Elizabeth **Bailey**,* b. England; d. England[2]

Samuel **Sherman**,* b. 1573, England; d. England, m. Philippa (Last Name Unknown),* b. England; d. England[2]

G-13

Henry **Baldwin**, b. England; d. England, m. Alice (Last Name Unknown),* b. England; d. England[2]

John **Alsop**, b. England; d. England, m. Anne **Alsop**, b. England; d. England[2]

Richard **Treat**,* b. England; d. England, m. Joanna (Last Name Unknown),* b. England; d. England[2]

Henry **Tracy**, b. England; d. England, m. Elizabeth **Bridges**, b. England; d. England[2]

Sir Thomas **Throckmorton**, b. England; d. England, m. Margaret **Whittington**, b. England; d. England[2]

Richard **Conway**, b. England; d. England, m. Agnes **Ratcliffe**,* b. England; d. England[2]

Fulke **Greville**, b. England; d. England, m. Elizabeth **Willoughby**, b. England; d. England[2]

Richard **Huntington**,* b. England; d. England, m. Alice **Loring**,* b. England; d. England[2]

G-14

Richard **Baldwin**, b. England; d. England, m. Ellen **Apuke**,* b. England; d. England[2]

Thomas **Alsop**,* b. England; d. England, m. Anne **Bassett**, b. England; d. England[2]

William **Tracy**,* b. England; d. England, m. Agnes **Digby**, b. England; d. England[2]

John **Bridges**, b. England; d. England, m. Elizabeth **Grey**, b. England; d. England[2]

William **Throckmorton**, b. England; d. England, m. Margaret **Mathew**,* b. England; d. England[2]

Thomas **Whittington**, b. England; d. England, m. Margaret **Needham**, b. England; d. England[2]

Sir Henry **Conway**, b. England; d. England, m. Angharad **Creuequer***[2]

Edward **Greville**, b. England; d. England, m. Agnes **Denton**, b. England; d. England[2]

Edward **Willoughby**, b. England; d. England, m. Margaret **Neville***[2]

G-15

Richard **Baldwin**, b. England; d. England[2]

William **Bassett**, b. England; d. England, m. Elizabeth **Maverell**, b. England; d. England[2]

Sigmond **Digby**, b. England; d. England, m. Alice **Walls**, b. England; d. England[2]

Gyles **Bridges**, b. England; d. England, m. Isabelle **Baynham**,* b. England; d. England[2]

Edmund **Grey**, b. England; d. England m.Florence **Hastings**,* b. England; d. England[2]

Christopher **Throckmorton**, b. England; d. England[2]

John **Whittington**,* b. England; d. England, m. Elizabeth **Milbourne**, b. England; d. England[2]

Sir William **Needham**, b. England; d. England, m. Isabel **Bromley**,* b. England; d. England[2]

Sir Hugh **Conway**, b. England; d. England[2]

John **Greville**,* b. England; d. England, m. Jane **Forster**, b. England; d. England[2]

John **Denton**, b. England; d. England, m. Isabel **Brome**,* b. England; d. England[2]

Robert **Willoughby**,* b. England; d. England, m. Elizabeth **De Beauchamp**, b. England; d. England[2]

G-16

William **Baldwin**,* b. England; d. England, m. Agnes **Dormer**, b. England; d. England[2]

Thomas **Maverell**,* b. England; d. England, m. Jane **Eyre**, b. England; d. England[2]

Everhard **Digby,*** b. England; d. England, m. Agnes **Clarke,*** b. England; d. England[2]

John **Walls,*** b. England; d. England[2]

Thomas **Bridges**, b. England; d. England[2]

Thomas **Baynham,*** b. England; d. England, m. Alice **Walwin,*** b. England; d. England[2]

John **Grey,*** b. England; d. England, m. Anne **Grey**, b. England; d. England[2]

John **Throckmorton**, b. England; d. England, m. Anne **Scargill,*** b. England; d. England[2]

Simon **Milbourne,*** b. England; d. England, m. Jane **Baskerville**, b. England; d. England[2]

Thomas **Needham**, b. England; d. England, m. Maud **Brereton,*** b. England; d. England[2]

John **Conway**, b. England; d. England[2]

Humphrey **Forster**, b. England; d. England, m. Alice **Popham,*** b. England; d. England[2]

Thomas **Denton**, b. England; d. England, m. Alice **Dauncey**, b. England; d. England[2]

Richard **De Beauchamp,*** b. England; d. England, m. Elizabeth **Stafford**, b. England; d. England[2]

G-17 ————————

William **Dormer**, b. England; d. England, m. Agnes **Lanneclyn,*** b. England; d. England[2]

Robert **Eyre,*** b. England; d. England, m. Elizabeth **Fitz William**, b. England; d. England[2]

Gyles **Bridges**, b. England; d. England, m. Catherine **Clyfford,*** b. England; d. England[2]

Edmund **De Grey**, b. England; d. England, m. Katherine **Percy**, b. England; d. England[2]

John **Throckmorton**, b. England; d. England, m. Elizabeth **Bridges,*** b. England; d. England[2]

Ralph **Baskerville**, b. England; d. England, m. Anne **Blackett,*** b. England; d. England[2]

Robert **Needham,*** b. England; d. England, m. Dorothy **Savage**, b. England; d. England[2]

Sir John **Conway,*** b. England; d. England[2]

Humphrey **Forster,*** b. England; d. England, m. Alice **Stoner**, b. England; d. England[2]

Thomas **Denton**, b. England; d. England, m. Agnes **Baldington**, b. England; d. England[2]

Humphrey **Stafford**,* b. England; d. England, m. Margaret **Beaufort**, b. England; d. England[2]

G-18

Geoffrey **Dormer**,* b. England; d. England, m. Ursula **Coleridge**, b. England; d. England[2]

Thomas **Fitz William**,* b. England; d. England, m. Margaret **Dymoke**, b. England; d. England[2]

Thomas **Bridges**,* b. England; d. England, m. Alice **Barkley**, b. England; d. England[2]

John **De Grey**, b. England; d. England, m. Constance **Holand**, b. England England[2]

Henry **Percy**, b. England; d. England, m. Eleanor **De Neville**, b. England; d. England[2]

John **Throckmorton**, b. England; d. England, m. Eleanor **Spinney**, b. England; d. England[2]

Sir John **Baskerville**, b. England; d. England, m. Elizabeth **Brugge**,* b. England; d. England[2]

John **Savage**, b. England; d. England, m. Dorothy **Vernon**, b. England; d. England[2]

Thomas **Stoner**, b. England; d. England, m. Alice **Kirkby**, b. England; d. England[2]

John **Denton**,* b. England; d. England, m. Johanne **De La Laundre***[2]

William **Baldington**,* b. England; d. England[2]

Edmund **Beaufort**, b. England; d. England, m. Eleanor **De Beauchamp**,* b. England; d. England[2]

G-19

Bartholomew **Coleridge**,* b. England; d. England, m. Alice **Fitz Alan**, b. England; d. England[2]

Thomas **Dymoke**,* b. 1427, England; d. 1470, England, m. Margaret **De Welles**, b. England; d. England[2]

Thomas **Barkley**,* b. England; d. England, m. Elizabeth **Chandos**, b. England; d. England[2]

Reynold **De Grey**, b. England; d. England, m. Margaret **De Roos**, b. England; d. England[2]

John **Holand**,* b. England; d. England, m. Elizabeth of Lancaster, b. England; d. England[2]

Henry **Percy**,* b. England; d. England, m. Elizabeth **Mortimer*** (Refer to Henry **Percy** G-15 Ellen **Arthur** to continue their lines.)[2]

Ralph **De Neville**, b. England; d. England, m. Joan of Lancaster, b. England; d. England[2]

Thomas **Throckmorton**, b. England; d. England, m. Agnes (Last Name Unknown),* b. England; d. England[2]

Sir Richard **Baskerville**, b. England; d. England, m. Joane **Everingham**,* b. England; d. England[2]

John **Savage**,* b. England; d. England, m. Catherine **Stanley**, b. England; d. England[2]

Ralph **Stoner**,* b. England; d. England, m. Eleanor **Butler**, b. England; d. England[2]

John **Kirkby**,* b. England; d. England[2]

Sir John **Beaufort**, b. 1371, Beaufort Castle, England; d. March 16, 1410, England, m. Margaret **De Holland**, b. England; d. England[2]

G-20

Ranulph **Fitz Alan**, b. Arundel, England; d. England[2]

Lionel **De Welles**, b. England; d. England, m. Joan **Waterton**,* b. England; d. England[2]

Thomas **Chandos**, b. England; d. England, m. Lucie (Last Name Unknown),* b. England; d. England[2]

Reginald **De Grey**,* b. England; d. England, m. Alinore **Le Strange**,* b. England; d. England[2]

Thomas **De Roos**,* b. England; d. England, m. Beatrice **Stafford**,* b. England; d. England[2]

John of Gaunt,* b. 1340, England; d. England, m. Blanche of Lancaster,* b. England; d. England (Refer to John of Gaunt G-14 Abigail **Adams** to continue his line.)[2]

Ralph **De Neville**,* b. England; d. England, m. Alice **De Audley**,* b. England; d. England (Refer to Ralph **De Neville** G-16 Ellen **Arthur** to continue their lines.)[2]

John of Gaunt,* m. Blanche of Lancaster* (Refer to John of Gaunt G-14 Abigail **Adams** to continue his line.)[2]

John **Throckmorton**,* b. England; d. England, m. Agnes **Abberbury**,* b. England; d. England[2]

Sir Richard **De Baskerville**, b. England; d. England, m. Isabel **Caveley**,* b. England; d. England[2]

Sir Thomas **Stanley**,* b. England; d. England, m. Joan **Goushill**,*

b. England; d. England (Refer to G-12 Abigail **Adams** to continue their lines.)[2]

James **Butler**, b. England; d. England, m. Elizabeth **Darcy**, b. England; d. England[2]

John of Gaunt,* m. Catherine **Roet,*** b. England; d. England (Refer to John of Gaunt G-14 Abigail **Adams** to continue their lines.)[2]

Thomas **De Holland,*** b. England; d. England *m*. Alice **Fitz Alan**, b. England; d. England[2]

G-21

William **Fitz Alan**, b. Arundel, England; d. England, m. Agnes (Last Name Unknown),* b. England; d. England[2]

Eudo **De Welles**, b. England; d. England, m. Maud **De Greystoke,*** b. England; d. England[2]

Roger **Chandos,*** b. England; d. England[2]

Richard **De Baskerville**, b. England; d. England, m. Jane **Poynings,*** b. England; d. England[2]

James **Butler,*** b. England; d. England, m. Eleanor **De Bohun**, b. England; d. England[2]

John **Darcy,*** b. England; d. England, m. Eleanor **Mennell**, b. England; d. England[2]

Richard **Fitz Alan,*** b. England; d. England, m. Eleanor **Plantagenet,*** b. England; d. England (Refer to Richard **Fitz Alan** G-15 Abigail **Adams** to continue their lines.)[2]

G-22

John **Fitz Alan,*** b. England; d. England, m. Alianore **Maltovers,*** b. England; d. England[2]

John **De Welles,*** b. England; d. England, m. Eleanor **De Mowbray**, b. England; d. England[2]

Walter **De Baskerville**, b. England; d. England, m. Sibill **Corbett,*** b. England; d. England[2]

Humphrey **De Bohun,*** b. England; d. England, m. Elizabeth **Plantagenet,*** b. England; d. England (Refer to Humphrey **De Bohun** G-16 Abigail **Adams** to continue their lines.)[2]

Nycolas **Mennell**, b. England; d. England[2]

G-23

John **De Mowbray**, b. England; d. England, m. Elizabeth **De Seagrave**, b. England; d. England[2]

Richard **De Baskerville**, b. England; d. England[2]

Nycolas **Mennell,*** b. England; d. England, m. Lucia **Thwynge**, b. England; d. England[2]

G-24

John **De Mowbray**, b. 1310, England; d. 1361, England, m. Joan of Lancaster, b. England; d. England[2]

John **De Seagrave**, b. England; d. England, m. Margaret **Plantagenet**, b. England; d. England[2]

Walter **De Baskerville**, b. England; d. England, m. Susan **Crigdon***. England; d. England[2]

Robert **Thwynge**, b. England; d. England[2]

G-25

Henry **Plantagenet,*** b. 1281, Grismond Castle, England; d. September 22, 1345, England, m. Maud **De Chaworth,*** b. 1282, Kidwelly, Wales; d. 1319, England (Refer to Henry **Pantagenet** G-16 Abigail **Adams** to continue their lines.)[2]

Stephen **De Seagrave***. 1280, England; d. 1375, England, m. Alice **De Arundel,*** b. Arundel, England; d. England[2]

Thomas **Plantagenet**, b. England; d. England, m. Alice **De Hale,*** b. England; d. England[2]

Roger **De Baskerville***. England; d. England[2]

Marmaduke **Thwynge,*** b. England; d. England, m. Lucia **Brus,*** b. England; d. England[2]

G-26

King Edward I,* b. June 17, 1239, London, England; d. July 7, 1307, m. August 5, 1254 Margaret of France,* b. France (Refer to King Edward I G-17 Abigail **Adams** to continue his line.)[2]

Abigail Fillmore

G+2

Abigail **Fillmore** had no grandchildren.

G+1

Millard **Fillmore**, b. April 25, 1828, East Aurora, New York; d. November 15, 1889, Buffalo, New York[11]

Mary **Fillmore**, b. March 27, 1832, Buffalo, New York; d. July 26, 1854, Buffalo, New York[11]

Abigail Powers, b. March 13, 1798, Stillwater, New York; d. March 30, 1853, Washington, D.C., m. February 5, 1826, Millard Fillmore, b. January 7, 1800, Kinderhook, New York; d. March 8, 1874, Buffalo, New York[2,8]

G-1

Lemuel **Powers**, b. June 15, 1756, Littleton, Mass.; d. May 18, 1800, Stillwater, New York, m. Abigail **Newland**, b. February 22, 1758, Mass.; d. February 21, 1838[2]

G-2

Lemuel **Powers**, b. April 9, 1714, Graton, Mass.; d. June 28, 1792, Littleton, Mass., m. January 4, 1742, Thankful **Leland**, b. June 26, 1724, Groydon, New Hampshire; d. February 19, 1805, Stillwater, New York[2]

Joseph **Newland**,* b. 1772, Mass., m. 1744, Bristol, Mass. Abigail **Babbitt**, b. January 25, 1725, Norton, Mass.[2]

G-3

William **Powers**, b. Mass.; d. ca. 1774, Sutton, Mass., m. Lydia **Per-**

ham, b. February 19, 1673, Chelmsford, Mass.; d. August 24, 1716, Groton, Mass.[2, 3]

John **Leland**, b. February 22, 1684, Sherborn, Mass., m. January 22, 1710, Hannah **Learned**, b. September 16, 1698, Sherbon, Mass.; d. Grafton, Mass.[2, 4]

Erasmus **Babbitt**, b. August 12, 1685, Dighton, Mass.; d. August 11, 1730, Norton, Mass., m. April 25, 1717, Abigail **Burt**, b. Mass.; d. Mass.[2, 5]

G-4

William **Powers**, b. March 16, 1661, Littleton, Mass; d. March 17, 1710; d. Mass., m. Mary **Bank**, b. Chelmsford, Mass.[2]

John **Perham**, b. January 27, 1667, Chelmsford, Mass.; d. July 29, 1743, Worcester, Mass., m. Lydia **Fletcher**, b. Mass.[3]

Ebenezer **Leland**, b. January 14, Mass., m. Deborah **Prescott***[4]

Benomi **Learned**, b. December 4, 1656, Chelmsford, Mass.; d. 1738, Newton, Mass., m. Sarah **Wright**, b. 1664; d. 1737[7]

Edward **Babbitt**, b. July 15, 1655, Taunton, Mass.; d. 1732, Bristol Co., Mass., m. Abigail **Tisdale**, b. July 15, 1667, Taunton, Mass.; d. 1732, Bristol Co., Mass.[4, 5]

Thomas **Burt**, b. 1661, Taunton, Mass.; d. 1717, Mass., m. 1694, Jemima **Phillips**,* b. 1661, Taunton, Mass.; d. March 28, 1718, Mass.[6]

G-5

Walter **Powers**,* b. 1639; d. February 22, 1707 or 1708, m. Trial **Shepard**, b. December 19, 1641, Weymouth, Mass.; d. February 22, 1708, Weymouth, Mass.[2, 3]

John **Perham**, b. 1640, Chelmsford, Mass.; d. January 23, 1720, Chelmsford, Mass., m. Liddish **Shipley**[3]

Samuel **Fletcher**, b. 1625 England; d. December 9, 1697, Chelmsford, Mass., m. Margaret **Hailstone**, b. England; d. Chelmsford, Mass.[3]

Henry **Leland**, b. 1655, Sherborn, Mass.; d. Sherborn, Mass., m. Margaret **Babcock**,* b. Mass.; d. May 21, 1705, Sherburn, Mass.[4]

Isaac **Learned**, b. 1624, England, m. Mary **Stearns**, b. England[7]

Edward **Babbitt**,* b. 1627, England; d. 1675, Taunton, Mass., m. Sarah **Tarne**, b. 1634, England; d. June 25, 1675, Bristol, Mass.[5]

John **Tisdale**, b. November 7, 1614, Yorkshire, England; d. June 27, 1670, Taunton, Mass., m. Sarah **Walker**, b. March 1, 1618, Weymouth, England; d. December 10, 1676, Taunton, Mass.[3]

James **Burt**,* b. 1622, England; d. 1680, m. Anne (Last Name Unknown)*[6]

G-6

Ralph **Shepherd**, b. 1603, Middlesex, England; d. August 10, 1693, Malden, Mass., m. Thankful or Thank Ye **Lord**, b. June 30, 1612, England; d. 1693, Malden, Mass.[3]

John **Perham**,* b. 1600, Coventry, England; d. Chelmsford, Mass., m. Ann (Last Name Unknown),* b. 1605, England[3]

John **Shipley**, b. May 9, 1607, Failsworth, England; d. September 10, 1678, Chelmsford, Mass., m. Ann (Last Name Unknown),* b. England; d. Chelmsford, Mass.[3]

Robert **Fletcher**,* b. 1583, Failsworth, England; d. April 3, 1677, Concord, Mass., m. Sarah **Hartwell**,* b. England[3]

William **Hailstone**, b. 1615, England; d. 1675, Taunton, Mass.[3]

William **Learned**, b. 1590, England; d. 1646, m. Judith **Gillman**,* b. England[7]

Isaac **Stearns**, m. Mary **Barker***[7]

Miles **Tarne**,* b. 1595, England; d. 1676, Boston, Mass., m. Sarah **Faulkner**,* b. England[5]

Thomas **Tisdale**,* b. 1596, Yorkshire, England; d. Yorkshire, England, m. Ruth (Last Name Unknown),* b. England[3]

James **Walker**,* b. 1590, England[3]

G-7

Isaac **Shepard**,* b. 1571, London, England[3]

Thomas **Lord**, b. 1585, Towcester, England; d. May 17, 1678, Hartford, Conn., m. Dorothy **Bird**, b. May 25, 1588, Towcester, England; d. August 2, 1676, Hartford, Conn.[3]

Robert **Shipley**,* b. 1581, Failsworth, England; d. Failsworth, England, m. Alice **Dunkerley**,* b. 1585, Manchester, England; d. 1644, Failsworth, England[3]

William **Hailstone**,* b. 1565, England; d. England[3]

William **Stearns**,* b. England, m. Emma **Ramsford**,* b. England[7]

G-8

Richard **Lord**,* b. 1555, Towcester, England; d. May 30, 1610, Towcester, England, m. Johanna **Mitchell**,* b. England; d. England[3]

Robert **Bird**,* b. 1558, Towcester, Mass.; d. July 18, 1622, Towcester, England, m. Amy **Hill**,* b. 1565, Herts, England; d. April 19, 1675, Towcester, England[3]

Caroline Fillmore

G+1

Caroline **Fillmore** had no children.

Caroline Carmichael born October 2, 1813, Morristown, New Jersey; d. August 11, 1881, Buffalo, New York, m. February 10, 1858, Albany, New York Millard Fillmore (Refer to Abigail Fillmore for information on Millard Fillmore)[1,2]

G-1

Charles **Carmichael,*** m. Temperance **Blatchley**[1]

G-2

Ebenezer **Blatchley**, b. 1735, m. Mary Cooper **Wick***[1]

G-3

Ebenezer **Blatchley**, b. 1709, m. Hannah **Miller**, b. 1709[1]

G-4

Ebenezer Blatchley, b. 1671[1]
Robert or John **Miller,*** m. Mary **Beckwith***[1]

G-5

Aaron **Blatchley**, b. 1644, New Haven, Connecticut, m. Mary **Dodd**, b. June 16, 1651, New Haven, Connecticut; d. 1686, New Haven, Connecticut[1,2]

G-6

Thomas **Blatchley**, b. 1615, m. Susannah **Ball**, b. 1622[1,3]

Daniel **Dodd**, b. October 15, 1615, England; d. 1666, New Haven, Connecticut, m. Mary **Wheeler**,* b. 1621, New Haven, Connecticut[2]

G-7

Thomas **Blatchley**,* b. 1589[1]

Alling **Ball**, b. 1595, London, England, m. Dorothy **Tuttle**,* b. 1594, London, England[3]

Thomas **Dodd**,* b. 1589, England, m. Katherine (Last Name Unknown)*[2]

G-8

William **Ball**, b. 1573, Wokingham, England; d. 1648, New Haven, Connecticut, m. Alice **Waltham**, b. 1573, Wiltshire, England[3]

G-9

John **Ball**, b. 1551, Wokingham, England; d. 1628, Wokingham, England, m. Elizabeth **Webb**, b. 1553, Ruscombe, England; d. 1595, Wokingham, England[3]

Richard **Waltham**,* b. England d. England[3]

G-10

John **Ball*** 1525, Wokingham, England; d. 1599, Wokingham, England, m. Agnes **Holloway**,* b. England; d. England[3]

Thomas **Webb**,* b. 1529, England; d. England[3]

ELIZABETH (BETTY) FORD

G+2

Children of Michael Gerald and Gayle Ann (Brumbaugh) Ford:

Sarah Joyce **Ford**, b. April 22, 1979, Pittsburgh, Pennsylvania, m. July 31, 1999, Blake **Goodfellow**[1]

Rebekah Elizabeth **Ford**, b. February 26, 1982, Winson-Salem, North Carolina[1]

Hannah Gayle **Ford**, b. September 17, 1985, Winston-Salem, North Carolina[1]

Children of John and Juliann (Felando) Ford:

Christian Gerald **Ford**, b. October 14, 1997[1]

Jonathan August **Ford**, b. November 29, 1999[1]

Children of Susan Elizabeth Ford and Charles Vance:

Tyne Mary **Vance**, b. August 15, 1980, Washington, D.C.[1]

Heather Elizabeth **Vance**, b. January 31, 1983, Washington, D.C.[1]

G+1

Michael Gerald **Ford**, b. March 15, 1950, m. Gayle Ann **Brumbaugh**[1]

John (Jack) **Ford**, b. March 16, 1952, m. Julianna **Felando**[1]

Steven Meigs **Ford**, b. May 19, 1956[1]

Susan Elizabeth **Ford**, b. July 6, 1957, m(1) Charles **Vance**, m(2) Vaden **Bales**[1]

Elizabeth Ann (Betty) Bloomer, b. April 8, 1918, Chicago, Illinois, m. October 15, 1948, Gerald Ford, b. July 14, 1913, Omaha, Nebraska[1,2]

G-1

William Stephenson **Bloomer**, b. 1894, Roanoke, Illinois, m. Hortense **Nehr***[3]

G-2

Peter **Bloomer**, m. Leah (Last Name Unknown)*[3]

G-3

Peter **Bloomer***[3]

Lucretia Garfield

G+2

Children of Harry August and Belle (Mason) Garfield:

Mason **Garfield**, b. October 5, 1892, Cleveland, Ohio, m(1) Anna **Scott**, m(2) Harriett **Pew**[1]

James **Garfield**, m. Edith **Townsend**[1]

Lucretia **Garfield**, b. January 18, 1894, m. John Preston **Comer**[1]

Stanton **Garfield**, b. August 3, 1895, Willoughby, Ohio, m. Lucy **Hodges**[1]

Children of James Rudolf and Helen (Hills) Garfield[1]:

John Newell **Garfield**, b. February 3, 1892, Chicago, Illinois; d. May 23, 1931, Mentor, Ohio, m. Janet **Dodge**[1]

James Abram **Garfield**, b. April 13, 1894, Chicago. Illinois, m. Edwina **Glenn**[1]

Newell **Garfield**, b. August 1, 1895, Chicago, Illinois[1]

Rudolph **Garfield**, b. September 13, 1899, Mentor, Ohio, m. Eleanor **Borton**[1]

Children of Mary Garfield and Joseph Stanley Brown:

Rudolph Stanley **Brown**, b. 1889, Mentor, Ohio; d. February 8, 1944, m. Catherine **Oliver**[1]

Ruth **Brown**, b. 1892, Mentor, Ohio[1]

Margaret **Brown**, b. 1895 Washington, D.C.; d. June 12, 1958, Conn., m. Max **Sellers**[1]

Children of Irvin McDowell and Susan (Emmons) Garfield:

Eleanor **Garfield**[1]

Jane **Garfield**[1]

Irvin McDowell **Garfield**[1]

Children of Abram and Sarah (Williams) Garfield:

Edward **Garfield**, b. 1899, m. Hope **Dillingham**[1]

Mary Louise **Garfield**, m. William Richard **Hallaran**[1]

G+1

Eliza Arabella **Garfield**, b. July 3, 1860, Hiram, Ohio; d. December 3, 1863, Hiram, Ohio[2]

Harry Augustus **Garfield**, b. October 11, 1863, Hiram, Ohio; d. December 12, 1942, Williamstown, Mass., m. Belle **Mason**[2]

James Rudolf **Garfield**, b. October 17, 1865, Hiram, Ohio; d. March 24, 1950, Cleveland, m. Helen **Hills**[2]

Mary **Garfield**, b. January 16, 1867, Washington, D.C.; d. December 30, 1947, Pasadena, Calif., m. Joseph Stanley **Brown**[2]

Irvin McDowell **Garfield**, b. August 3, 1870, Hiram, Ohio; d. July 19, 1907, Boston, Mass., m. Susan **Emmons**[2]

Abram **Garfield**, b. November 21, 1872, Washington, D.C.; d. October 16, 1908, m(1) Sarah **Williams**, m(2) Helen **Matthews**[2]

Edward **Garfield**, b. December 25, 1874, Hiram, Ohio; d. October 25, 1876, Washington, D.C.[2]

Lucretia Rudolph, b. April 19, 1832, Garretsville, Ohio; d. March 14, 1918, m. November 11, 1858, James Abram Garfield, b. November 19, 1831, Orange, Ohio; d. September 19, 1881, Elberon, New Jersey[3, 9]

G-1

Zebulon **Rudolph**, b. February 28, 1803, Frederick Co., Va.; d. Hiram, Ohio, m. Arabella **Mason**, b. ca. 1805, Watertown, Mass.; d. Hiram, Ohio[3]

G-2

John **Rudolph**, b. 1760, Frederick Co., Va.; d. Hiram, Ohio, m. Elizabeth **Lantz***[3]

Elijah **Mason**, b. February 27, 1760, Watertown, Mass.; d. January 27, 1808, Walpole, New Hampshire, m. September 13, 1787, Lucretia **Greene**[2, 3]

G-3

George **Rudolph**, b. Va.; d. Frederick Co., Va.[3]

Peleg **Mason**, b. April 6, 1716, Stonington, Conn.; d. February 10, 1764, Conn., m. Mary **Stanton**, b. Westerly, Rhode Island[2]

John **Greene**, m. Azubah **Ward**, b. October 30, 1737, Worcester, Mass.; d. Tolland, Conn.[2]

G-4

John Adam **Rudolph***[3]

John **Mason**, b. 1673; d. 1736, m. Anne **Sanford**, b. 1680[2]

Joseph **Stanton**, b. 1674, Westerly, Rhode Island; d. 1751, Stonington, Conn., m. Esther **Gallup**, b. November 1, 1685, Stonington, Conn.[2]

Nathaniel **Greene**,* m. Elizabeth **Taylor**[2]

Daniel **Ward**, b. September 3, 1700; d. May 21, 1777, m. Mary **Stone***[4]

G-5

John **Mason**,* b. 1646; d. September 18, 1676, m. Abigail **Fitch**,* b. August 5, 1650[2]

Peleg **Sanford**, b. May 10, 1639, Portsmouth, Rhode Island; d. February 28,1701, Newport, Rhode Island, m. Mary **Coddington**, b. May 16, 1654, Newport, Rhode Island; d. 1683, Portsmouth, Rhode Island[2, 5]

Joseph **Stanton**, b. Hartford, Conn.; d. March 21, 1714, Stonington, Conn., m. Hannah **Mead**,* b. 1648, Mass.; d. 1676, Stonington, Conn.[5]

Benadam **Gallup**,* m. Hester **Prentice**, b. July 20, 1660; d. May 17, 1751[8]

John **Taylor**,* m. Anne **Winslow**[2]

Obadiah **Ward**, b. April 19, 1663, Sudbury, Mass.; d. December 17, 1717, Worcester, Mass., m. Joanna **Mixer**, b. November 14, 1666, Watertown, Mass.[4]

G-6

John **Sanford**, b. England, m. Bridget **Hutchinson**, b. 1618, England; d. 1698[2]

William **Coddington**,* b. 1601, Boston, England; d. January 4, 1678, Newport, Rhode Island, m. Anne **Brinley**, b. September 30, 1628, Newport, Rhode Island; d. May 9, 1708, Newport, Rhode Island[5]

Thomas **Stanton**,* b. 1595, Wolverton, England; d. Wolverton, England, m. Katherine **Washington**,* b. 1595, Radway, England; d. Wolverton, England[5]

John **Prentice**, b. May 6, 1678; d. 1691, m. Hester **Nichols***[8]

Edward **Winslow**, m. Elizabeth **Hutchinson**, b. 1639; d. 1728[2]

Richard **Ward**, b. April 1, 1635, England; d. March 31, 1666, Sudbury, England, m. Mary **Moore**, b. England[4]

Isaac **Mixer**, m. Mary **Coolidge**, b. October 14, 1637, Watertown, Mass.; d. March 2, 1659, Watertown, Mass.[4]

G-7

Samuel **Sanford**,* b. England; d. England, m. Eleanor (Last Name Unknown),* b. England[2]

William **Hutchinson**,* b. 1586, Alford, England; d. 1642, England, m. Anne **Marbury**, b. 1591, Alford, England; d. 1643, In an Indian massacre[2]

Thomas **Brinley**,* b. England, m. Ann **Wise**,* b. England[5]

Valentine **Prentice**,* b. 1598, England; d. 1633, England, m. Alice **Bredde**,* b. England[8]

John **Winslow***b. 1597, England; d. 1674, Mass., m. 1624, Mary **Chilton**, b. 1605, England; d. 1679, Mass.[2]

Edward **Hutchinson**, b. 1613, England; d. 1675, m. Catherine **Hamby**, b. England[2]

William **Ward**,* b. 1603, England; d. August 16, 1687, Marlborough, Mass., m. Elizabeth (Last Name Unknown),* b. England[4]

John **Moore**,* b. England, m. Elizabeth **Whale***[4]

Isaac **Mixer**,* b. England, m. Sarah **Thurston***[4]

John **Coolidge**,* b. England, m. Mary **Ravens***[4]

G-8

Rev. Francis **Marbury**, b. 1555, London, England; d. 1611, London, England, m. Bridget **Dryden**, b. 1565, Northampton, England; d. April 2, 1645, England[2]

James **Chilton*** (Mayflower Pilgrim), b. England; d. 1620, Mass., m. Susanna (Last Name Unknown)*[2]

William **Hutchinson**,* m. Anne **Marbury***[2]

Robert **Hamby**, b. England, m. Elizabeth **Arnold**,* b. England[2]

G-9

William **Marbury**, b. England; d. England, m. Agnes **Linton**,* b. England; d. England[2]

John **Dryden**, b. 1525, Staffe Hill, England; d. September 3, 1584, England, m. Elizabeth **Cope**, b. 1524, Northampton, England; d. England[2]

William **Hamby**, b. 1543, England; d. 1613, England, m. Margaret **Blewett**, b. England; d. England[2]

G-10

Robert **Marbury**, b. England; d. England, m. Elizabeth (Last Name Unknown),* b. England; d. England[2]

David **Dryden**, b. 1500, Staffe Hill, England; d. England, m. Isabel **Nicholson**, b. 1501 Climberland, England[2]

John **Cope**, b. England; d. England, m. Bridget **Raleigh**, b. England; d. England[2]

Edward **Hamby**, b. 1512, England; d. 1559, m. Eleanor **Booth**, b. 1510, England; d. 1547, England[2]

Edmond **Blewett**,* b. 1512, England; d. 1559, England[2]

G-11

William **Marbury**, b. England; d. England, m. Ann **Blount**, b. England; d. England[2]

William **Dryden**,* b. England; d. England[2]

William **Nicholson**,* b. England; d. England[2]

Sir William **Cope**,* b. England; d. England, m. Jane **Spencer**,* b. 1465, England; d. 1525, England[2]

Edward **Raleigh**, b. England; d. England, m. Anne **Chamberlayne**, b. England; d. England[2]

George **Hamby**,* b. England; d. England[2]

John **Booth**, b. England; d. England, m. Anne **Thimbleby**, b. Eng; d. England[2]

G-12

John **Marbury**,* b. England; d. England, m. Eleanor (Last Name Unknown),* b. England; d. England[2]

Thomas H. **Blount**, b. 1414, England; d. 1468, England, m. Anne **Hawley*** b. 1423, England; d. 1462, England[2]

Sir Edward **Raleigh**, b. England; d. England, m. Margery **Verney**, b. England; d. England[2]

Richard **Chamberlayne**,* b. 1438, England; d. 1497, England[2]

William **Booth**,* b. England; d. England, m. Elizabeth **Ayscough**, b. England; d. England[2]

Richard **Thimbleby**,* b. England; d. England, m. Elizabeth **Hilton**, b. England; d. England[2]

G-13

Thomas **Blount**, b. 1373, England; d. 1456, England, m. Margaret **Gresley,*** b. England; d. England[2]

William **Raleigh,*** b. England; d. England, m. Elizabaeth **Greene,** b. England; d. England[2]

John **Ayscough,*** b. England; d. England, m. Margaret **Talboys,** b. England; d. England[2]

Godfrey **Hilton,** b. England; d. England, m. Margery (Last Name Unknown),* b. England; d. England[2]

G-14

Walter **Blount,** b. 1348, England; d. 1403, England, m. Sacha **De Ayala,*** b. 1356; d. 1418[2]

Sir Thomas **Greene,** b. England; d. England, m. Philippa **Ferriers,*** b. England; d. England[2]

John **Talboys,** b. England; d. England, m. Katherine **Cabthorpe,*** b. England; d. England[2]

Sir Godfrey **Hilton,*** b. England; d. England, m. Hawise **Luttrell,** b. England; d. England[2]

G-15

John **Le Blount,** b. 1298, England; d. 1358, England, m. Isolde **De Montjoy,*** b. England; d. England[2]

Sir Thomas **Greene,*** b. England; d. England, m. Mary **Talbot,** b. England; d. England[2]

Sir John **Talboys,** b. England; d. England, m. Agnes **Cokefield,*** b. England; d. England[2]

Andrew **Luttrell,** b. England; d. England, m. Joan **Talboys,*** b. England; d. England[2]

G-16

Sir Walter **Le Blount,** b. 1277, England; d. 1315, England, m. Joan **Sodington,*** b. England; d. England[2]

Richard **Talbot,*** b. England; d. England, m. Anharet **Le Strange,** b. England; d. England[2]

Walter **Talboys,** b. England; d. England, m. Margaret (Last Name Unknown),* b. England; d. England[2]

Sir Andrew **Luttrell,*** b. England; d. England, m. Hawise **Le De Spencer,** b. 1345, England; d. 1414, England[2]

G-17

William **Le Blount**, b. 1233, England; d. 1280, England, m. Isabel **De Beauchamp**, b. England; d. England[2]

John **Le Strange,*** b. England; d. England, m. Isabel **Fitz Alan**, b. England; d. England[2]

Henry **Talboys,*** m. England; d. England, m. Eleanor **De Boroughdon**, b. England; d. England[2]

Sir Philip **Le De Spencer**, b. 1313, Lincolnshire, England; d. 1349, England, m. Joan **De Cobham,*** b. England; d. England[2]

G-18

Robert **Le Blount**, b. 1197, England; d. 1188, England, m. Isabel **De Odinsels,*** b. England; d. England[2]

Lord William **De Beauchamp,*** m. Isabel **Mauduit*** (Refer to William **De Beauchamp** G-18 Abigail **Adams** to continue their lines.)[2]

Richard **Fitz Alan,*** b. England; d. England, m. Isabel **Le De Spencer**, b. England; d. England[2]

Gilbert **De Boroughdon,*** b. England; d. England, m. Elizabeth **De Umfreville**, b. England; d. England[2]

Hugh **Le De Spencer**, b. 1260, England; d. 1326, England, m. Isabelle **De Beauchamp,*** b. 1266, Warrick, England; d. May 30, 1306, Elmley Castle, England[2]

G-19

Stephen **Le Blount**, b. 1166, England; d. 1135, England, m. Marie **Le Blount**, b. England; d. England[2]

Hugh **Le De Spencer,*** b. England; d. England, m. Eleanor **De Clare**, b. England; d. England[2]

Robert **De Umfreville**, b. England; d. England, m. Lucy **Kyme,*** b. England; d. England[2]

Hugh **Le De Spencer**, b. 1223, Rhyshall, England; d. 1265, Killed in Battle of Evesham, Yorkshire, England, m. Aliva **Bassett**, b. England; d. England[2]

G-20

Gilbert **Le Blount,*** b. England; d. England, m. Agnes **Le Isle***[2]

William **Le Blount,*** b. England; d. England[2]

Gilbert **De Clare,*** m. Joan **Plantagenet*** (Refer to Gilbert **De Clare** G-19 Ellen **Arthur** to continue Gilbert's line.)[2]

Gilbert **De Umfreville,*** b. England; d. England, m. Elizabeth **Comyn**, b. England; d. England[2]

Sir Hugh **Le De Spencer,*** b. 1197, Rhyshall, England; d. 1237, Lincolnshire, England[2]

G-21

King Edward I,* m. Eleanor **De Castille*** (Refer to King Edward I G-17 Abigail **Adams** to continue their lines.)[2]

Alexander **Comyn,*** b. England; d. England, m. Elizabeth **De Quincy**, b. England; d. England[2]

G-22

Roger **De Quincy**, b. 1174, Winchester, England; d. April 25, 1264, England, m. Helen **McDonald**[2]

G-23

Saier **De Quincy**, b. 1150, Winchester, England; d. November 3, 1219, Damietta, Palestine, m. 1173, Margaret **De Beaumont**, b. 1170, England; d. January 12, 1236[6]

Alan **McDonald**, Lord of Galloway, b. 1170, Runnemede, Scotland; d. ca. 1234, m. Helen **De Lisle**[7]

G-24

Robert **De Quincy**, b. 1125, m. Orable **De Leuchars**[6]

Robert **De Beaumont**, b. 1130, Leicester, England; d. August 31, 1190, England Permel **De Grandmesnil**[6]

Robert **McDonald**, b. Scotland; d. Scotland, m. Eleanor **De Morville**[7]

Reginald, Lord of the Isles, m. Ponia **De Moray**[7]

G-25

Saier **De Quincy,*** b. England; d. England, m. Maud **De Lis***[6]

Nes **De Leuchars***[6]

Robert **De Beaumont**, b. Normandy, France, m. Amice **De Gael***[6]

Hugh **De Grandmesnil***[6]

Uchtred, Lord of Galloway, b. Scotland; d. Scotland, m. Gunnilda of Dunbar*[7]

Richard **De Morville,*** m. Avice **De Lancaster,*** b. 1134, England[7]

G-26

Roger **De Beaumont**, b. Normandy, France; d. Normandy, France, m. Adeline **De Meulan**, b. Normandy, France; d. Normandy, France[6]

Hugh "The Great," b. 1057, France; d. October 18, 1106, France, m. Isabelle (Last Name Unknown)*[6]

Fergus, Lord of Galloway,* b. Scotland; d. Scotland, m. Elizabeth of England, b. England[7]

G-27

Humphrey **De Beaumont**,* b. Normandy, France; d. Normandy, France[6]

Waleran **De Meulan**,* b. France; d. France, m. Oda **De Comteville**, b. Comteville, France; d. France[6]

King Henry I of France, b. 1005, Paris, France; d. August 4, 1060, Paris, France, m. Anne of Russia, b. Russia; d. France[6]

King Henry I of England, m. Mathilda, Princess of Scotland (Refer to King Henry I G-22 Abigail **Adams** to continue their lines.)[6]

G-28

Jean **De Comteville**, b. Comteville, France; d. France[6]

Robert II, b. 970, France; d. July 10, 1031, France, m. Constance **De Toulouse**, b. 977, Toulouse, France; d. July 25, 1032, France[6]

Yaroslav I, b. Russia; d. Russia, m. Ingegard of Sweden, b. Sweden[6]

G-29

Baldwin II, b. Blois, France; d. France[6]

Hugues **Capet**, b. 938, France; d. October 24, 996, France, m. Adelaide **De Poitiers**, b. Poitiers, France; d. France[6]

Guillaume I **De Arles**, b. 947, Toulouse, France; d. 994, France, m. 982, Adlis-Blanche **De Anjou**, b. Anjou, France; d. France[6]

Vladimir 1 "The Great," b. Russia; d. Russia, m. Rogneda **Von Pololek***[6]

King Olaf III, b. Sweden; d. Sweden[6]

G-30

Baldwin I, b. Blois, France; d. France[6]

Hugues "Le Grand,"* b. 900, France; d. June 16, 956, France, m. Avoi-Hatbruide **De Saxe**,* b. Germany[6]

Guillaume III,* b. 910, Poitiers, France; d. 966, France, m. 933, Gerlac-Adele **De Normandy**,* b. Normandy, France[6]

Boso III,* b. France; d. France, m. Constance (Last Name Unknown)*[6]

Foulques II, b. France; d. France, m. Gerberge **De Gatanais**,* b. Gatanais, France[6]

Sviatoslav I,* b. Russia; d. Russia, m. Malfredd **Von Lubeck***[6]

Eric VI "The Victorious,"* b. 935, Sweden; d. Sweden, m. Sigrid "The Haughty"*[6]

G-31

Godfrey **De Neustria**, b. France; d. France[6]

G-32

Rowland **De Neustria**, b. France; d. France[6]

G-33

Charles "The Younger," b. France; d. France[6]

G-34

Charlemagne, b. April 2, 742, France; d. France, m. Hildegarde **De Veinzzau***[6]

G-35

King Pepin "The Short,"* b. 714, France; d. France, m. Bertha, Countess De Laon*[6]

Julia Grant

G+2

Children of Frederick Dent and Ida Marie (Honore) Dent:

Julia **Grant**, b. June 7, 1876, at the White House, m. September 25, 1899, Prince Michael Mikhailovich **Cantacuzene**[1]

Ulysses S. **Grant**, b. July 4, 1881; d. August 29, 1968, Clinton, New York, m. November 27, 1907, Edith **Root**[1]

Children of Ulysses and Fannie Josephine (Chaffee) Grant:

Miriam **Grant**, b. September 8, 1881, New York, New York, m(1) September 17, 1904, Ulysses **Macy**, m(2) John **Rice**[1]

Chaffee **Grant**, b. September 28, 1883, New York, New York, m(1) Ellen **Wrenshall**, m(2) Marion **Farnsworth**[1]

Julia **Grant**, b. April 15, 1885, New York, New York, m. October 8, 1910, Edmund **King**[1]

Fanny **Grant**, b. August 11, 1889, Salem Center, New York; d. 1943, m. October 16, 1911, Isaac Hart **Purdy**[1]

Ulysses **Grant**, b. May 23, 1893, m(1) Matilda **Bartikofsky**, m(2) Frances **Dean**[1]

Children of Algernon and Ellen (Grant) Sartoris:

Grant Greville **Sartoris**, b. July 11, 1875, Washington, D.C.[1]

Algernon Edward **Sartoris**, b. March 17, 1877; d. 1907, m. 1904, Cecile **Goufflard**[1]

Vivian May **Sartoris**, b. April 7, 1879, London, England; d. 1933, m. Frederick Roosevelt **Scovell**[1]

Rosemary Alice **Sartoris**, b. November 30, 1880, London, England; d. 1914, m. 1906, George **Woolston**[1]

Children of Jesse Root and Elizabeth (Chapman) Grant:

Nellie **Grant**, b. August 5, 1881, Elberon, New Jersey; d. 1972, m. May 15, 1903, William Piggott **Cronan**[1]

Chapman **Grant**, b. March 22, 1887, Salem Center, New York, m. November 21, 1917, Mabel **Ward**[1]

G+1

Frederick Dent **Grant**, b. May 30, 1850, St. Louis, Missouri; d. April 11, 1912, New York, m. October 20, 1874, Chicago Ida Marie **Honore**[2]

Ulysses Simpson **Grant**, b. July 22, 1852, Bethel, Ohio; d. September 26, 1929, San Diego, Calif., m(1) November 1, 1880, New York City Fannie Josephine **Chaffee**, m(2) America **Workman**[2]

Ellen Wrenshall **Grant**, b. July 4, 1855; d. August 30, 1972, Chicago, Illinois, m(1) Algernon Charles **Sartoris**, m(2) Frank **Jones**[2]

Jesse Root **Grant**, b. February 6, 1858; d. June 8, 1934, Los Altos, Calif., m(1) Elizabeth **Chapman**, m(2) Lillian **Burns**[2]

Julia Dent, b. February 16, 1826; d. December 14, 1902, Washington, D.C., m. August 22, 1848, Ulysses S. Grant, b. April 27, 1822, Ohio; d. July 23, 1885, Mt. McGregor, New York[3, 8]

G-1

Frederick Fayette **Dent**, b. October 6, 1786, Cumberland Co., Maryland; d. December 15, 1873, St. Louis, Missouri, m. December 22, 1804, Ellen **Wrenshall**, b. 1793, Halifax, England; d. January 9, 1857, St. Louis, Missouri[3]

G-2

George **Dent**, b. May 23, 1755, Whitehaven, Maryland; d. Alleghany Co., Pa., m. April 28, 1785, Susanna **Dawson**, b. 1740, Prince George Co., Maryland; d. 1807, Alleghany Co., Pa.[3]

John **Wrenshall**, b. December 27, 1761, Preston, England; d. September 24, 1821, Pa., m. Mary **Bennington**, b. 1761, England; d. July 1, 1812, Pittsburgh, Pa[3]

G-3

Peter **Dent**, b. January 10, 1728, Prince George Co., Maryland; d. March 26, 1765, Maryland, m. June 19, 1754, Mary Eleanor (Last Name Unknown),* b. 1730, Charles Co., Maryland; d. June 28, 1758, Prince George Co., Maryland[3]

John **Dawson**, b. 1706, Charles Co., Maryland, m. Martha Ann **Marbury**, b. September 11, 1715, Talbot Co., Maryland; d. June 28, 1795[3]

Thomas **Wrenshall**, b. 1735, Preston, England; d. March 2, 1790, Preston, England, m. May 3, 1756, Margaret **Bray**,* b. 1738, Preston, England; d. England[3]

Matthew **Bennington**, b. October 6, 1737, Halifax, England, m. May 25, 1760, Sarah **Spencer**,* b. 1739, Preston, England[3]

G-4

Peter **Dent**, b. 1693; d. October 24, 1757, m. Mary **Brooke**, b. October 8, 1709; d. January 10, 1779[3]

Nicholas **Dawson**, b. 1670; d. 1727, m. Mary **Doyne**[3]

William **Wrenshall**,* b. England; d. England[3]

Matthew **Bennington**,* b. England; d. England[3]

G-5

William **Dent**, b. 1660, St. Mary's Co., Maryland; d. February 17, 1704–1705, m. February 8, 1685, Elizabeth **Fawke**, b. 1668, Charles Co., Maryland[3]

Thomas **Brooke**, b. 1683, Nottingham, Maryland; d. December 18, 1744, Prince George's Co., Maryland, m. May 9, 1704, Lucy **Smith**, b. 1686, Calvert Co., Maryland; d. April 15, 1770[3, 4]

John **Dawson**,* m. Rebecca **Doyne***[3]

Robert **Doyne**,* m. Mary **Stone***[3]

Francis **Marbury**,* m. Eliza (Last Name Unknown)*[3]

G-6

Thomas **Dent**, b. 1630, Gisborough, England; d. April 22, 1676, St. Mary's Co., Maryland, m. Rebecca **Wilkinson**, b. 1633; d. 1726, Prince George Co., Maryland[3]

Gerard **Fawke**, b. 1634, Gunston, England; d. October 30, 1669, m. Ann **Thoroughgood**, b. 1630, Staffordshire, England[3]

Thomas **Brooke**, b. 1660; d. 1730, m. Anna **Baker***[3, 4]

Walter **Smith**, b. 1667, Calvert Co., Maryland; d. June 4, 1711, m. 1686, Rachel **Hall**, b. 1671, Calvert Co., Maryland; d. October 28, 1730, Calvert Co., Maryland[3, 4]

G-7

Peter **Dent**,* b. 1605, Gisborough, England, m. Margaret **Nicholson**,* b. England[3]

William **Wilkinson**,* b. 1612, Gabriel, England; d. September 21, 1663, St. Mary's Co., Maryland, m. Naomi **Hughes**, b. 1616, England; d. Norfolk Co., Va.[3,4,5]

Roger **Fawke**, b. 1602, Stafford, England, m. Mary **Bailey**, b. 1606, Stafford, England[3]

Adam **Thoroughgood**, b. 1603, Grimston, England, m. July 18, 1627, Sarah **Offley**, b. April 16, 1609, London, England; d. 1657, Princess Anne Co., Maryland[5]

Thomas **Brooke**, b. June 23, 1632, Bettel, England; d. 1676, Maryland, m. Eleanor **Hatton**, b. 1642; d. 1725, Prince George Co., Maryland[4]

Richard **Smith**,* b. 1640, England; d. 1714, England, m. Eleanor **Morgan**, b. England[4]

Richard **Hall**, b. 1635, England; d. August 28, 1688, Calvert Co., Maryland[4]

G-8

Gabriel **Wilkinson**,* b. England[3]

John **Fawke**, b. 1552, England; d. England, m. Dorothy **Cupper**, b. 1556, England; d. England[2,3]

William **Thoroughgood**,* b. 1560, England; d. May 19, 1626, England, m. Anne **Edwards**,* b. England[2,5]

Robert **Offley**, b. 1550, England; d. 1625, England, m. Ann **Osborne**, b. 1570, England; d. England[2,5]

Robert **Brooke**, b. June 2, 1602, London, England; d. July 20, 1655, m. 1627, Mary **Baker**,* b. 1606, Battel, England; d. 1633, England[4]

Richard **Hatton**,* b. England, m. Margaret (Last Name Unknown),* b. England[4]

Henry **Morgan**,* b. England[4]

G-9

Francis **Fawke**, b. 1527, Stafford, England; d. England, m. Joan **Raynsford**, b. 1530, Brewood, England; d. England[3]

John **Cupper**,* b. England; d. England, m. Audrey **De Peto**, b. England; d. England[2]

Robert **Offley**, b. 1520, London, England; d. England[5]

Sir Edward **Osborne**, b. 1539, London, England; d. February 15, 1592, England, m. 1562, Anne **Hewett**, b. 1543, England; d. July 14, 1585, London, England[5]

Thomas **Brooke**, b. 1561, Hampshire, England; d. 1612, White

Church, England, m. Susan **Forster**, b. London, England; d. White Church, England[4]

G-10

John **Fawke**, b. 1498, Brewood, England; d. England, m. Anne **Bradshaw**, b. 1503, Windley, England[3]

John **Raynsford**,* b. England; d. England[3]

John **De Peto**, b. 1478, England; d. 1542, England[2]

William **Offley**, b. 1490, Stafford, England; d. England, m. Elizabeth **Wright**,* b. 1485, Stafford, England; d. England[5]

Richard **Osborne**, b. 1513, Ashford, England; d. August 11, 1581, m. Jane **Broughton**, b. 1517, Broughton, England[5]

Sir William **Hewitt**, b. 1514, England; d. January 25, 1565, England, m. Alice Elizabeth **Leveson**, b. 1523, Halling, England; d. April 8, 1561, England[7]

Richard **Brooke**,* b. Hampshire, England; d. England, m. Elizabeth **Twyne**,* b. England; d. England[4]

Sir Thomas **Forster**, b. August 10, 1548, England; d. May 18, 1612, England, m. Susan **Foster**, b. England; d. England[5]

G-11

Roger **Fawke**,* b. England; d. England, m. Cassandra **Humfries**,* b. England; d. England[3]

John **Bradshaw**,* b. England; d. England, m. Isabel **Kinnersley**, b. England; d. England[3]

Edward **De Peto**, b. England; d. England[2]

John **Offley**,* b. 1450, Stafford, England; d. England, m. Margery (Last Name Unknown),* b. England; d. England[5]

Richard **Osborne**,* b. England; d. England, m. Elizabeth **Fyldens**,* b. England; d. England[5]

John **Broughton**,* b. England; d. England, m. Jane (Last Name Unknown),* b. England; d. England[5]

Edmund **Hewitt**,* b. 1493, England; d. England[7]

Nicholas **Leveson**, b. 1495, London, England; d. October 13, 1539, England, m. Denyse **Bodley**, b. 1498, England; d. September 10, 1561[7]

Thomas **Forster**, b. England; d. England, m. Margaret **Browning**,* b. England; d. England[5]

Thomas **Foster**,* b. England; d. England[5]

G-12

John **Kinnersley*** b.England; d. England, m. Margaret **Aston**, b. England; d. England[3]

John **De Peto**,* b. England; d. England[2]

Richard **Leveson**, b. 1457, England; d. England, m. Hielana **Wyllenhall***[7]

Thomas **Bodley**,* b. 1473, England; d. England, m. Joan **Leech**,* b. 1478, England; d. England[7]

Sir Roger **Forster**, b. England; d. England, m. Joan **Hussey**,* b. England; d. England[5]

G-13

John **Aston**, b. England; d. England, m. Elizabeth **Delves**, b. England; d. England[3]

Richard **Leveson**, b. 1431, Prestwood, England; d. England, m. Joanna **De Knightley**, b. England; d. England[7]

Thomas **Forster**, b. England; d. England, m. Elizabeth **De Fetherstonehaugh**,* b. England; d. England[5]

G-14

Sir Robert **Aston**, b. England; d. England, m. Isabella **Brereton**,* b. England; d. England[2]

Nicholas **Leveson**, b. 1405, England; d. England, m. Mathilda **Prestwood**, b. 1409, England; d. England[7]

John **De Knightley**, b. 1369, England; d. 1416, England, m. Joan **De Thornbury**, b. England; d. England[7]

Thomas **Forster**, b. England; d. England[5]

G-15

Sir Roger **Aston**,* b. England; d. England, m. Joyce **De Umfreville**, b. England; d. England[2]

Richard **Leveson**, b. 1378, England; d. England, m. Joanna **De Rushall**, b. 1382, England; d. England[7]

John **Prestwood**, b. 1380, England; d. England[7]

John **De Knightley**, b. 1339, England; d. 1414, England, m. Elizabeth **De Burgh**, b. 1343, England; d. England[7]

John **De Thornbury**,* b. England; d. England[7]

Thomas **Forster**,* b. England; d. England, m. Joan **Elmeden**, b. England; d. England[5]

G-16

Sir Baldwin **De Umfreville**, b. England; d. England, m. Maud (Last Name Unknown),* b. England; d. England[2]

John **Leveson,*** b. 1346, England; d. England, m. Agnes (Last Name Unknown),* b. England; d. England[7]

John **De Rushall,*** b. 1356, England; d. England[7]

John **Prestwood,*** b. England; d. England[7]

Robert **De Knightley,*** b. 1315, England; d. 1395, England, m. Julianne (Last Name Unknown),* b. England; d. England[7]

Adam **De Burgh,*** b. 1320, England; d. England, m. Alilitha **Harcourt,*** b. England; d. England[7]

William **Elmeden,*** b. England; d. England, m. Elizabeth **De Umfreville**, b. England; d. England[5]

G-17

Sir Baldwin **De Umfreville,*** b. England; d. England, m. Joyce **De Botetorte**, b. England; d. England[3]

Sir Thomas **De Umfreville**, b. England; d. England, m. Agnes **De Umfreville**, b. England; d. England[3]

G-18

John **De Botetorte**, b. 1318, England; d. 1385, England, m. Joyce **La Zouche**, b. 1327, England; d. 1372, England[2]

Robert **De Umfreville,*** m. Lucy **De Kyme*** (Refer to Robert **De Umfreville** G-19 Lucretia **Garfield** to continue their lines.)[2]

G-19

Thomas **De Botetorte**, b. 1285, England; d. 1322, England, m. Joan De **Somery,*** b. England; d. England[2]

Lord William **La Zouche**, b. Ashby, England; d. February 28, 1336, England, m. 1327, Eleanor **De Clare**, b. 1292, England; d. 1337, England[2]

G-20

John **De Botetorte**, b. 1265, England; d. November 25, 1324, England, m. Maud **Fitz Thomas,*** b. England; d. England[2]

Robert **La Zouche,*** b. England; d. England, m. Joyce **La Zouche**, b. 1240, England; d. 1290, England[2]

Gilbert **De Clare**, b. September 2, 1243, Hampshire, England; d. December 7, 1292, England, m. Joan of Acre,* b. 1272, England; d. 1307, England[2]

G-21

King Edward I,* m. Alice **Lusignan*** (Refer to King Edward I G-17 Abigail **Adams** to continue his line.)[2]

William **La Zouche,** b. 1209, England; d. England, m. Maude **De Mortimer,*** b. 1213, England; d. England[2]

Richard **De Clare,** b. England; d. England, m. Margaret **De Lacy,*** b. England; d. England[2]

G-22

Roger **La Zouche,** b. England; d. England, m. Margaret (Last Name Unknown),* b. England; d. England[2]

Gilbert **De Clare,*** b. England; d. England, m. Isabell **Marshall,*** b. England; d. England (Refer to Gilbert **De Clare** G-21 Ellen **Arthur** to continue their lines.)[2]

G-23

Alan **La Zouche,*** b. 1141, England; d. 1190, England, m. Alix **De Beaumez***[2]

Florence Harding

G+2

Children of Eugene Marshall De Wolfe and Esther (Neely) De Wolfe:

Jean **De Wolfe**, b. 1909; d. 1971[5]

George **De Wolfe**, b. 1912; d. 1968[5]

G+1

Children of Florence Kling and Henry De Wolfe:

Eugene Marshall **De Wolfe**[1]

Florence Mabel Kling, b. August 16, 1860, Marion, Ohio; d. November 21, 1924, m(1) Henry De Wolfe, m(2) July 8, 1891, Warren Gamaliel Harding, b. November 2, 1865, Corsica, Ohio; d. August 2, 1923, San Francisco, California[1, 5]

G-1

Amos **Kling**, b. June 15, 1833, Lancaster Co., Pa., m. Louisa, m. **Bouton**, b. September 2, 1835, New Canaan, Conn.; d. 1887, Marion. Ohio[1]

G-2

Michael **Kling**, b. Pa., m. Elizabeth **Vitalis**,* b. Pa.[1]

Harvey **Bouton**, b. February 13, 1803, New Canaan, Conn.; d. 1881, Plainsville, Ohio, m. October 18, 1826, Emily **Hanford***[1]

G-3

John Ludwig **Kling**, b. 1750, Stone Arabia, New York; d. February 15, 1823, Schorhasie Co., New York, m. November 15, 1772, Anne **France**, b. October 30, 1753, on board a ship enroute to America; d. Schorhasie, New York[1]

Jakin **Bouton**, b. 1767, Norwalk, Conn., m. Rhoda **Richards***[1]

G-4

Heindrick **Kling***[1]

Sebastian **France,*** b. Wurtenberg, Germany, m. Anne **Fritz,*** b. Wurtenberg, Germany[1]

Ezra **Bouton**, b. November 18, 1723, Stamford, Conn., m. Mary **Bouton**, b. 1732, Norwalk, Conn.[1, 2]

G-5

Eleazer **Bouton**, b. 1696, Norwalk, Conn., m. Elizabeth **Seymour**, b. 1708, Danbury, Conn.[1, 2]

Jackin **Bouton**, b. 1694, Norwalk, Conn.; d. 1779, Conn.[2]

G-6

Joseph **Bouton**, b. 1674, m. Mary **Hayes,*** b. ca. 1667; d. Norwalk, Conn.[2]

Matthew **Seymour**, b. 1669, Norwalk, Conn.; d. 1734, Norwalk, Conn., m. Sarah **Hayes**, b. September 19, 1673, Norwalk, Conn.; d. 1711, Norwalk, Conn.[3]

Joseph **Bouton,*** m. Mary **Hayes*** (Refer to Joseph **Bouton** G-6 Florence **Harding** to continue his line.)[2]

G-7

John **Bouton**, b. 1636, m. Abigail **Marvin**, b. 1640; d. 1672[2]

Thomas **Seymour**, b. July 15, 1632, Sawbridgeworth, England; d. Norwalk, Conn., m. Hannah **Marvin**, b. October 1, 1634, Essex, England; d. 1680[3]

Samuel **Hayes,*** b. 1642; d. 1712, m. Elizabeth **Moore***[3]

G-8

John **Bouton**, b. 1605, England; d. ca. 1645, m. Alice **Kellogg,*** b. March 26, 1600, England; d. December 1, 1680[2]

Matthew **Marvin**, b. March 26, 1600, England; d. December 20, 1678, m. Elizabeth **Gregory**, b. 1603, England; d. January 24, 1681, Hartford, Conn.[2]

Richard **Seymour,*** b. 1604, England, m. Mercy **Ruscoe,*** b. 1610, Sawbridgeworth, England[3]

Matthew **Marvin,*** m. Elizabeth **Gregory*** (Refer to Matthew **Marvin** G-8 Florence **Harding** to continue their lines.)[2, 3]

G-9

Nicholas **Bouton**,* b. England[2]

Edward **Marvin**, b. 1545, England; d. November 15, 1615, England, m. Margaret (Last Name Unknown)*[2]

Henry **Gregory**, b. England; d. England[2]

G-10

Reinhold **Marvin**, b. 1513, England; d. October 14, 1561, England, m. Mary (Last Name Unknown)*[2]

John **Gregory**, b. 1556, England, m. Alice **Alton**,* b. 1564, Nottingham, England[4]

G-11

Thomas **Gregory**, b. England; d. England, m. Dorothy **Beeston**, b. England; d. England[4]

G-12

Hugh **Gregory**, b. England; d. England, m. Mary (Last Name Unknown)*[4]

George **Beeston**, b. England; d. England, m. Alicia **Davenport**,* b. England; d. England[4]

G-13

William **Gregory**, b. 1470, England; d. England, m. Dorothy **Parre**,* b. 1478, England; d. England[4]

John **Beeston**,* b. 1478, England; d. England, m. Katherine **Calveley**,* b. 1482, England; d. England[4]

G-14

Adam **Gregory**, b. England; d. England, m. Adae **Ormston**, b. England; d. England[4]

G-15

Nicholas **Gregory**, b. England; d. England[4]

Adam **Ormston**,* b. England; d. England[4]

G-16

John **Gregory**,* b. England; d. England, m. Mary **Moton**,* b. England; d. England[4]

Anna Harrison

G+2

Children of John Scott and Lucretia (Johnson) Harrison:

Elizabeth **Harrison**, b. 1825; d. 1904, m. George **Eaton**[1]

William Henry **Harrison**, b. 1827; d. 1829[1]

Sarah Lucretia **Harrison**, b. 1829, m. Thomas Jefferson **Devin**[1]

Children of John Scott and Elizabeth (Irwin) Harrison:

Archibald Irwin **Harrison**, b. 1832; d. 1870, m. Elizabeth **Sheets**[1]

Benjamin **Harrison**, b. August 20, 1833, North Bend, Ohio; d. March 13, 1901, Indianapolis, Indiana, m(1) October 20, 1853, Oxford, Ohio Caroline Lavinia **Scott**, m(2)April 6, 1896, Mary Scott Dimmick **Lord**[1]

Mary Jane **Harrison**, b. 1835; d. 1867[1]

Anna Symmes **Harrison**, b. 1837; d. 1838[1]

John Irwin **Harrison**, b. 1839; d. 1839[1]

Carter Bassett **Harrison**, b. 1840; d. 1905, m. Sophia **Dashide**[1]

Anna Symmes **Harrison**, b. 1842; d. 1926[1]

John Scott **Harrison**, b. 1844; d. 1926, m. Sophia Elizabeth **Lytle**[1]

James Findlay **Harrison**, b. 1847; d. 1848[1]

Children of John Cleves Symmes and Clarissa (Pike) Harrison:

John Cleves **Harrison**[2]

Rebecca **Harrison**, b. August 29, 1821; d. June 14, 1849, m. John **Hunt**[2]

Anna Marie **Harrison**, m. James Madison **Roberts**[2]

Clara Louise **Harrison**, b. 1824; d. 1883, m(1) Tomlin Miller **Banks**, m(2) Oliver Perry **Morgan**[2]

William Henry **Harrison**, b. 1828; d. 1900, m(1) Mary Ann **McIntyre**, m(2) Elvira (Last Name Unknown)[2]

Montgomery Pike **Harrison**, b. 1829; d. October 7, 1849, Texas[2]

G+1

Elizabeth Bassett **Harrison**, b. September 29, 1796, Cincinnati, Ohio; d. September 27, 1846, m. June 29, 1814, John Cleves **Short**[1]

John Cleves Symmes **Harrison**, b. October 28, 1798, Cincinnati, Ohio; d. October 30, 1830, m. Clarissa **Pike**[1]

Lucy **Harrison**, b. September 5, 1800, Richmond, Va.; d. April 7, 1826, Cincinnati, Ohio, m. September 30, 1819, David K. **Estes**[1]

William Henry **Harrison**, b. September 3, 1802, Vincennes, Indiana; d. February 6, 1838, North Bend, Ohio, m. February 18, 1824, Jane **Irwin**[1]

John Scott **Harrison**, b. October 4, 1804, Vincennes, Indiana; d. May 25, 1878, North Bend, Ohio, m(1) Lucnetia Knapp **Johnson**, m(2) August 12, 1831, Elizabeth **Irwin**[1]

Benjamin **Harrison**, b. May 5, 1806, Vincennes, Indiana; d. June 9, 1840, m(1) Louisa **Bonner**, m(2) Mary **Raney**[1]

Mary Symmes **Harrison**, b. December 8, 1809, Vincennes, Indiana; d. March 5, 1879, m. John Henry **Thornton**[1]

Carter Bassett **Thompson**, b. October 26, 1811, Vincennes, Indiana; d. June 16, 1836, m. Mary Ann **Sutherland**[1]

Anna **Harrison** October 28, 1813, North Bend, Ohio, m. William Henry Harrison **Taylor**[1]

James Findlay **Harrison**, b. May 14, 1814, North Bend, Ohio; d. April 6, 1819[1]

Anna Symmes, b. July 25, 1775, Morristown, New Jersey; d. February 25, 1864, North Bend, Ohio, m. November 25, 1795, William Henry Harrison, b. February 9, 1773, Berkeley, Virginia; d. April 4, 1841, Washington, D.C.[3, 12]

G-1

John Cleve **Symmes**, b. July 21, 1742, Suffolk Co., New York; d. February 26, 1814, North Bend, Ohio, m. Anna **Tuthill**, b. June 17, 1749, Suffolk Co., New York; d. 1776[3]

G-2

Timothy **Symmes**, b. May 27, 1714, Scituate, Mass.; d. April 6, 1756, Suffolk Co., New York, m. Mary **Cleves**, b. June 17, 1749, Suffolk Co., New York; d. 1776[3]

Daniel **Tuthill**, b. June 18, 1715, Suffolk Co., New York; d. November 18, 1798, Suffolk Co., New York, m. Phoebe **Horton**, b. 1722, Suffolk Co., New York; d. 1793, Suffolk Co., New York[3, 4]

G-3

Timothy **Symmes**, b. 1683, Charlestown, Mass., m. July 31, 1710, Elizabeth **Collamore**[3]

John **Cleves**, b. 1704, Suffolk Co., New York, m. Mary **Hallock**, b. Suffolk Co., New York; d. January 14, 1785, Suffolk Co., New York[4]

Daniel **Tuthill**, b. January 23, 1679, Suffolk Co., New York; d. December 9, 1762, Suffolk Co., New York, m. Mehitable **Horton**[3]

Caleb **Horton**, b. December 23, 1687, Southold, New York; d. August 6, 1722, Roxbury, New York, m. Phoebe **Terry**, b. June 5, 1690, Southold, New York; d. December 14, 1776, Roxbury, New York[4]

G-4

William **Symmes**, b. 1626 or 1628; d. July 13, 1705, m. Mary **Chickering**, b. November 2, 1643, Wrentham, England; d. March 12, 1721, Weymouth, Mass.[3, 7]

Anthony **Collamore**, b. England; d. December 16, 1693, at sea, m. 1666, Sarah **Chittenden**, b. February 25, 1647, Scituate, Mass.; d. October 25, 1703, Scituate, Mass.[3]

John **Cleves**,* m. Eliza (Last Name Unknown)*[3]

William **Hallock**, b. 1667, Suffolk, New York; d. June 19, 1736, Southold, New York, m. Mary (Last Name Unknown),* b. 1667, Suffolk, New York; d. January 26, 1752, Southold, New York[8]

John **Tuthill**, b. May 1, 1665, Southold, New York; d. January 7, 1749, New York[3]

Jonathan **Horton**, b. May 23, 1647, Southold, New York; d. July 23, 1707, Southold, New York, m. Bethia **Wells**, b. 1655, Southold, New York; d. April 14, 1733, Southold, New York[4]

Barnabas **Horton**, m. Sarah **Wines**, b. 1667, Southampton New York[4]

Nathaniel **Terry**,* b. January 7, 1656, Southold, New York; d. October 22, 1723, Southold, New York, m. Mary **Horton**, b. 1666, Suffolk, New York; d. September 6, 1720, Southold, New York[4]

G-5

Zachariah **Symmes**, b. April 5, 1599, Canterbury, New York; d. February 4, 1671, m. Sarah **Baker**, b. 1605, England; d. June 10, 1673, Charlestown, Mass.[10]

Francis **Chickering** April 14, 1606, Suffolk, England; d. October

10, 1658, Dedham, Mass., m. Ann **Fiske**, b. April 1, 1610, Suffolk, England; d. December 5, 1649, Dedham, Mass.[7]

John **Collamore**, b. 1608, England; d. 1657, Mass., m. Mary **Nicholls**, b. 1612, England; d. Mass.[1]

Isaac **Chittenden**, b. 1625, England; d. May 2, 1676, Mass., m. 1646, Mary **Vinal**, b. 1628, England; d. Mass.[3]

John **Tuthill**, b. 1635, m. Deliverance **King**, b. August 31, 1641, Salem, Mass.; d. January 24, 1689, Oyster Ponds, New York[9]

Barnabas **Horton**, b. July 13, 1600, Mousley. England; d. July 13, 1684, Southold, New York, m. Mary **Langston**, b. England[4]

William **Wells**, b. England, m. Mary **Youngs**, b. England[4]

Caleb **Horton**, b. England, m. Abigail **Hallock**, b. England[4]

Barnabas **Wines**, b. England, m. Mary **Benjamin**, b. England[4]

G-6

William **Symmes**,* b. 1570, Canterbury, England; d. 1621, Canterbury, England, m. Mary **Ingleram**,* b. 1577, Canterbury, England; d. Canterbury, England[4]

Henry **Chickering**,* b. England, m. Mary (Last Name Unknown),* b. England[7]

John **Fiske**, b. 1580, England, m. Anne **Lawter**, b. England[7]

Thomas **Collamore**, b. September 20, 1570, Devonshire, England; d. January 11, 1608, Devonshire, England, m. Agnes **Adams**, b. England; d. England[11]

Thomas **Chittenden**, b. 1584, Kent, England; d. 1669, Scituate, Mass., m. Rebecca (Last Name Unknown),* b. 1595, Kent, England; d. Scituate, England[12]

Stephen **Vinal**, b. England; d. Mass., m. Ann (Last Name Unknown),* b. England; d. Mass.[12]

Henry **Tuthill**, b. England, m. Bridget (Last Name Unknown),* b. England[3]

William **King**, b. 1595, Weymouth, England; d. 1650, Southold, England, m. February 17, 1616, Dorothy **Hayne**, b. 1601, England; d. Southold, New York[9]

Joseph **Horton**, b. 1578, Mousley, England; d. 1640, Springfield, Mass., m. Mary **Schuyler**, b. England[4]

William **Wells**,* b. England, m. Elizabeth (Last Name Unknown),* b. England[4]

John **Youngs**, b. England, m. Mary (Last Name Unknown),* b. England[4]

Barnabas **Horton**, m. Mary **Langston*** (Refer to Barnabas **Horton** G-5 Anna **Harrison** to continue his line.)[4]

William Peter **Hallock,*** b. England, m. Margaret **Howell,*** b. England[4]

Barnabas **Wines**, b. England, m. Anna **Eddy**, b. England[4]

Richard **Benjamin,*** b. England, m. Anna (Last Name Unknown),* b. England[4]

G-7

William **Fiske**, b. 1550, England; d. England, m. Anna **Austeye**, b. 1560, England; d. England[7]

Robert **Lawter,*** b. 1555, England; d. England, m. Mary **Fiske**, b. England; d. England[7]

Peter **Collamore**, b. Devonshire, England; d. Devonshire, England, m. Edith (Last Name Unknown),* b. England; d. England[1]

John **Adams**, b. Somersetshire, England; d. Somersetshire, England, m. Margery **Squire,*** b. Somersetshire, England; d. Somersetshire, England[11]

Robert **Chittenden,*** b. 1559, Kent, England; d. England, m. Eleanor **Hatch,*** b. 1559, Kent, England; d. 1628, England[12]

John **Vinal**, b. England; d. England[12]

Henry **Tuthill**, b. England; d.England, m. Alice **Gooch**, b. England; d. England[13]

William **King,*** b. 1574, Weymouth, England; d. 1625, Hawkchurch, England, m. Ann **Bowdridge,*** b. 1575, Weymouth, England; d. Hawkchurch, England[9]

Walter **Hayne,*** b. 1575, England; d. England[9]

William **Horton,*** b. 1550, Firthouse, England; d. England, m. Elizabeth **Hanson,*** b. 1552, Mousley, England; d. England[4]

Christopher **Youngs,*** b. 1545, Reyden, England; d. June 14, 1626, Reyden, England, m. Margaret **Elvin,*** b. England; d. England[4]

Charles **Wines,*** b. England; d. England, m. Prudence **Beacon,*** b. England; d. England[4]

William **Eddy,*** b. England; d. England, m. Mary **Fosten,*** b. England; d. England[4]

G-8

Robert **Fiske**, b. 1521, England; d. 1602, England, m. Sibella **Gold,*** b. England; d. England[7]

Walter **Austeye,*** b. England; d. England[7]

William **Fiske**, b. 1525, England; d. England[7]

John **Collamore**,* b. England; d. England, m. Margery **Hext**, b. England; d. England[1]

John **Adams**,* b. England; d. England, m. Catherine **Stebbing**,* b. England; d. England[11]

John **Tuthill**,* b. England; d. England, m. Elizabeth (Last Name Unknown),* b. England; d. England[13]

John **Gooch**,* b. 1558, Suffolk, England; d. Suffolk, England, m. Margaret **Rau**,* b. 1562, Suffolk, England; d. Suffolk, England[13]

G-9

Richard **Fiske**, b. 1493, England; d. England[7]

Richard **Fiske*** (Refer to Richard **Fiske** G-9 Anna **Harrison** to continue his line.)[7]

Thomas **Hext**, b. 1478, England; d. England, m. Wilnot **Poyntz**, b. 1487, England; d. 1558[1]

G-10

Simon **Fiske**,* b. England; d. England[7]

Thomas **Hext**,* b. England; d. England, m. Joan **Fortescue**, b. England; d. England[1]

G-11

John **Fortescue**, b. 1420, England; d. 1480, England, m. Jane **Preston**,* b. England; d. England[1]

G-12

William **Fortescue** , b. 1385, England; d. England, m. Isabel **Falwell**,* b. England; d. England[1]

G-13

William **Fortescue**, b. 1345, England; d. England, m. Elizabeth **De Beauchamp**, b. England; d. England[1]

G-14

William **Fortescue** , b. England; d. England, m. Alice **Strechleigh**,* b. England; d. England[1]

Sir John **De Beauchamp**, b. England; d. England, m. Margaret **Whalesburgh***[1]

G-15

Adam **Fortescue**, b. England; d. England, m. Anna **De La Port***[1]

Sir John **De Beauchamp**, b. 1285, England; d. 1346, England, m. Alice **De Nonant**,* b. England; d. England[1]

G-16

Adam **Fortescue**, b. England; d. England[1]

Sir Humphrey **De Beauchamp**, b. 1274, England; d. 1316, England, m. Sibyl **Oliver**, b. England; d. England[1]

G-17

Sir Adam **Fortescue**, b. England; d. England[1]

Robert **De Beauchamp**, b. 1224, England; d. 1266, England, m. Alice De **Mohun**, b. 1224, England; d. 1285, England[1]

G-18

Richard **Fortescue**, b. England; d. England[1]

Reginald **De Mohun**, b. 1206, Dunster, England; d. January 20, 1258, Devonshire, England, m. Hawise **Fitz Geoffrey**, b. England; d. England[1]

G-19

Sir John **Fortescue**, b. England; d. England[1]

Geoffrey **De Mandeville**,* b. England; d. England, m. Aveline **De Clare**, b. England; d. England[1]

G-20

William **Fortescue**, b. England; d. England[1]

Roger "The Good" **De Clare**, b. England; d. England, m. Maud **De St. Hilary**, b. England; d. England[1]

G-21

Richard **Fortescue**,* b. England; d. England[1]

Richard **De Clare**, b. England; d. England, m. Alice **De Meschines**, b. England; d. England[1]

G-22

Lord Gilbert **De Clare**,* b. England; d. England, m. Adelaide **De Clermont**,* b. England; d. England[1]

Ranulf III **De Meschines**,* b. 1070, Chester, England; d.

1129, England, m. Lucy **Taillebois**, b. 1072, Mercia, England; d. 1136, England[1]

G-23

Ivo **De Taillebois,*** b. England; d. England, m. Lucy of Mercia, b. 1040, Mercia, England; d. England[1]

Alfgar III, b. England; d. England, m. Elfgifu,* b. England; d. England[1]

G-24

Leofric III,* b. England; d. England, m. Lady Godiva,* b. October 10, 1067; d. England[1]

Caroline Harrison

G+2

Children of Russell Benjamin and Mary Angeline (Saunders) Harrison:

Marthena **Harrison**, b. January 18, 1890; d. February 22, 1973, m. Harry **Williams**, Jr.[1]

William Henry **Harrison**, b. August 10, 1896; d. October 8, 1990, m. Mary Elizabeth **Newton**[1]

Children of James Robert and Mary(Harrison) McKee:

Mary **McKee**[1]

Benjamin Harrison **McKee**[1]

G+1

Russell Benjamin **Harrison**, b. August 12, 1854, Oxford, Ohio; d. December 13, 1936, Indianapolis, Indiana, m. January 9, 1884, Omaha, Nebraska Mary Angeline **Saunders**[1]

Mary **Harrison**, b. April 3, 1858, Indianapolis, Indiana; d. October 28, 1930, Greenwich, Conn., m. November 5, 1884, Indianapolis, Indiana James Robert **McKee**[1]

Caroline Lavinia Scott, b. October 1, 1832, Oxford, Ohio; d. October 25, 1892, Washington, D.C., m. October 20, 1853, Benjamin Harrison, b. August 20, 1833, North Bend, Ohio; d. March 13, 1901, Indianapolis, Indiana[2,4]

G-1

John Witherspoon **Scott**, b. January 22, 1800, Beaver Co., Pa.; d. November 27, 1892, Washington, D.C., m. Mary **Neal**, b. 1803, Philadephia, Pa.; d. March 1, 1876, Oxford, Ohio[2]

G-2

Alexander **Scott**, b. December 26, 1763, Peach Bottom, Pa., m. November 18, 1790, Rachel **McDowell***[3]

John **Neal**,* m. Mary **Potts***[2]

G-3

Josiah **Scott**, b. 1735, Pa.; d. February 20, 1819, Pa., m. Violet **Foster**, b. 1739, Washington Co., Pa.; d. 1819, Washington Co., Pa.[3]

John **McDowell**,* m. Rachel **Bradford***[3]

G-4

Abraham **Scott**,* b. Pa.; d. Pa.[3]

Alexander **Foster**,* b. 1710, Londonderry, Ireland; d. 1767, Lancaster Co., Pa., m. Mary **Conner**,* b. 1710[3]

Mary Harrison

G+2

Benjamin Harrison **Walker**, m. Elizabeth **Sillcock**[1]
Mary Jane **Walker**, m. Newell **Garfield**[1]

G+1

Elizabeth **Harrison**, b. February 21, 1897, Indianapolis, Indiana; d. December 25, 1955, New York, New York, m. James Blaine **Walker**, b. January 20, 1889, Helena, Montana; d. 1921, New York, New York[1]

Mary Scott Lord, b. April 30, 1858, Honesdale, Pennsylvania; d. January 5, 1948, New York, New York, m. April 6, 1896, New York, New York, Benjamin Harrison (Refer to Caroline Harrison for information on Benjamin Harrison)[1,2]

G-1

Russell Farnham **Lord,*** m. Elizabeth Mayhew **Scott**[2]

G-2

John Witherspoon **Scott,*** m. Mary **Neal*** (Refer to G-2 Caroline **Harrison** to continue their lines.)[2]

Lucy Hayes

G+2

Children of Sardis Birchard and Mary Nancy (Sherman) Hayes:

Rutherford Birchard **Hayes**, b. October 2, 1887, Toledo, Ohio[1]
Sherman Otis **Hayes**, b. October 11, 1888, Toledo, Ohio[1]
Webb Cook **Hayes**, b. September 25, 1890, Toledo, Ohio[1]
Walter **Hayes**, b. July 27, 1893, Toledo, Ohio[1]
Scott Russell **Hayes**, b. September 23, 1894, Toledo, Ohio[1]

Children of Rutherford Platt and Lucy (Platt) Hayes:

Rutherford **Hayes**, b. February 20, 1896, Columbus, Ohio[1]
William Platt **Hayes**, b. December 8, 1897, Columbus, Ohio[1]
Birchard **Hayes**, b. July 4, 1902, Falconhurst, North Carolina[1]

Children of Frances Hayes and Harry Eaton Smith:

Dalton **Smith**, b. June 22, 1898, Spiegel Grove, Ohio[1]

G+1

Sardis Birchard **Hayes**, b. November 4, 1853, Cincinnati, Ohio; d. January 24, 1926, Toledo, Ohio, m. December 30, 1886, Mary Nancy **Sherman**, b. May 15, 1859, Ohio; d. June 22, 1924, Toledo, Ohio[1]

James Webb **Hayes**, b. March 20, 1856, Cincinnati, Ohio; d. July 26, 1935, Marion, Ohio, m. Mary **Miller**, b. April 11, 1856, Fremont, Ohio; d. March 3, 1935, Phoenix, Arizona[1]

Rutherford Platt **Hayes**, b. June 24, 1858, Cincinnati, Ohio; d. July 3, 1927, Tampa, Florida, m. October 24, 1894, Lucy **Platt**[1]

Joseph Thompson **Hayes**, b. December 21, 1861, Cincinnati, Ohio; d. June 24, 1863[1]

George Cook **Hayes**, b. September 29, 1864, Chillicothe, Ohio; d. May 24, 1866, Chillicothe, Ohio[1]

Frances **Hayes**, b. September 2, 1867, Cincinnati, Ohio; d. March 18, 1950, Lewiston, Maine, m. September 1, 1897, Harry **Smith**[1]

Scott Russell **Hayes**, b. February 28, 1871, Columbus, Ohio; d. May 6, 1923, Croton-On-Hudson, New York, m. Maude **Anderson**, b. July 7, 1873; d. November 19, 1966[1]

Manning Force **Hayes**, b. August 4, 1873, Fremont, Ohio; d. August 28, 1874, Fremont, Ohio[1]

Lucy Webb, b. August 28, 1831, Chillicothe, Ohio; d. June 25, 1889, Fremont, Ohio, m. December 30, 1852, Rutherford Birchard Hayes, b. October 4, 1822, Delaware, Ohio; d. January 17, 1893, Fremont, Ohio[1,2]

G-1

Dr. James **Webb**, b. March 17, 1795, Lexington, Kentucky; d. July 1, 1833, Lexington, Kentucky, m. April 18, 1826, Maria **Cook**, b. March 9, 1801, Chillicothe, Ohio; d. September 14, 1866[2]

G-2

Isaac **Webb**, b. January 19, 1758, Richmond, Virginia; d. June 26, 1833, Lexington, Kentucky, m. December 23, 1790, Lucy **Ware**, b. November 12, 1773, Frederick Parish, Virginia; d. June 22, 1833, Lexington, Kentucky[2]

Isaac **Cook**, b. July 16, 1768, Wallingford, Conn.; d. January 22, 1842, Ross Co., Ohio, m. December 25, 1792, Margaret **Scott**, b. June 15, 1772, Pa.; d. September 28, 1833, Lexington, Kentucky[2]

G-3

Isaac **Webb**, b. September 25, 1709, Richmond, Virginia; d. July 10, 1760, Kentucky, m. Frances **Barber**, b. 1720, Richmond, Virginia; d. Kentucky[2]

James **Ware**, b. March 13, 1741, Gloucester Co., Virginia; d. 1820, Kentucky, m. Virginia Catherine **Todd**, b. February 9, 1753, Fayette Co., Kentucky[2]

Isaac **Cook**, b. July 28, 1739, Wallingford, Conn.; d. 1810, Conn., m. 1760, Martha **Cook**, b. October 26, 1741, Wallingford, Conn.[2]

Matthew **Scott**, b. 1740, Meshaminy, Pa.; d. May 20, 1798, m. January 11, 1764, Elizabeth **Thompson**[2]

G-4

Giles **Webb**, b. 1677, England; d. 1731, m. Elizabeth **Spann*** (2)(3) William **Barber***[2]

James **Ware**, b. November 15, 1714, King and Queen Co., Virginia; d. September 25, 1796, Franklin Co., Kentucky, m. Agnes **Pace**, b. October 14, 1714[2, 4]

James **Todd***[2]

Isaac **Cook**, b. July 22, 1710, Conn., m. Jerusha **Sexton***[2]

Benjamin **Cook**,* m. Hannah **Munson**[2]

John **Scott**,* b. 1700, m. 1722, Jane **Mitchell***[2]

William **Thompson**,* b. 1736, Ireland; d. September 3, 1781, Pa., m. Catherine **Ross***[2]

G-5

John William **Webb**, b. 1649; d. 1694, m. Mary **Samford**, b. 1650[3]

Edward **Ware**, b. Virginia, m. Elizabeth **Garrett**, b. Virginia[4]

Isaac **Cook**, b. 1681, m. Sarah **Curtis**[2]

Waitstill **Munson**, b. December 12, 1697, m. Phoebe **Merriman**, b. September 16, 1699; d. December 11, 1772[5]

G-6

Giles **Webb**, b. 1620, England; d. 1692, m. Judith **Bland***[3]

James **Samford**, b. England, m. Mary (Last Name Unknown),* b. England[3]

Valentine **Ware**, b. 1640, King and Queen Co., Va.; d. 1693[4]

John **Garrett**, b. February 2, 1634, Leicester, England; d. 1706, m. 1664, Elizabeth **Ware**, b. February 7, 1635, Leicester, England[4]

Samuel **Cook**, b. 1663, Mass.; d. 1725, Mass., m. Hope **Parker**[2]

Isaac **Curtis**,* m. Sarah **Foote***[2]

Samuel **Munson**, b. February 28, 1668; d. November 23, 1741, m. Martha **Farnes***[5]

Caleb **Merriman**, b. May 16, 1665; d. July 19, 1703, m. Mary **Preston**[5]

G-7

Richard **Webb**, b. 1603, England[3]

Peter **Ware**, b. England, m. Joan **Valentine***[4]

John **Garrett**,* b. Leicester, England; d. August 31, 1680, Upper Darby, Pa., m. Mary (Last Name Unknown),* b. England[4]

Nicholas **Ware**,* b. 1625, Ratcliffe, England; d. 1662, m. 1650, Anna **Vassall**, b. April 20, 1628, Ratcliffe, England; d. 1657[4]

Samuel **Cook**, b. 1641, Mass.; d. 1702, Mass.[2]

Edward **Parker**[2]

Samuel **Munson**, b. June 7, 1643; d. March 2, 1693, m. Martha **Bradley**, b. 1648; d. January 7, 1707[5]

Nathaniel **Merriman**,* b. England, m. Joan (Last Name Unknown),* b. England[5]

Eliasaph **Preston**,* b. England, m. Mary (Last Name Unknown),* b. England[5]

G-8

William Micajah **Webb**, b. January 9, 1582, England[3]

Peter **Ware**, b. 1597, England, m. Mary **Hickes**,* b. England[4]

William **Vassall**, b. August 27, 1592, Ratcliffe, England; d. July 13, 1655, Plymouth, Mass., m. Anna **King**, b. December 1, 1594, Woodham, England; d. Barbados[4]

Henry **Cook**,* b. 1615, England; d. 1661, m. 1639, Judith **Burdsall**,* b. England[2]

Thomas **Munson**, b. September 13, 1612, England; d. May 7, 1685, m. Joanna **Mew**, b. England[5]

William **Bradley**, b. June 27, 1609, England; d. May 29, 1691, m. Alice **Pritchard**, b. 1624, England; d. 1692[5]

G-9

Alexander **Webb**, b. August 20, 1559, England; d. England, m. Mary **Wilson**, b. England[3]

Robert **Ware**, b. England, m. Elizabeth (Last Name Unknown),* b. England[4]

John **Vassall**, b. 1544, Normandy, France; d. September 13, 1625, Stepney, England, m. Anne **Russell**,* b. 1556, Ratcliffe, England; d. May 5, 1593, Stepney, England[4]

George **King**,* b. 1567, Essex, England; d. December 7, 1625, Essex, England, m. Jean **Lorram**,* b. 1571, Essex, England[4]

John **Munson**, b. October 14, 1577, England, m. Elizabeth **Sparke**, b. England[5]

Daniel **Bradley**, b. January 26, 1588, England; d. November 27, 1641, m. Elizabeth **Atkinson**, b. England[5]

Roger **Pritchard**, b. 1600, England; d. 1670, m. Frances (Last Name Unknown),* b. England[5]

G-10

Alexander **Webb**, b. December 24, 1534, England; d. 1573, England, m. Margaret **Arden,*** b. England; d. England[3]

James **Ware,*** b. Yorkshire, England; d. May 14, 1632, Dublin, Ireland, m. 1590, Mary **Briden,*** b. December 23, 1566, Dublin, Ireland; d. December 5, 1632, Dublin, Ireland[4]

John **Vassall,*** b. 1572, Normandy, France; d. England[4]

Richard **Munson**, m. Margery **Barnes***[5]

William **Bradley**, b. 1545, England; d. July 19, 1600, m. Agnes **Margates,*** b. England; d. England[5]

Benjamin **Pritchard,*** b. England, m. Rebecca **Jones,*** b. England[5]

G-11

Henry Alexander **Webb**, b. May 11, 1510, England, m. Grace **Arden,*** b. England[3]

Thomas **Munson**, b. England; d. England[5]

William **Bradley**, b. 1505, England; d. 1577, England[5]

G-12

John Alexander **Webb**, b. January 11, 1484, England; d. England[3]

John **Munson**, b. 1505, England; d. England[5]

John **Bradley**, b. 1475, England; d. England[5]

G-13

John **Webb,*** b. July 9, 1450, England; d. England[3]

John **Munson,*** b. 1485, England; d. England[5]

Thomas **Bradley,*** b. 1450, England; d. England[5]

Lou Hoover

G+2

Children of Herbert Charles and Margaret Eve (Watson) Hoover:

Margaret Ann **Hoover**[1, 2]
Herbert **Hoover**[1, 2]
Joan Leslie **Hoover**[1, 2]

Children of Allan Henry and Marion (Cutler) Hoover:

Allan Henry **Hoover**[1, 2]
Andrew **Hoover**[1, 2]
Lou **Hoover**[1, 2]

G+1

Herbert Charles **Hoover**, b. March 28, 1905, San Francisco; d. July 9, 1969, Pasadena, California, m. June 25, 1925, Margaret Eve **Watson**[1, 2]

Allan Henry **Hoover**, b. July 17, 1907, London, England; d. March 17, 1937, Los Angeles, California, m. Marion **Cutler**[1, 2]

Lou Henry, b. March 29, 1874, Waterloo, Iowa; d. January 7, 1944, m. February 10, 1899, Herbert Clark Hoover, b. August 10, 1874, West Branch, Iowa; d. October 26, 1964, New York, New York[3, 9]

G-1

Charles Delano **Henry**, b. July 20, 1845, Wooster, Ohio; d. July 21, 1928, Palo Alto, California, m. June 17, 1873, Florence Ida **Weed**, b. 1849, Waterloo, Iowa; d. June 24, 1927, Palo Alto, California[3]

G-2

William **Henry**, b. November 13, 1816, Wooster, Ohio; d. 1856, Amanda, Ohio, m. October 10, 1844, Mary Ann **Dwire**, b. 1828, Ashland, Ohio; d. 1912, Massillon, Ohio[3]

Phineas Kimberley **Weed**, b. March 7, 1821, Wayne Co., Ohio; d. November 13, 1895, Shell Rock, Iowa, m. Philomel **Scobey**, b. August 18, 1829; d. June 24, 1897, Palo Alto, California[3]

G-3

William **Henry**, b. 1780, Maryland; d. March 23, 1862, m. September 4, 1804, Abigail **Hunt**, b. January 29, 1781, Beaver Co., Pa.; d. November 29, 1843, Wayne Co., Ohio[3]

Rev. William **Dwire**, b. 1786; d. December 10, 1847, Wooster, Ohio, m. Rebecca **Pittinger**, b. 1788, Culpeper Co., Virginia; d. 1833[3]

Joshua **Weed***; d. December 29, 1828, Wayne Co., Ohio, m. 1810, Abigail **Kimberley**,* b. December 10, 1801, Georgetown, Pa.; d. January 30, 1881, Norwolk, Ohio[3]

Dr. John **Scobey**, b. April 18, 1800, Francistown, New Hampshire; d. July 21, 1846, Shell Rock, Iowa, m. 1825, Nancy **Wallace**, b. May 1, 1806; d. 1890[3]

G-4

William **Henry**, b. 1753, m. Jane **Patton***[3]

Robert **Hunt**, b. June 1, 1745, New Jersey; d. November 2, 1845, Ohio, m. Abigail **Pancoast**,* b. February 24, 1743, Pa.; d. 1827, Millersburg, Ohio[4, 5]

Isaac **Dwire**, b. 1761, Washington Co., Pa.; d. 1851, m. Susannah **Ellis***[3]

Henry Jacob **Pittinger**, b. April 11, 1764; d. June 17, 1837, m. Mary **Barcus**,* b. 1760, Hunterdon, New Jersey; d. May 1, 1837[3]

John **Scobey**[3]

Josiah **Wallace**,* b. 1769; d. April 6, 1843, m. Polly **Goffe**, b. June 23, 1771; d. October 25, 1854[3]

G-5

Samuel **Henry***[3]

Robert **Hunt**, b. February 21, 1708, Burlington Co., New Jersey; d. February 29, 1764, m. Abigail **Wood**, b. 1715, New Jersey; d. February 22, 1747, Burlington Co., New Jersey[3]

William **Dwire**,* m. Sarah **Ellis**[3]

Henrick **Pittinger**, b. February 25, 1735, Hunterdon Co., New Jersey; d. 1825, New Jersey, m. October 30, 1759, Myrtle Maria **Wyckoff**, b. November 20, 1738, Hunterdon Co., New Jersey; d. Culpeper Co., Va.[3]

David **Scobey***[3]

John **Goffe**, b. February 16, 1727, New Hampshire; d. February 3, 1813, New Hampshire, m. September 17, 1749, Jemima **Holden***[3]

G-6

Robert **Hunt**,* m. 1708, Elizabeth **Woolman**[3]

Benjamin **Wood**, b. New Jersey; d. 1738, m. January 3, 1707, Elizabeth Mary **Key**, b. New Jersey[5]

Simeon **Ellis**, b. 1698, Newton, Jersey; d. 1773, Haddonfield, New Jersey, m. Sarah **Collins**, b. 1703, Newport, Rhode Island[3, 6]

Hendrick **Pittinger**,* b. 1695, Somerset, New Jersey; d. April 25, 1775, Bridgewater, New Jersey, m. 1725, Mary **Lowe**,* b. September 15, 1703, New Jersey; d. New Jersey[3]

Nicholas **Wyckoff**, b. 1707, Freehold, New Jersey, m. Maria **Wall**, b. 1712, Middletown, New Jersey[3]

Joseph **Scobey**[3]

John **Goffe**, m. Hannah **Griggs**[7]

G-7

John **Woolman**, b. 1655, m. Elizabeth **Borton**, b. July 27, 1664, Aynhoe, England; d. September 30, 1718, New Jersey[5]

Henry **Wood**,* b. Gloucester, New Jersey; d. 1691, Gloucester, New Jersey, m. Hannah **Yokley**,* b. 1686, Gloucester, New Jersey; d. Gloucester, New Jersey[5, 8]

John **Kay**,* m. Elizabeth (Last Name Unknown)*[5]

Simeon **Ellis**, b. September 16, 1656, Woodale, England; d. January 29, 1715, Haddonfield, England, m. Sarah **Bates**[6]

Joseph **Collins**, b. November 18, 1672, Ratcliffe, England, m. Katherine **Huddleston**, b. 1679, Newport, England[6]

Jacob **Wyckoff**, b. 1676, Albany, New York, m. October 16, 1706, Willpyje Jansen **Van Voorhees**, b. 1684, Monmouth, New Jersey[3]

John **Wall**,* m. Mary **Hubbard***[3]

David **Scobey**[3]

John **Goffe**,* m. Hannah **Parrish**[7]

Ichabod **Griggs**, b. September 27, 1675; d. February 20, 1718, Roxbury, Mass., m. Margaret **Bishop**[9]

G-8

William **Woolman*** b. England[5]

John **Borton,*** b. England, m. Anne **Kinton,*** b. England[5]

Thomas **Ellis,*** b. 1628, Burlington, England; d. 1682, Burlington, New Jersey, m. Hannah (Last Name Unknown)*; d. 1678, Burlington, New Jersey[6]

William **Bates,*** b. 1635, Wickloe, Ireland; d. 1700, Newton, New Jersey, m. Mary **Ball***[6]

Francis **Collins***b. 1650, Ratcliffe, England; d. 1720, Northampton, New Jersey, m. Sarah **Mayham***[6]

Valentine **Huddleston,*** b. 1628, England; d. June 8, 1727, New Bedford, Mass., m. Katherine **Chatham,*** b. London, England[6]

Nicholas **Wyckoff,*** b. 1646; d. 1715, m. 1672, Sarah **Monfoort***[3]

Jansen **Van Vorhees**[3]

Joseph **Scobey**, b. Ireland[3]

Robert **Parrish**, b. 1644, Cambridge, Mass.; d. 1694, Chelsea, Mass., m. Mercy **Crispe***[7]

Joseph **Griggs**, m. Hannah **Davis***[7]

Samuel **Bishop,*** m. Hester **Cogswell**[7]

G-9

Thomas **Parrish,*** b. 1612, England; d. April 18, 1668, Groton, Mass., m. Mary **Danforth**, b. England[7]

Ichabod **Griggs**, b. England; d. Margaret **Bishop,*** b. England[9]

William **Cogswell**, b. 1619, Kent, England; d. December 15, 1700, Chebacco, Mass., m. 1649, Susanna **Hawke**, b. 1633, Charlestown, Mass.; d. January 13, 1676, Sangus, Mass.[9]

G-10

Nicholas **Danforth**, b. England, m. Elizabeth **Symmes,*** b. England[7]

Joseph **Griggs**, b. 1624, England; d. February 10, 1714, m. Hannah **Davis,*** b. England[9]

John **Cogswell**, b. 1593, Westbury, England; d. November 29, 1669, Mass., m. September 10, 1615, Elizabeth **Thompson,*** b. 1094, Westbury, England; d. June 2, 1676, Mass.[9]

Adam **Hawke,*** b. 1608, Westbury, England; d. March 13, 1672, Sangus, Mass., m. Anne **Browne**, b. 1609, England; d. December 4, 1669, Lynn, Mass.[9]

G-11

Thomas **Danforth**,* b. 1560, Framlingham, England; d. April 20, 1621, Framlingham, England, m. Jane **Sudbury**,* b. England; d. England[7]

Thomas **Griggs**,* b. September 2, 1585, England; d. June 23, 1646, England, m. Mary (Last Name Unknown)*[9]

Edward **Cogswell**,* b. 1554, Westbury, England; d. 1616, England, m. Alice (Last Name Unknown)*[9]

Edward **Browne**, b. September 9, 1586, England; d. England, m. Jane **Leids**,* b. England; d. England[9]

G-12

Thomas **Browne**, b. England; d. England, m. Joan **Gabb**,* b. England; d. England[9]

G-13

Christopher **Browne**, b. 1482, England; d. July 3, 1538, England[9]

G-14

Christopher **Browne**, b. 1450, England; d. 1526, England, m. Agnes **Beddingfield**, b. England; d. England[9]

G-15

John **Browne**,* b. England; d. England[9]

Edmund **Beddingfield**, b. England; d. England, m. Margaret **Scott**,* b. England; d. England[9]

G-16

Thomas **Beddingfield**, b. England; d. England, m. Anne **Waldegrave**,* b. England; d. England[9]

G-17

Edmund **Beddingfield**,* b. England; d. England, m. Margaret **Tudenham**,* b. England; d. England[9]

Rachel Jackson

G+1

Rachel **Jackson** had no children.

Rachel Donelson, b. June 15, 1767, Halifax Co., Va.; d. December 22, 1828, Nashville, Tennessee, m. August 1, 1791, Andrew Jackson, b. March 15, 1767, South Carolina; d. June 8, 1845, Nashville, Tennessee[1,3]

G-1

John **Donelson**, b. 1720, Somerset Co., Maryland; d. April 11, 1786, Nashville, Tennessee, m. Rachel **Stockley**, b. 1722, Accomack Co., Va.; d. 1801, Nashville, Tennessee[1]

G-2

John **Donelson**, b. 1696, Maryland; d. 1736, Maryland, m. Catherine **Davis**, b. 1696, Somerset Co., Maryland; d. Somerset Co., Maryland[2]

Alexander **Stockley**, b. 1696, Accomack Co., Va.; d. September 27, 1762, Accomack Co., Va., m. Jane **Matthews**[2]

G-3

Patrick **Donelson**,* b. 1670, Somerset Co., Maryland; d. 1725, m. Jean (Last Name Unknown)*[1,2]

Rev. Samuel **Davis**, m. Mary **Simpson***[2]

Joseph **Stockley**, b. 1658, Accomack Co., Va.; d. May 3, 1731, Accomack Co., Va., m. Rachel **Beaston***[2]

Thomas **Matthews***[2]

G-4

Patrick **Davis***[2]

John **Stockley**,* b. 1621, Accomack Co., Va.; d. August 18, 1673, m. Elizabeth **Woodman**,* b. 1624, Accomack Co., Va.[2]

Martha Jefferson

G+2

Children of Martha Jefferson and Thomas M. Randolph, Jr.

Anne Cary **Randolph**, b. 1791[1]
Thomas Jefferson **Randolph**, b. 1792[1]
Ellen Wayles **Randolph**, b. 1792[1]
Cornelia **Randolph**, b. 1799[1]
Virginia **Randolph**, b. 1801[1]
Mary **Randolph**, b. 1803[1]
James Madison **Randolph**, b. 1806[1]
Benjamin Franklin **Randolph**, b. 1808[1]
Meriwether Lewis **Randolph**, b. 1810[1]
Septimia Anne **Randolph**, b. 1814[1]
George Wythe **Randolph**, b. 1818[1]

G+1

Children of Martha Wayles and Thomas Jefferson:

Martha **Jefferson**, b. September 1772, Monticello, Charlottesville, Va.; d. October 10, 1836, Edgehill, Va., m. February 23, 1790, Monticello to Thomas Mann **Randolph**, b. May 17, 1768, Tuckahoe, Va.; d. June 20, 1828, Monticello.[2]

Jane **Jefferson**, b. April 3, 1774, Monticello; d. 1775, Monticello[2]

Unnamed **Jefferson**, b. May 28, 1777, Monticello; d. June 14, 1777, Monticello[2]

Maria (Polly) **Jefferson**, b. August 1, 1778, Monticello; d. April 15, 1871, Monticello, m. October 13, 1797, Monticello John Wayles **Eppes**, b. April 7, 1773, City Point, Va.; d. September 5, 1873, Millbrook, Va.[2,3,4]

Lucy Elizabeth **Jefferson**, b. November 3, 1780, Monticello; d. April 17, 1804, Monticello[3,4]

Lucy Elizabeth **Jefferson**, b. May 8, 1782, Monticello; d. 1784, Monticello[3,4]

Martha Wayles, b. October 19, 1748, Chesterfield Co., Va.; d. September 6, 1782, Monticello, Charlottesville, Va., m(1) Bathurst Skelton, m(2) January 1, 1772, Thomas Jefferson, b. April 13, 1743, Virginia; d. Monticello[3, 4]

G-1

John **Wayles**,* b. January 31, 1715, Lancaster, England; d. May 23, 1773, Charles City Co., Va., m. May 3, 1746, Martha **Eppes**, b. April 10, 1712, Chesterfield Co., Va. November 5, 1748, Va.[2, 3]

G-2

Francis **Eppes**, b. 1685, Henrico Co., Va.; d. November 7, 1733 or 1734, Nottoway Co., Va., m. Sarah **Kennon**, b. 1689, Chesterfield Co., Va.; d. 1746, Charles City Co., Va.[2, 3, 4]

G-3

Francis **Eppes**, b. 1659, Shirley Hundred, Va.; d. 1718 or 1719, Henrico Co., Va., m. Anne **Isham**, b. Henrico Co., Va.; d. Va.[2, 3, 4]

Richard **Kennon**,* b. 1650, Henrico Co., Va.; d. August 20, 1696, Henrico Co., Va., m. Elizabeth **Worsham**, b. 1656, Chesterfield Co., Va.; d. 1705, Henrico Co., Va.[4]

G-4

Francis **Eppes**, b. November 29, 1627, England; d. December 2, 1678, m. Frances **Wells**,* b. England[3]

Henry **Isham**, b. 1628, England; d. 1675, m. Katherine **Banks**,* b. 1632, England[5]

John William **Worsham**,* b. 1625, Charles City Co., Va.; d. 1660, Henrico Co., Va., m. Elizabeth **Littleberry**,* b. 1623, Henrico Co., Va.; d. September 23, 1678, Henrico Co., Va.[4]

G-5

Francis **Eppes**, b. May 15, 1597, Ashford, England; d. September 30, 1674, m. Maria **Pawlett**, b. 1601, England[3]

William **Isham**, b. March 20, 1587 or 1588, Pytchley, England; d. 1631, Pytchley, England, m. Mary **Brett**, b. 1603, Toddington, England; d. 1675[5]

G-6

John **Eppes**, b. 1566, Ashford, England; d. November 19, 1627, Ashford, England, m. Thomazine **Fisher**, b. 1573, England; d. England[3]

Thomas **Pawlett**,* b. England; d. England[3]

Eusby **Isham**, b. February 26, 1582, England; d. June 11, 1626, England, m. Anne **Borlase**, b. 1556, England; d. January 6, 1628, England[5]

William **Brett**, b. 1578, England; d. 1624, England[6]

G-7

John **Eppes**,* b. 1526, Ashford, England; d. England, m. Agnes **Harle**,* b. England; d. England[3]

Alexander **Fisher**, b. 1532, England; d. 1590, England, m. Katherine **Maplesden**, b. 1543, England; d. England[3]

Gregory **Isham**, b. 1520, Braunston, England; d. September 4, 1558, England, m. Elizabeth **Dale**, b. England; d. England[4]

Sir John **Borlase**, b. England; d. England, m. Anne **Lytton**, b. England; d. England[5]

Robert **Brett**, b. England; d. England, m. Elizabeth **Highgate**, b. England; d. England[6]

G-8

Peter **Maplesden**,* b. England; d. England[3]

Eusby **Isham**, b. 1491, England; d. December 11, 1546, England, m. Ann **Pulton**,* b. England; d. England[4]

Matthew **Dale**,* b. England; d. England[4]

Edmund **Borlase**,* b. England; d. England, m. Susannah **Isham**,* b. England; d. England[5]

Sir Robert **Lytton**, b. England; d. England, m. Frances **Cavalery**,* b. England; d. England[5]

Robert **Brett**,* b. England; d. England, m. Elizabeth **Bush**,* b. England; d. England[6]

Reginald **Highgate**,* b. England; d. England[6]

G-9

Thomas **Isham**, b. 1456, Pytchley, England; d. England, m. Ellen **De Vere**, b. 1464, Addington, England; d. England[4]

Sir William **Lytton**,* b. England; d. England, m. Audrey **Booth**, b. England; d. England[5]

G-10

William **Isham**, b. England; d. England, m. Elizabeth **Branspeth,*** b. England; d. England[4]

Richard **De Vere,*** b. England; d. England, m. Isabella **Greene**, b. England; d. England[2, 4]

Sir Philip **Booth**, b. 1433, England; d. England, m. Margaret **Hopton**, b. 1433, England; d. England[5]

G-11

Robert **Isham**, b. England; d. England, m. Elizabeth **Knoston,*** b. England; d. England[4]

John **De Greene**, b. England; d. England, m. Margaret **Greene**, b. England; d. England[2]

George **Booth,*** b. 1400, England; d. England[5]

Sir William **Hopton,*** b. England; d.England, m. Margaret **Wentworth**, b. 1430, Nettlestead, England; d. England[5]

G-12

Sir Henry **De Greene*** (Father of John **De Greene**), b. England; d. England, m. Matilda **De Mauduit,*** b. England; d. England[2]

Sir Roger **Wentworth**, b. England; d. England, m. Margery **De Spencer**, b. England; d. England[5]

G-13

Sir Thomas **De Greene**, b. England; d. England, m. Catherine **De Drayton,*** b. England; d. England[2]

John **Wentworth**, b. England; d. England, m. Agnes **Dronsfield,*** b. England; d. England[5]

Sir Philip **De Spencer,*** b. 1355, England; d. 1424, England, m. Elizabeth **De Tibbett**, b. England; d. England[5]

G-14

Sir Thomas **De Greene,*** b. England; d. England, m. Lucy **La Zouche**, b. England; d. England[2]

John **Wentworth**, b. England; d. England, m. Jane **Le Tyas**[5]

Robert **De Tibbett**, b. 1330, England; d. 1372, England, m. Margaret **Diencourt**, b. 1340, England; d. England[5]

G-15

Eudes **La Zouche**, b. England; d. England, m. Millicent **De Cantelupe,*** b. England; d. England[2]

William **Wentworth**, b. England; d. England, m. Isabel **Pollington**,* b. England; d. England[5]

John **De Tibbett**,* b. England; d. England, m. Margaret **Badlesmere**, b. England; d. England[5]

William **Diencourt**,* b. 1300, England; d. England, m. Margaret **De Welle**,* b. England; d. England[5]

G-16

Alan **La Zouche**, b. 1205, England; d. August 10, 1270, England, m. Helen **De Quincy**[5]

William **Wentworth**,* b. England; d. England, m. Dionipia **Rotherfield**,* b. England; d. England[5]

Bartholomew **Bartlesmere**,* b. England; d. England, m. Margaret **De Clare**, b. England; d. England[5]

G-17

Roger **La Zouche**, b. 1175, Molton, England; d. England, m. Margaret (Last Name Unknown),* b. England; d. England[2]

Roger **De Quincy**,* m. Helen **McDonald*** (Refer to Roger **De Quincy** G-22 Lucretia **Garfield** to continue their lines.)[2]

Thomas **De Clare**,* m. Juliana **Fitz Mauris*** (Refer to Thomas **De Clare** G-18 Abigail **Adams** to continue their lines.)[7]

G-18

Alan **La Zouche**, b. 1141, Harringworth, England; d. 1190, England, m. Adelicia **De Belmeis**, b. 1138, England; d. England[2]

G-19

Geoffrey **La Zouche**, b. England; d. England, m. Hawise **Fergant**, b. England; d. England[2]

Philip **De Belmeis**, b. England; d. England, m. Maud **De Meschines**, b. England; d. England[2]

G-20

Eudon I,* m. Anne (Last Name Unknown)*[2]

Alain IV,* m. Ermengarde **De Anjou***[2]

Walter **De Belmeis***[2]

William **De Meschines**,* b. 1100, England; d. England, m. Lady Cicely **De Romilly***[2]

Claudia Alta (Lady Bird) Johnson

G+2

Children of Lynda Bird Johnson and Charles Robb:

Lucinda Desha **Robb**[1]
Catherine Lewis **Robb**[1]
Jennifer Wickliffe **Robb**[1]

Children of Lucy Baines Johnson and Patrick John Nugent:

Patrick Lyndon **Nugent**, m. Nicole **Tatum**[1]
Nicole Marie **Nugent**, m. Richard Brent **Covert**[1]
Rebekah Johnson **Nugent**, m. Jeremy Charles **McIntosh**[1]
Claudia Taylor **Nugent**, m. Steven Howard **Brod**[1]

G+1

Lynda Bird **Johnson**, b. March 19, 1944, m. December 9, 1967, at White House, Charles **Robb**[2]

Lucy Baines **Johnson**, b. July 2, 1947, m. August 6, 1966, Washington, D.C., Patrick John **Nugent**[1, 2]

Claudia Alta "Lady Bird" Taylor, b. December 22, 1912, Karnack, Texas, m. November 17, 1934, Lyndon Baines Johnson, b. August 27, 1908; d. January 22, 1973, Stonewall, Texas[2, 7]

G-1

Thomas Jefferson **Taylor**, b. August 29, 1874, Augusta Co., Alabama; d. October 22, 1960, Karnack, Texas, m. November 28, 1900, Minnie Lee **Pattillo**, b. 1874, Billingsly, Alabama; d. September 14, 1918, Karnack, Texas[2]

G-2

Thomas Jefferson **Taylor**, b. 1846, Alabama; d. 1874, m. July 30, 1867, Emma Louisa **Bates**, b. October 6, 1848, Columbia, South Carolina; d. December 5, 1924, Autauga Co., Alabama[2]

Luther **Pattillo**, b. 1842, Muskogee Co., Georgia, m. Sarah Jane **Myrick**, b. March 21, 1841, Autauga Co., Alabama[2]

G-3

William **Taylor**, b. 1815; d. 1867, m. Sarah Jane **Ponsonby**,* b. 1817[2]

Elihu **Bates**,* m. Elizabeth **Parr***[2]

Alfred Cato **Pattillo**, b. 1804, Muskogee Co., Ga., m. Catherine **Shelbach**,* b. 1805, South Carolina[2, 3]

George **Myrick**,* b. January 15, 1810, Hancock, Georgia; d. October 14, 1890, m. November 21, 1833, Nancy **Temple**, b. October 19, 1814; d. October 28, 1892[4]

G-4

William **Taylor**,* m. Nancy **Collins**[5]

Littleberry **Pattillo**, b. 1775, Prince George Co., Va.; d. October 19, 1814, Muskogee Co., Georgia, m. Mary Ann **Simpson**[2]

Benjamin **Temple**, b. March 22, 1777, Prince George Co., Va.; d. 1843, Autauga Co., Alabama, m. Jincy **Stembridge**, b. November 7, 1785, Hancock Co, Georgia; d. March 15, 1833, Autuga Co., Alabama[4]

G-5

John **Collins**,* m. Judith **Word**, b. 1748, New Kent Co., Va.; d. February 1, 1828, Halifax Co., Va.[5]

James **Pattillo**, b. 1750, Prince George Co., Va., b. 1818, Brunswick Co., Va., m. 1774, Elizabeth **Floyd***[3]

Peter **Temple**, b. 1750; d. April 24, 1802, Hancock Co., Georgia, m. Nancy Ann **Eppes**,* b. 1758; d. June 2, 1823, Hancock Co., Georgia[4]

William **Stembridge**,* m. Kindness **Breedlove***[4]

G-6

Charles **Word**, b. March 14, 1709; d. 1792, m. Sarah **Collins**[5]

James **Pattillo**, b. December 23, 1725, Prince George Co., Va.; d. 1785, Brunswick Co., Va., m. Elizabeth **Littleberry***[3]

Samuel **Temple**, m. Mary **Williams***[4]

G-7

John **Word**,* b. 1680, m. Ann **Chiles**, b. 1680[5]

James **Pattillo** Scotland; d. 1760, Dinwiddie Co., Va., m. Mary **Littleton***[3]

Samuel **Temple**, m. Elizabeth **Leath***[4]

G-8

Henry **Chiles**, b. November 13, 1698; d. March 20, 1746, m. Ann **Harrelson**[6]

James **Pattillo**, b. July 8, 1659, Scotland; d. Scotland, m. Mary (Last Name Unknown)*[3]

William **Temple**,* m. Rebecca **Tatum***[4]

G-9

Henry **Chiles**, m. Margaret **Littlepage**, b. 1673; d. 1732[6]

Paul **Harrelson**,* m. Rebecca **Burgess***[6]

Robert **Pattillo**,* b. Scotland, m. Catherine **Blair*** Scotland[3]

G-10

Walter **Chiles**,* b. 1630, m. Susannah **Brooks***[6]

Richard **Littlepage**,* b. 1650; d. March 20, 1717, m. Frances **De Rochelle***[6]

ELIZA JOHNSON

G+2

Children of Martha Johnson and David Trotter Patterson:

Andrew Johnson **Patterson**, b. February 25, 1857, Greeneville, Tenn.; d. June 25, 1932, Greeneville, Tenn., m. Martha Ellen **Barkley**[1]

Mary Belle **Patterson**, b. November 11, 1859, Greeneville, Tenn.; d. July 9, 1891, Auburn Lake Trails, Calif., m. John **Landstreet**[1]

Children of Mary Johnson and Daniel Stover:

Eliza **Stover**[1]

Lillie **Stover**[1]

Sarah **Stover**, b. 1857; d. March 22, 1886, m. William **Bachman**[1]

Andrew Johnson **Stover**, b. March 6, 1860; d. January 25, 1923[1]

G+1

Martha **Johnson**, b. October 15, 1828, Greenville, Tennessee; d. July 10, 1901, Greenville, Tennessee, m. December 13, 1855, Greenville, Tennessee David Trotter **Patterson**, b. February 29, 1818, Cedar Creek, Tennessee; d. November 3, 1891, Afton, Tennessee[2]

Charles **Johnson**, b. February 19, 1830, Greenville, Tennessee; d. April 4, 1863, Nashville, Tennessee[2]

Mary **Johnson**, b. May 8, 1832, Greenville, Tennessee; d. April 19, 1883, Bluff City, Tennessee, m(1) April 27, 1852, Daniel **Stover**, b. November 14, 1826, Carter Co., Tennessee; d. December 18, 1864, Nashville, Tennessee, m(2) April 20, 1869, William Ramsay **Brown**[2]

Robert **Johnson**, b. February 22, 1834, Greenville, Tennessee; d. April 22, 1869, Greenville, Tennessee[2]

Andrew **Johnson**, b. August 5, 1852 Greenville, Tennessee; d. March 12, 1879, Elizabethton, Tennessee, m. November 25, 1875, Hot Springs, North Carolina Kate May **Rumbough**[2]

Elizabeth (Eliza) McCardle, b. October 4, 1810, Leesburg, Tennessee; d. January 15, 1876, Carter's Station, Tennessee, m. 1827, Andrew Johnson, b. December 29, 1808, Raleigh, North Carolina; d. July 31, 1875, Tennessee[3,5]

G-1

John **McCardle,*** m. Sarah **Phillips**, b. January 29, 1789, Marshfield, Mass.[3]

G-2

Benjamin **Phillips**, b. August 14, 1758, Marshfield, Mass., m. Sarah **Thomas**, b. September 20, 1761, Marshfield, Mass.[3,4]

G-3

John **Phillips**, b. 1722, m. Grace **Holloway***[3,4]

John **Thomas,*** b. 1721, m. Sarah **Pitney**, b. January 2, 1722, Marshfield, Mass.[3,4]

G-4

John **Phillips,*** m. Faith **Doten***[4]

James **Pitney**, b. 1683; d. March 14, 1763, m. Sarah **Smith,*** b. Marshfield, Mass.[4]

G-5

Jeremiah **Pitney**[4]

G-6

Michael **Pitney,*** m. Elizabeth (Last Name Unknown)*[4]

Jacqueline Kennedy

G+2

Children of Edwin Arthur and Caroline (Kennedy) Schlossberg:

Rose **Schlossberg**, b. June 25, 1988, New York, New York[1]

Tatiana Celia **Schlossberg**, b. May 5, 1990, New York, New York[1]

John Bouvier **Schlossberg**, b. January 19, 1993, New York, New York[1]

G+1

Unnamed **Kennedy**, b. 1955; d. 1955[2]

Caroline **Kennedy**, b. November 27, 1957, New York, New York, m. July 19, 1987, Centerville, Mass., Edwin **Schlossberg**[2]

John Fitzgerald **Kennedy**, b. November 25, 1960, Washington, D.C.; d. July 17, 1999, Plane crash off Martha's Vineyard, m. September 21, 1996, Cumberland Island, Georgia Carolyne **Bessette**[2]

Patrick Bouvier **Kennedy**, b. August 7, 1963, Otis Air Force Base, Mass.; d. August 9, 1963, Boston, Mass.[2]

Jacqueline Lee Bouvier, b. July 28, 1929, Southampton, Long Island, New York; d. May 19, 1994, New York, New York, m. September 12, 1953, John Fitzgerald Kennedy, b. May 29, 1917, Brookline, Mass.; d. November 22, 1963, Dallas, Texas[3,4]

G-1

John Vernou **Bouvier**, b. May 19, 1891, East Hampton, Mass.; d. 1957, m. July 7, 1928, Janet **Lee**[3]

G-2

John Vernou **Bouvier** August 12, 1865, Torresdale, Pa.; d. January 14, 1948, m. Maud Frances **Sergeant**, b. 1865; d. April 3, 1940[3]

James Thomas **Lee**, b. 1877; d. 1972, m. Margaret A. **Merritt***[3]

G-3

John Vernou **Bouvier**, b. 1843; d. 1926, m. Caroline Maslin **Ewing***[3]

William R. **Sergeant**,* m. Edith **Leaman***[3]

Dr. James **Lee**, m. Mary **Norton**[3]

G-4

Michael **Bouvier**, b. February 2, 1792; d. 1874, m. Louise C. **Vernou**, b. 1811; d. October 5, 1872[3]

Thomas **Lee**,* b. Ireland, m. Frances **Smith**,* b. Ireland[3]

John **Norton**,* b. Ireland, m. Mary **Shelley**,* b. Ireland[3]

G-5

Eustache **Bouvier**, b. May 29, 1758, Grenoble, France; d. 1835, m. February 3, 1789, Therese **Mercier**, b. August 12, 1766; d. 1828, Provencial, France[3]

John **Vernou**,* b. 1781; d. 1837, m. Elizabeth **Lindsay**[3]

G-6

Francois **Bouvier**, b. January 30, 1728, France, m. April 26, 1753, m. Benoite **Repelin***[3]

Joseph **Mercier**, m. Anne **Trintignant**[3]

William Alexander **Lindsay**,* m. Elizabeth **Clifford***[3]

G-7

Georges **Bouvier**,* b. 1705, Savoy, France; d. France[3]

Melkior **Mercier***[3]

Jean **Trintignant**,* m. Therese **Paulin***[3]

Mary Lincoln

G+2

Children of Robert Todd and Mary Eunice (Harlan) Lincoln:

Jack **Lincoln**[1]

Mary **Lincoln**, b. October 15, 1869, Springfield, Illinois; d. 1938, m. Charles **Isham**, b. 1853; d. 1919[1]

Abraham **Lincoln**, b. August 14, 1873, Chicago, Illinois; d. March 5, 1890[1]

Jessie **Lincoln**, b. November 6, 1875; d. January 5, 1948, Bennington, Vermont m(1) Frank **Johnson**, m(2) Robert **Randolph**, m(3) Warren **Beckwith**[1]

G+1

Robert Todd **Lincoln**, b. 1843, Springfield, Illinois; d. 1926, Manchester, Vermont, m. September 24, 1868, Washington, D.C. Mary Eunice **Harlan**, b. August 25, 1846, Iowa[2]

Edward Baker **Lincoln**, b. 1846; d. 1850[2]

William Wallace **Lincoln**, b. 1850; d. February 19, 1863, Washington, D.C.[2]

Thomas (Tad) **Lincoln**, b. 1853; d. 1871[2]

Mary Ann Todd, b. December 13, 1818, Lexington, Kentucky; d. July 16, 1882, Springfield, Illinois, m. November 4, 1842, Abraham Lincoln, b. February 12, 1809, Hardin Co., Kentucky; d. April 15, 1865, Washington, D.C.[3, 13]

G-1

Robert Smith **Todd**, b. February 25, 1791, Lexington, Kentucky;

d. July 15, 1849, Springfield, Illinois, m. November 26, 1812, Eliza Ann **Parker**, b. 1794 or 1795, Lexington, Kentucky; d. July 6, 1825[3]

G-2

Levi **Todd**, b. 1757, Lancaster Co., Pa.; d. 1807, Fayette Co., Kentucky, m. February 25, 1779, Jane **Briggs**, b. 1764, Lincoln Co., Kentucky; d. July 15, 1849, Springfield, Illinois[3]

Robert P. **Parker**, b. October 12, 1760, Montgomery Co., Pa.; d. March 4, 1800, Lexington, Kentucky, m. March 16, 1789, Elizabeth **Porter**, b. September 27, 1769, Norristown, Pa.; d. 1851, Lexington, Kentucky[3]

G-3

David Levi **Todd** Longford Co., Ireland; d. February 8, 1785, Fayette Co., Kentucky, m. April 7, 1749, Hannah **Owens**,* b. 1729, Montgomery Co., Pa.; d. May 10, 1814, Fayette Co., Ky.[3]

Samuel **Briggs**,* b. 1744; d. 1795, Kentucky, m. Sarah **Logan**, b. 1745, Orange Co., Va.[3]

James **Parker**,* b. 1735, Montgomery Co., Pa.; d. December 12, 1797, Kentucky, m. Mary **Todd**, b. May 8, 1732, New Haven, Conn.[3]

Andrew **Porter**, b. September 24, 1743, Norristown, Pa.; d. November 16, 1813, Norristown, Pa., m. March 10, 1767, Elizabeth **McDowell**, b. 1747, Norristown, Pa.; d. April 9, 1773, Norristown, Pa.[3]

G-4

Robert **Todd**, b. 1697; d. 1775, m. Ann **Smith**,* b. 1697[3]

James **Logan**[3]

Gersham **Todd**, b. October 12, 1695, New Haven, Conn.; d. 1748, New Haven, Conn., m. Elizabeth **Merriman**, b. July 2, 1703, Wallingford, Conn.; d. 1732, New Haven, Conn.[3,4]

Robert **Porter**, b. 1698; d. July 14, 1770, m. Lilliouo **Christy**, b. 1707; d. 1750[3]

Samuel **McDowell**, b. Scotland; d. 1750, m. Mary **McClung**, b. October 6, 1709; d. 1789[3]

G-5

John **Todd**,* b. 1667, Armagh Co., Ireland; d. 1719, Armagh Co., Ireland[3]

James **Logan**, b. October 30, 1674, Lurgen, Ireland; d. October 31, 1751, m. Sarah **Read***[3]

Michael **Todd**, b. January 18, 1653, New Haven, Conn.; d. 1713, m. Elizabeth **Brown**[3]

John **Merriman**, b. February 28, 1660, New Haven, Conn.; d. 1741, Wallingford, Conn., m. November 20, 1690, Elizabeth **Peck**, b. December 29, 1673, Wallingford, Conn.; d. 1709, Wallingford, Conn.[4]

Robert **Porter**,* b. 1663, Londonderry, Ireland; d. 1780, m. 1684, Eleanor **Rogers**,* b. 1668, Londonderry, Ireland; d. 1750[3]

John **Christy**,* m. Jane **Smith***[3]

John **McDowell**, b. 1703; d. 1742, m. Magdalen **Woods**, b. 1706, Ireland; d. 1810, Va.[5]

William **McClung***[3]

G-6

Patrick **Logan**; d. February 4, 1700, m. Isabella **Hume**[3]

Christopher **Todd**, b. January 11, 1617, Pontefract, England; d. April 23, 1686, New Haven, Conn., m. Grace **Middlebrook**, b. 1620, Hold Hills, England; d. New Haven, Conn.[3, 4]

Eleazer **Brown**, b. October 10, 1642, New Haven, Conn.; d. October 23, 1714, New Haven, Conn., m. Sarah **Bulkeley**, b. August 12, 1640, Concord, Mass.; d. June 12, 1723, New Haven, Conn.[6, 7]

Nathaniel **Merriman**, b. 1613, London, England; d. February 13, 1694, Wallingford, Conn., m. Joan **Lines**,* b. 1628, New Haven, Conn.; d. December 8, 1709, Wallingford, Conn.[8]

John **Peck**, b. November 17, 1640, New Haven, Conn.; d. October 4, 1694, Wallingford, Conn., m. Mary **Moss**, b. 1644; d. November 16, 1725[9]

Ephraim **McDowell**, b. 1672; d. 1774, Augusta, Va., m. Margaret **Irvine**, b. 1672, Ireland; d. 1728, Ireland[5]

Michael **Woods**, m. Margaret **Campbell**[5]

G-7

Alexander **Logan**, b. 1590[3]

James **Hume**, b. 1585, m. Bethia **Dundas**, b. 1595[7]

William **Todd**, b. 1593, Yorkshire, England; d. May 8, 1677, Yorkshire, England, m. Katherine **Ward**, b. November 29, 1596, Yorkshire, England; d. England[4]

Michael **Middlebrook**, b. 1594, Yorkshire, England[4]

Francis **Brown**, b. 1610, Yorkshire, England; d. April 13, 1668, New Haven, Conn., m. Mary **Edwards**, b. 1615, England; d. December 7, 1693, New Haven, Conn.[7]

Thomas **Bulkeley**, b. April 13, 1617, England; d. 1658, Conn., m. Sarah **Jones**, b. 1620, England; d. 1683, Fairfield, Conn.[6]

George **Merriman**, b. 1559, Witney, England; d. 1655, London, England[8]

William **Peck**, b. 1601; d. October 14, 1694, m. Elizabeth (Last Name Unknown),* b. 1608; d. December 5, 1683[9]

John **Moss**,* b. 1604; d. March 31, 1707, m. Abigail **Charles***[9]

Abraham **McDowell**,* b. 1631, Scotland; d. Ireland[5]

James **Irvine**,* b. 1645, Ireland; d. Ireland, m. Mary **Wylie**,* b. 1650, Ireland; d. Ireland[5]

John **Woods**, b. 1650, Ireland; d. 1724, Ireland, m. Elizabeth **Worsop**[5]

James **Campbell**,* m. Susan (Last Name Unknown)*[5]

G-8

Sir Robert **Logan**,* m. Lady Jane **Kerr***[3]

Patrick **Hume**,* b. 1545, England; d. England, m. Elizabeth **Montgomery**, b. 1545, England; d. England[7]

James **Dundas**,* b. England; d. England, m. Isabel **Maule**, b. England; d. England[7]

William **Todd**,* b. 1569, Yorkshire, England; d. 1617, England, m. Isabel **Rogerson**,* b. 1571, Yorkshire, England; d. England[4]

John **Ward**,* b. 1570, Yorkshire, England; d. England, m. Isabel **Brustar**,* b. 1574, Yorkshire, England[4]

John **Edwards**, b. 1584, England; d. May 8, 1676, m. Elizabeth **Whitfield**,* b. 1588, England; d. England[6]

Rev. Peter **Bulkeley**, b. England; d. England, m. Jane **Allen**,* b. England; d. England[6, 10]

Gregory **Merriman**,* b. 1530, Witney, England; d. 1596, London, England, m. Mary **Ring**,* b. 1534, Witney, England; d. England[8]

William **Peck**, b. England; d. England[9]

David **Irvine**, b. England; d. England, m. Sophia **Gault**,* b. England; d. England[5]

John **Woods**,* b. England; d. England, m. Isabelle **Bruce**, b. England; d. England[5]

Thomas **Worsop**,* b. England; d. England, m. Elizabeth **Parsons**, b. England; d. England[5]

G-9

Neil **Montgomery**, b. 1500, England; d. 1547, England, m. Margaret **Mure**, b. England; d. England[7]

William **Maule**, b. 1545, England; d. April 19, 1619, England, m. Bethia **Guthrie**, b. England ; d. England[11]

John **Edwards**,* b. 1549, England; d. England, m. Martha **Blundell**, b. England; d. England

Edward **Bulkeley**, b. 1540, England; d. June 5, 1620, England, m. Olive **Irby**, b. 1547, England; d. 1614[2, 6, 12]

Stephen **Peck**,* b. England; d. England, m. Mary **Cave**,* b. England; d. England[8]

Robert **Irvine**, b. England; d. England, m. Elizabeth **Wylie**,* b. England; d. England[5]

Patrick **Bruce**, b. England; d. England, m. Janet **Jackson**,* b. England; d. England[5]

Richard **Parsons**,* b. England; d. England, m. Anna Letitia **Loftus**, b. England; d. England[5]

G-10

Hugh **Montgomery**, b. 1460, England; d. September 3, 1546, England, m. Helen **Campbell**, b. England; d. England[7]

Robert **Maule**,* b. England; d. England, m. Isabel **Arbuthnott**,* b. England; d. England[11]

Thomas **Bulkeley**, b. ca. 1515, England; d. 1591, m. Elizabaeth **Grosvenor***[6]

John **Irby**, b. 1520, England; d. April 10, 1553, England, m. Rose **Overton**,* b. 1526; d. June 17, 1579, England[12]

Alexander **Irvine**,* b. England; d. England, m. Magdelene **Scrimgrour***[5]

William **Bruce**, b. England; d. England, m. Jane **Fleming**,* b. England; d. England[5]

Adam **Loftus**,* b. England; d. England, m. Jane **Vaughn**,* b. England; d. England[5]

G-11

Alexander **Montgomery**,* b. England; d. England, m. Catherine **Kennedy**, b. England; d. England[17]

Colin **Campbell**, b. England; d. England, m. Isabel **Stewart**,* b. England; d. England[7]

William **Bulkeley**, b. 1490, England; d. 1571, England, m. Beatrice **Hill**,* b. England; d. England[6]

Anthony **Irby**,* b. 1500, England; d. June 21, 1552, England, m. Alice **Bountyne**,* b. 1500, England; d. 1551, England[12]

Alexander **Bruce**,* b. 1530, Scotland, m. Janet **Livingston**, b. England; d. England[5]

G-12

Gilbert **Kennedy**, b. England; d. England, m. Catherine **Maxwell**,* b. England; d.England[7]

Alexander **Campbell**, b. England; d. England, m. Elizabeth **Somerville**,* b. England; d. England[7]

Alexander **Livingston**,* b. England; d. England, m. Anne **Douglas**, b. England; d. England[5]

G-13

James **Kennedy**,* b. 1380, England; d. England, m. Mary **Stewart**, b. England; d. England[7]

Duncan **Campbell**,* b. 1360, England; d. 1453, England, m. Margaret **Stewart**, b. England; d. England[7]

John **Douglas**, b. England; d. England, m. Janet **Crichton**,* b. England; d. England[5]

G-14

Robert III, m. Annabelle **Drummond**[7]

Robert III, m. Margaret **Graham***[7]

James **Douglas**,* m. Joan, Princess of Scotland[5]

G-15

Robert II,* m. Elizabeth **Mure***[7]

Robert II,* m. Elizabeth **Mure***[7]

James I, King of Scotland, m. Joan **De Beaufort**[5]

G-16

Robert III, King of Scotland, m. Annabelle **Drummond***[5]

John **De Beaufort**, m. Margaret **De Holland***[5]

G-17

Robert II,* King of Scotland, m. Elizabeth **Muir***[5]

John of Gaunt,* m. Catherine **Roet*** (Refer to John of Gaunt G-14 Abigail **Adams** to continue their lines.)

Dorothea (Dolley) Madison

G+2

Dolley **Madison** had no grandchildren.

G+1

Children of Dolley Payne and John Todd:

John Payne **Todd**, b. September 30, 1790, Philadelphia, Pa.[1]

William Temple **Todd**, b. 1793, Philadelphia, Pa.; d. October 24, 1793, Philadelphia, Pa.[1]

Dolley Payne, b. May 20, 1772, Hanover Co., Va.; d. July 8, 1849, Washington, D.C., m(1) John Todd, m(2) September 15, 1794, James Madison, b. March 16, 1751, Prince George Co., Va.; d. June 28, 1836, Montpelier, Orange Co., Va.[1,11]

G-1

John **Payne**, b. 1736, Goochland Co., Va.; d. Philadelphia, Pa., m. Mary **Coles**, b. 1744, Hanover Co., Va.; d. February 8, 1808, Clarksburg, West Virginia[1,2]

G-2

Josiah **Payne**, b. October 30, 1705, Goochland Co., Va.; d. 1784, Goochland Co., Va., m. 1732, Ann **Fleming**, b. 1712, Jamestown, Va.; d. 1784, Goochland Co., Va.[1,2]

William **Coles**, b. ca. 1703, Enniscarthy, Ireland; d. 1781, m. Lucy **Winston**, b. ca. 1724, Hanover Co., Va.[1]

G-3

George **Payne**, b. 1679, Goochland Co., Va.; d. 1744, Goochland Co., Va., m. 1704, Mary **Woodson**, b. 1678, Henrico Co., Va.; d. February 1, 1766, Goochland Co., Va.[1,2]

Charles **Fleming,*** b. 1667, New Kent Co., Va., m. Susanna **Tarleton,*** b. 1663, New Kent Co., Va.[3,4,5,6,7]

Walter **Coles,*** b. 1670, Enniscarthy, Ireland; d. January 7, 1740, Dublin, Ireland, m. Alice **Philpot,*** b. 1670, Ireland; d. 1750, Dublin, Ireland[1]

Isaac **Winston,*** b. 1676, Hanover Co., Va., m. Sarah **Dabney,*** b. Albemarle Co., Va.[1]

G-4

William **Payne**, b. 1645, Goochland Co., Va.; d. September 9, 1700, Lancaster Co., Va., m. Susanna **Merriman**, b. 1663, Lancaster Co., Va.[1,2]

Robert "Potato Hole" **Woodson**, b. ca. 1633, Prince George Co., Va.; d. 1709.

Prince George Co., Va., m. Elizabeth **Ferris**, b. 1638, Henrico Co., Va.; d. 1689, Henrico Co., Va.[1,2]

John **Fleming**, b. 1627, Cumberland, Scotland; d. April 29, 1686, New Kent Co., Va., m. Mercy or Mary (Last Name Unknown),* b. 1637, York, Va.; d. New Kent Co., Va.[3,4,5,6,7]

Stephen **Tarleton,*** b. 1637, New Kent Co., Va.; d. 1688, New Kent Co., Va., m. Susannah **Bates**, b. 1641, New Kent Co., Va.; d. New Kent Co., Va.[3,4,5,6,7]

Abraham **Coles,*** b. Dublin, Ireland[1]

Anthony **Winston**, b. New Kent Co., Va.; d. December 14, 1725, Hanover Co., Va., m. Kezziah **Jones***[1]

Cornelius **Dabney**, m. Sarah **Jennings**, b. 1686, Hanover Co., Va.; d. Hanover Co., Va.[1]

G-5

John **Payne,*** b. 1615, England; d. 1690, Rappahannock Co., Va., m. Margaret (Last Name Unknown),* b. Essex Co., Va.[1,2]

Richard **Merriman,*** m. Susan **Campian,***[1,2]

Dr. John **Woodson**, b. 1585/1586, Devonshire, England; d. April 18, 1644, Prince George Co., Va., m. Sarah **Winston**, b. 1590, Devonshire, England; d. January 17, 1660, Henrico Co., Va.[2,8]

Richard **Ferris**, b. 1596, London, England; d. 1637, Henrico Co., Va., m. Sarah **Hambaleton***[8]

Alexander **Fleming**, b. Ambernauld, Scotland, m. Elizabeth **Anderson**, b. Glasgow, Scotland; d. October 6, 1656, Rappahannock Co., Va.[3, 4, 5, 6, 7]

John **Bates,*** b. 1601, Kent, England; d. January 24, 1667, York Co., Va., m. 1624, Elizabeth **Winston**, b. 1599, England; d. March 30, 1661, York Co., Va.[3, 4, 5, 6, 7]

William **Winston,*** b. 1630, England; d. 1702, New Kent Co., Va., m. Sarah (Last Name Unknown),* b. 1642, New Kent Co., Va.; d. 1719, Hanover Co., Va.[1]

Cornelius **Dabney,*** b. 1640, France; d. New Kent Co., Va., m. Susanna **Swan**, b. 1644, France[9]

Charles **Jennings**, b. July 28, 1662, England, m. Mary **Cary***[9]

G-6

John **Woodson**, b. 1542, England; d. England[8]

Isaac **Winston**, b. Devonshire, England, m. Mary Elizabeth **Dabney***[8]

Nicholas **Ferris,*** b. 1560, Yorkshire, England; d. 1620, London, England,* m. Mary **Woodenoth**, b. 1562, Shavington, England; d. 1634, Huntingdonshire, England[8]

John **Fleming**, b. England; d. England, m. Lady Margaret **Livingston,*** b. England; d. England[3, 4, 5, 6, 7]

William **Anderson,*** b. England; d. England, m. Marion **Bell,*** b. England; d. England[3, 4, 5, 6, 7]

Isaac **Winston,*** b. 1584, England[3, 4, 5, 6, 7]

Humphrey **Jennings**, b. August 23, 1629, England; d. July 6, 1689, Warrickshire, England, m. Mary **Millward**, b. 1636, Birmingham, England; d. 1708, Warrickshire, England[10]

G-7

Reginald **Woodson,*** b. England; d. England, m. Alice **Hammon,*** b. England; d. England[8]

George **Woodennoth**, b. 1528, Shavington, England; d. England, m. Anne **Starkey,*** b. 1530, England; d. England[8]

John **Fleming**, b. 1535, England; d. September 6, 1572, England[3, 4, 5, 6, 7]

John **Jennings,*** b. August 8, 1579, England; d. December 25, 1653, England, m. 1602, Joyce **Weaman,*** b. England; d. England[10]

John **Millward,** * b. February 10, 1603, Warwickshire, England; d. Warwickshire, England, m. Ann **Whitchalgh,*** b. 1606, Warwickshire, England; d. England[10]

G-8

Lawrence **Woodennoth**, b. Shavington, England, m. Joyce **Wilbram,*** b. England; d. England[8]

Malcolm **Fleming**, b. England; d. England, m. Janet **Stewart**, b. England; d. England[3, 4, 5, 6, 7]

G-9

George **Woodennoth (Woodnett)**, b. 1476, England; d. England, m. Anne **Corbett,*** b. 1477, England; d. England[8]

John **Fleming**, b. 1465, England; d. 1524, England, m. Eupheme **Drummond**, b. England; d. England[3, 4, 5, 6, 7]

King James IV of Scotland, b. Scotland; d. Scotland, m. Lady Isabel **Stewart**[3, 4, 5, 6, 7]

G-10

John **Woodennoth (Woodnett)**, b. 1450, England; d. England, m. Margery **Weaver,*** b. 1452, England; d. England

Malcolm **Fleming**, b. England; d. England, m. Eupheme **Livingston,*** b. England; d. England[3, 4, 5, 6, 7]

King James III of Scotland, b.Scotland; d. Scotland, m. Margaret **Von Oldenburg***[3, 4, 5, 6, 7]

James **Stewart,*** m. Margaret **Oglivie**[3, 4, 5, 6, 7]

G-11

John **Woodennoth (Woodnett)**, b. 1428, England; d. England, m. Margery **Trobbleshall,*** b. 1430, England; d. England[8]

Sir Robert **Fleming**, b. England; d. England, m. Janet **Douglas**, b. England; d. England[3, 4, 5, 6, 7]

King James II of Scotland, b. Scotland; d. Scotland, m. Marie **Gueldern***[3, 4, 5, 6, 7]

Alexander **Olgivie***[3, 4, 5, 6, 7]

G-12

Randall **Woodennoth (Woodnett),*** b. 1404, England; d. England, m. Eva **Brow,*** b. 1406, England; d. England[8]

Sir Malcolm **Fleming,*** b. 1383, England; d. November 24, 1440, (Executed) England, m. Elizabeth **Stewart**, b. 1384, England; d. 1413, England[3, 4, 5, 6, 7]

Sir James **Douglas,*** b. Scotland; d. Scotland, m. Beatrix **Sinclair**, b. England; d. England[3, 4, 5, 6, 7]

King James I of Scotland, b. Scotland; d. Scotland, m. Joan **Beaufort**, b. England; d. England[3, 4, 5, 6, 7]

G-13

Robert **Stewart**, b. Scotland; d. Scotland, m. Muriella **De Keith***[3, 4, 5, 6, 7]

Sir Henry **Sinclair**, b. 1375; d. February 1, 1426, m. Egidia **Douglas**[3, 4, 5, 6, 7]

King Robert III of Scotland, b. Scotland; d. Scotland, m. Annabelle **Drummond***[3, 4, 5, 6, 7]

G-14

King Robert II, b. Scotland; d. Scotland, m. Elizabeth **Mure**[3, 4, 5, 6, 7]

Henry **Sinclair**,* m. Jean **Haliburton***[3, 4, 5, 6, 7]

Sir William **Douglas**,* m. Egidia **Stewart***[3, 4, 5, 6, 7]

King Robert II, b. Scotland; d. Scotland, m. Elizabeth **Mure**[3, 4, 5, 6, 7]

G-15

Walter 6th High Steward of Scotland, b. Scotland; d. Scotland, m. Margaret **Bruce**[3, 4, 5, 6, 7]

Sir Adam **Mure**,* m. Janet **Mure***[3, 4, 5, 6, 7]

Walter 6th High Steward of Scotland, m. Margaret **Bruce**[3, 4, 5, 6, 7]

G-16

James 5th High Steward of Scotland,* b. Scotland; d. Scotland, m. Cecilia **Dunbar***[3, 4, 5, 6, 7]

King Robert I,* b. Scotland; d. Scotland, m. Isabel (Last Name Unknown)*[3, 4, 5, 6, 7]

James 5th Steward of Scotland,* m. Cecilia **Dunbar***[3, 4, 5, 6, 7]

Ida McKinley

G+2

Ida McKinley had no grandchildren.

G+1

Katherine **McKinley**, b. January 25, 1871, Canton, Ohio; d. June 25, 1876, Canton, Ohio[1]

Ida **McKinley**, b. April 1, 1872, Canton, Ohio; d. August 22, 1873, Canton, Ohio[1]

Ida Saxton, b. June 8, 1847, Canton, Ohio; d. May 26, 1907, Canton, Ohio, m. January 25, 1871, William McKinley, b. January 29, 1843, Canton, Ohio; d. September 14, 1901, Canton, Ohio[2, 6]

G-1

James Asbury **Saxton**, b. May 1, 1816, Canton, Ohio; d. March 16, 1887, Canton, Ohio, m. Katherine **De Walt**, b. August 18, 1827, Canton, Ohio; d. March 14, 1873, Canton, Ohio[2, 3]

G-2

John **Saxton**, b. September 28, 1792, Huntingdon Co., Pa.; d. April 16, 1871, Canton, Ohio, m. Margarite **Laird**, b. December 17, 1792, Northumberland Co., Pa.; d. March 28, 1858, Canton, Ohio[2, 3]

George **De Walt**, b. Hanover, Pa.; d. October 29, 1850, Canton, Ohio, m. Christiana **Harter**, b. 1800, Lancaster Co., Pa.; d. October 27, 1870, Canton, Ohio[2, 3]

G-3

James **Saxton**, b. February 12, 1768, Frederick, Maryland; d.

December 29, 1845, Huntingdon, Pa., m. Hannah **Ashbaugh**,* b. 1773, Huntingdon Co., Pa.; d. July 14, 1872, Huntingdon Co., Pa.[2, 3]

Jacob **Laird**,* b. 1755, Scotland; d. 1791, Huntingdon Co., Pa., m. Jane **Johnston**,* b. 1746, Scotland[2, 3]

Philip **De Walt**, b. 1761, on a ship coming from Germany; d. November 15, 1844, Canton, Ohio, m. Eva (Last Name Unknown)*[2, 3]

Michael **Harter**,* b. Wurtenberg, Germany, m. Catherine **Markley**,* b. 1774; d. March 29, 1847, Stark Co., Ohio[2, 3]

G-4

George **Saxton**,* b. 1745, Broadrun, Maryland; d. Frederick Co., Maryland, m. Sarah **Harlan**, b. 1748, Frederick Co., Maryland; d. Frederick Co., Maryland[2, 3]

G-5

John **Harlan**, b. January 2, 1216, Chester Co., Pa.; d. Frederick Co., Maryland, m. Martha **Ashby***[3]

G-6

James **Harlan**, b. August 19, 1692, New Castle, Delaware; d. Frederick Co., Maryland[4]

G-7

George **Harlan**, b. March 11, 1649; d. 1714, m. 1678, Elizabeth **Duck**[4]

G-8

James **Harlan**, b. 1625, England, m. Rebecca **Kirk**,* b. England[4]

Ezekaliek **Duck**,* b. 1628, m. Hannah **Hoopes**, b. England[4]

G-9

William **Harlan**,* b. 1600, England, m. Deborah (Last Name Unknown)*[4]

John **Hoopes**, b. July 2, 1598, England; d. February 1, 1636, m. Isabelle **Calvert**[4]

G-10

Robert **Hoopes**, b. July 8, 1675, m. August 18, 1636, Margaret **Harrison**,* b. England[4]

John **Calvert**, b. 1580, m. Grace (Last Name Unknown),* b. England[5]

G-11

John **Hoopes,*** b. 1554, England; d. April 22, 1608, England, m. Jane **Stainhouse***

Leonard **Calvert,*** m. Grace Alicia **Crossland***[5]

Elizabeth Monroe

G+2

Children of Samuel Lawrence and Maria Hester (Monroe) Gouverneur:

James Monroe **Gouverneur**, b. 1822; d. 1885, Baltimore, Maryland[1]

Elizabeth **Gouverneur**, b. 1824; d. 1868, m(1) Monroe **Bilby**, m(2) Henry **Heiskill**, m(3) G.D. **Sparrier** (1) Samuel **Gouverneur**[1]

Children of George and Eliza (Monroe) Hay:

Hortense **Hay**[1]

G+1

Eliza **Monroe**, b. December 5, 1787, Fredericksburg, Va.; d. January 27, 1840, Paris, France, m. October 17, 1808, Fredericksburg, Va. George **Hay**, b. December 15 1765, Williamsburg, Virginia; d. September 21, 1830, Richmond, Virginia[2]

James Spence **Monroe**, b. 1799; d. September 28, 1800, Richmond, Va[1]

Maria Hester **Monroe**, b. 1803, Paris, France; d. 1850, Oak Hill, Va., m. March 9, 1820, White House Samuel Lawrence **Gouverneur**, b. 1799; d. 1867[1]

Elizabeth Kortright, b. June 30, 1768, New York, New York; d. September 23, 1830, m. February 16, 1786, James Monroe, b. April 28, 1758, Virginia; d. July 4, 1831, New York, New York[3, 6]

G-1

Lawrence **Kortwright**, b. May 21, 1706, New York, New York; d. May 6, 1755, New York, New York, m. Hannah **Aspinwall**, b. 1729, Hempstead, Long Island, New York[3]

G-2

Cornelius **Kortright**, b. 1704, New York, New York; d. April 15, 1745, New York, New York, m. 1726, Hester **Cannon**, b. April 21, 1706, New York, New York; d. February 12, 1784[3]

John **Aspinwall**, b. October 28, 1704, New York, New York, m. August 28, 1728, Mary **Sands**, b. 1708, Oyster Bay, Long Island, New York; d. December 4, 1765, New York, New York[3]

G-3

Lawrence Cornelius **Kortright**, b. 1681, Harlem, New York; d. 1726, New York, m. 1703, Helena **Benson**; d. April 27, 1707, New York, New York[2]

John **Cannon**, b. 1677, Staten Island, New York; d. October 7, 1746, m. September 20, 1697, Marie **Le Grand**; d. April 16, 1751, Staten Island, New York[3]

Joseph **Aspinwall**, b. August 12, 1673, New York, New York; d. May 9, 1692, New York, m. Hannah **Deane**, b. 1680[3]

James **Sands**, b. 1662, Oyster Bay, Long Island, New York; d. Oyster Bay, New York, m. Mary **Cornell**, b. 1679[3, 4]

G-4

Cornelius **Kortright**, b. 1645; d. 1689, m. Metje **Elyessen**, b. 1645[3]

Johannes **Benson**, b. February 8, 1655; d. 1715, m. Lysbeth **Van Deusen**[3]

Andrew **Cannon**,* b. 1651, Staten Island, New York; d. 1710, Staten Island, New York, m. Jane **Pearce***[3]

Pierre **Le Grand**,* m. Jeanne **Demendel***[1]

Peter **Aspinwall**, b. 1638, m. Remembrance **Palfrey**, b. September 16, 1638[3]

Christopher **Deane**, b. 1643; d. 1689, m. Hannah **Simms**[3]

James **Sands**, b. 1622; d. March 13, 1695, m. Sarah **Walker**, b. 1626; d. 1709[3]

John **Cornell**, b. 1637; d. 1704, m. 1669, Mary **Russell***[3]

G-5

Jan **Kortright**,* b. 1610, Leerdom, Holland; d. 1673[3]

Bazstien **Elyessen**,* b. 1615, Holland[3]

Derrick **Benson**,* b. 1625, Groningen, Holland; d. February 12, 1659, Albany, New York, m. Catalina **Berck**, b. 1625, Amsterdam, Holland; d. April 14, 1633, Holland[3]

Matthew **Van Deusen**,* m. Helena **Roberts***[3]

Thomas William **Aspinwall**,* b. 1577, Liverpool, England, m. Elizabeth (Last Name Unknown)*[3]

Peter **Palfrey**,* b. 1598, New Castle, England; d. 1663, Reading, Mass., m. Edith (Last Name Unknown)*[3]

Stephen **Deane**,* b. 1620, England; d. Mass., m. Elizabeth **Ring**, b. England; d. 1689, Mass.[3]

John **Simms**, b. 1610, England, m. Ruth (Last Name Unknown),* b. 1615, England; d. Mass.[3]

Henry **Sands**, b. September 30, 1572, England, m. Elizabeth **Goffer**, b. England[3]

John **Walker**,* b. England, m. Catherine **Hutchinson**,* b. England[3]

Thomas **Cornell**, b. 1575; d. 1656, m. Rebecca **Briggs**, b. England[3]

G-6

Sampson **Berck**,* m. Trijontje **Van Rechteren***[3]

Andrew or William **Ring**,* b. 1580, England; d. Plymouth, Mass., m. Mary **Durrant**,* b. 1587, England; d. July 15, 1631, Plymouth, Mass.[5]

Archbishop Edwin **Sands**,* b. England; d. England, m. Cecilia **Wilford**,* b. England; d. England[3]

Thomas **Goffer**,* b. England; d. England[3]

THELMA CATHERINE (PAT) NIXON

G+2

Children of Trisha Nixon and Edward Cox:

Christopher Nixon **Cox**[1, 2]

Children of Julie Nixon and Dwight David Eisenhower:

Jennie Elizabeth **Eisenhower**[1, 2]
Alex Richards **Eisenhower**[1, 2]
Melanie Catherine **Eisenhower**[1, 2]

G+1

Patricia "Tricia" **Nixon**, b. February 21, 1946, Washington, D.C., m. June 12, 1971, White House, Edward **Cox**[1]

Julie **Nixon**, b. February 5, 1948, m. December 22, 1968, Dwight David **Eisenhower**[1]

Thelma Catherine "Pat" Ryan born March 16, 1912, Ely, Nevada; d. June 22, 1993, Park Ridge, New Jersey, m. June 21, 1940, Richard Milhaus Nixon, b. January 9, 1913, Yorba Linda, Calif.; d. April 23, 1994, New York, New York[3, 4]

G-1

William **Ryan,*** b. 1875, Storey Co., Nevada, m. Katherine **Halberstadt,*** b. Germany[3]

JANE PIERCE

G+2

Jane **Pierce** had no grandchildren.

G+1

Franklin **Pierce**, b. February 2, 1836, Hillsborough, New Hampshire; d. February 5, 1836, Hillsborough, New Hampshire[1]

Frank Robert **Pierce**, b. August 27, 1839, Concord, New Hampshire; d. November 14, 1843, Concord, New Hampshire[1]

Benjamin **Pierce**, b. April 13, 1841, Concord, New Hampshire; d. January 6, 1853, Andover, Mass.[1]

Jane Appleton, b. March 12, 1806, Hillsborough, New Hampshire; d. December 2, 1863, Concord, New Hampshire, m. November 19, 1834, Franklin Pierce, b. November 23, 1804, New Hampshire; d. October 8, 1869, New Hampshire[2,6]

G-1

Rev. Jesse **Appleton**, b. 1772, Hillsborough, New Hampshire; d. November 24, 1815, Hillsborough, New Hampshire, m. April 25, 1800, Elizabeth **Means**, b. 1779 or 1780, Amherst, New Hampshire; d. October 29, 1844, Boston, Mass.[2]

G-2

Francis **Appleton**, b. March 25, 1733, Ipswich, Mass.; d. January 29, 1816, m. March 5, 1758, Elizabeth **Hubbard**, b. 1730, Ipswich, Mass.; d. November 7, 1815, Hillsborough, New Hampshire[2]

Robert **Means**, b. August 28, 1742, Stewartstown, Ireland; d. January 24, 1823, New Hampshire, m. November 24, 1774, Mary **McGregore**, b. December 6, 1752; d. January 14, 1828, Hampshire[2]

G-3

Isaac **Appleton**, b. May 30, 1704, Ipswich, Mass.; d. December 18, 1794, Ipswich, Mass., m. April 25, 1731, Elizabeth **Sawyer**, b. September 5, 1709, Wells York, Maine; d. April 29, 1785[2]

John **Hubbard**, b. 1664, Ipswich, Mass.; d. 1747, Ipswich, Mass., m. April 22, 1710, Mary **Browne***[2]

Thomas **Means**,* b. Ireland[2]

David **McGregore**,* m. Elizabeth (Last Name Unknown)*[2]

G-4

Isaac **Appleton**, b. 1664, Ipswich, Mass.; d. May 22, 1745, m. 1695, Priscilla **Baker**, b. 1675, Topsfield, Mass.; d. May 26, 1731[2]

Francis **Sawyer**, b. November 3, 1670, Wells York, Maine; d. August 31, 1756, Ipswich, Mass., m. October 6, 1705, Eliza **Dennis***[2]

Richard **Hubbard**, b. 1631, Ipswich, Mass.; d. May 3, 1681, m. 1658, Sarah **Bradstreet**; d. 1636, Andover, Mass.[2]

G-5

Samuel **Appleton**, b. February 27, 1624, Wallingford, England; d. May 15, 1696, m. December 8, 1650, Mary **Oliver**, b. June 7, 1640, Ipswich, Mass.; d. February 16, 1698[2]

Thomas **Baker**, b. September 13, 1636, Norwich, Conn.; d. March 18, 1718, Topsfield, Mass., m. March 26, 1672, Priscilla **Symonds**, b. 1648, Ipswich, Mass.; d. January 2, 1734, Ipswich, Mass.[2]

William **Sawyer**, b. February 1, 1656, Newbury, Mass.; d. June 7, 1718, m. Sarah **Littlefield**, b. November 16, 1649, Wells York, Maine; d. April 27, 1743, Wells York, Maine[2]

William **Hubbard**,* b. 1595, Cambridge, England; d. August 19, 1670, m. Judith **Knapp**, b. 1600, Ipswich, Mass.[2]

Gov. Simon **Bradstreet**, b. 1603 or 1604, Horbling, England; d. March 27, 1697, Salem, Mass., m. 1628, Ann **Dudley**, b. 1612, Northampton, England; d. September 16, 1672, Andover, Mass.[2]

G-6

Samuel **Appleton**, b. August 13, 1586, Wallingfield, England; d. 1670, m. January 24, 1615 or 1616, Judith **Everard**, b. 1587, Preston, England[2]

John **Oliver**, b. 1613, Bristol, England; d. September 17, 1640, m. 1639, Joanne **Lowell**, b. 1620, Bristol, England; d. June 14, 1677, Newbury, England[2]

John **Baker**,* b. 1598, Norwich, England; d. 1680, Topsfield, Mass., m. Elizabeth (Last Name Unknown),* b. England[2]

Samuel **Symonds**, b. 1595, Essex, England; d. October 11, 1678, Boston, Mass., m. 1637, Martha **Read**, b. England[2]

William **Sawyer**, b. 1613, Lincoln, England; d. 1702, Newbury, Mass., m. 1644, Ruth **Bidfield**, b. England[2]

Francis **Littlefield**, b. June 17, 1619, Littlefield, England; d. January 15, 1712, m. Rebecca **Rust**,* b. January 31, 1630, Wells York, Maine; d. March 29, 1685[2]

John **Knapp**, b. 1560, Ipswich, Mass., m. Martha **Blois**, b. Bures, England[2]

Rev. Simon **Bradstreet**, b. 1580, Horbling, England; d. February 9, 1621, Horbling, England, m. Margaret (Last Name Unknown),* b. 1584, Horbling, England[2]

Gov. Thomas **Dudley**, b. 1576, Northampton, England; d. July 31, 1653, Roxbury, England, m. Dorothy **Yorke**, b. 1582, England[2]

G-7

Thomas **Appleton**, b. 1539, Wallingfield, England; d. May 16, 1603, London, England, m. Mary **Isaac**, b. 1549, Patrickbourne, England; d. June 11, 1613, London, England[2]

John **Everard** b.1545, Mashbury, England; d. 1598, m. 1574, Judith **Bourne**, b. England[2]

Percival **Lowell**, b. 1571, Kingston, England; d. January 8, 1664 or 1665, Newbury, Mass., m. Rebecca (Last Name Unknown),* b. England[2]

Richard **Symonds**, b. 1556, Shrapshire, England; d. July 8, 1627, Essex, England, m. Elizabeth **Plumbe**, b. December 9, 1560, Essex, England; d. 1611, England[2]

Edmund **Read**, b. May 23, 1563, Essex, England; d. 1623, England, m. Elizabeth **Cooke**, b. 1572, Essex, England; d. England[2]

John **Sawyer**, b. 1582, England; d. July 15, 1660, m. Agnes **Sharpe**, b. 1583, England; d. January 2, 1635[2]

William **Bidfield**,* b. England, m. Elizabeth (Last Name Unknown),* b. England[2]

Edmund **Littlefield**, b. June 22, 1592, Exeter, England; d. December 11, 1661, Wells York, Maine, m. Agnes **Austin**, b. February 1, 1596, Exeter, England; d. December 12, 1677[2]

Robert **Knapp**,* b. 1537, Dedham, England; d. October 14, 1617, England, m. Margaret **Poley**, b. 1540, Suffolk, England; d. England[2]

Symond **Bradstreet**,* b. 1542, Gislingham, England; d. England[2]

Sir Roger **Dudley**, b. ca. 1548, London, England; d. 1590, England, m. Susanna **Thorne**, b. 1559, London, England; d. England[2]

Edmund **Yorke**, b. England; d. England, m. Katherine (Last Name Unknown),* b. England; d. England[2]

G-8

William **Appleton**, b. 1513, Waldingfield, England, m. Rose **Sexton**, b. England; d. England[2]

Edward **Isaac**, b. 1510, England; d. 1573, England, m. Margery **Whitehall**, b. 1510, England; d. England[2]

Thomas **Everard**, b. 1517, England; d. England, m. Margery **Wiseman**, b. 1521, England; d. England[2, 4]

John **Bourne**,* b. England; d. England[2]

Richard **Lowell**,* b. England; d. England[2]

John **Symonds**,* b. England; d. England, m. Anne **Bendbow**,* b. England; d. England[2]

Robert **Plumbe**,* b. 1530, England; d. England, m. Elizabeth **Purchase**,* b. 1534, England; d. June 25, 1596, England[2]

William **Read**, b. 1540, England; d. 1630, England, m. Mary **Church**,* b. 1541, England; d. 1577, England[2]

Thomas **Cooke**,* b. 1543, England; d. England, m. Elizabeth **Brand**,* b. 1548, England; d. England[2]

Francis **Littlefield**,* b. 1565; d. October 21, 1618, m. Mary (Last Name Unknown),* b. England; d. England[2]

Richard **Austin**,* b. February 28, 1548, England; d. February 15, 1623, England, m. Agnes (Last Name Unknown),* b. 1575, England; d. England[2]

Edmund **Poley**, b. 1485, England; d. December 31, 1548, England, m. Myrabell **Garneys**,* b. England; d. England[2, 5]

Thomas **Dudley**, b. England; d. England, m. Elizabeth **Threkeld**,* b. England; d. England[2, 3]

Thomas **Thorne**,* b. England; d. England, m. Mary **Purefoy**,* b. England; d. England[2]

Gilbert **Yorke**,* b. England; d. England, m. Amye **Bond**,* b. England; d. England[2]

G-9

Robert **Appleton**, b. 1478, Waldingfield, England; d. 1526, England, m. Mary **Mountney**,* b. England; d. England[2]

Robert **Sexton**,* b. 1470, England d England, m. Agnes **Jermyn**,* b. England; d. England[2]

William **Isaac**, b. 1483, Patrickbourne, England; d. 1518,

England, m. Margery **De Haute**, b. 1485, Kent, England; d. 1540, England[2]

Sir Richard **Whitehall**, b. 1465, England; d. 1537, England, m. 1491, Lady Elizabeth **Muston**,* b. England; d. England[2]

Henry **Everard**,* b. 1495, Mashbury, England; d. England[2, 4]

John **Wiseman**,* b. 1495, England; d. August 17, 1558, England, m. Agnes **Josselyn**, b. 1500, England; d. England[2]

Roger **Read**,* b. 1509, Wickford, England; d. 1558, England, m. Elizabeth (Last Name Unknown),* b. England; d. England[2]

Henry **Poley**, b. England; d. England, m. Constance **Gedding**, b. England; d. England[2, 5]

Sir Edmund **Dudley**, b. Dudley Castle, England; d. England, m. Maud **Clifford**, b. England; d. England[2]

G-10

Thomas **Appleton**,* b. Waldingfield, England; d. England, m. Margaret **Crane**,* b. England; d. England[2]

James **Isaac**, b. 1461, Kent, England; d. 1501, England, m. 1482, Alice **Guilford**, b. England; d. England[2]

Sir Thomas **De Haute**, b. 1466, Waltham, England; d. November 28, 1502, England, m. 1485, Isabel **De Frowick**, b. 1466, Gunnersburg, England; d. England[2]

Adrian **Whitehall**, b. 1435, England; d. 1503, London, England, m. Margaret **Worsley**; d. 1505, London, England[2]

Thomas **Everard**, b. 1460, Mashbury, England; d. 1529, England, m. 1485, Mary or Joane **Cornish**, b. 1465, Mashbury, England; d. England[2, 4]

Symon **Poley**, b. 1429, Stokes, England; d. England[2, 5]

William **Gedding**,* b. England; d. England, m. Marjorie **Watkins**,* b. England; d. England[2]

John **Dudley**, b. December 25, 1407, Dudley Castle, England; d. September 30, 1487, Dudley Castle, England, m. Elizabeth **De Berkeley**, b. Gloucester, England; d. Dudley Castle, England[2, 3]

Thomas **Clifford**, b. March 22, 1414, Westmoreland, England; d. May 25, 1455, St. Albans, England, m. Joan **Dacre**, b. 1418, Haworth Castle, England[2, 3]

G-11

John **Isaac**, b. 1422, England; d. 1501, England, m. Joan **Toke**, b. 1438, England; d. England[2]

Sir John **Guilford**, b. 1428, England; d. 1493, England, m. Alice **Waller**, b. England; d. England[2]

Sir William **De Haute**, b. 1430, Waltham, England; d. July 2, 1497, England, m. Joan **Horne**, b. 1439, Waltham, England; d. England[2]

Sir Thomas **Frowick**, b. 1423, Gunnersburg, England; d. September 26, 1485, m. 1447, Joan **Sturgeon**, b. England; d. England[2]

Richard **Whitehall**,* b. 1410, England; d. England, m. Joan (Last Name Unknown),* b. England; d. England[2]

Otewell **Worsley**, b. 1410, England; d. England, m. Rose **Trevor**, b. England; d. England[2]

John **Everard**,* b. 1432, Mashbury, England; d. England, m. Catherine (Last Name Unknown),* b. England; d. England[2, 4]

John **Cornish**, b. England; d. England[2, 4]

Richard **Poley**, b. 1400, Stokes, England; d. England, m. Mary **Blyant**, b. England; d. England[2, 5]

Sir John **Dudley**, b. 1380, Malpas, England; d. Dudley Castle, England, m. Constance **Blount**, b. 1385, Staffordshire, England; d. Dudley Castle, England[3]

Sir John **De Berkeley**, b. January 21, 1351, Worton, England; d. 1428, England, m. Elizabeth **Bettishouse**, b. England; d. England[3]

John **Clifford**,* b. England; d. England, m. Elizabeth **Percy**,* b. England; d. England[3]

Lord Thomas **Dacre**, b. England; d. England, m. Philippa **De Neville**, b. England; d. England[3]

G-12

John **Isaac**, b. 1380, England; d. England, m. Cecily (Last Name Unknown),* b. England; d. England[2]

Ralph **Toke**,* b. 1410, England; d. 1451, England[2]

Edward **Guilford**, b. 1380, England; d. 1449, England, m. Julien **De Pitlesden**,* b. England; d. England[2]

Richard **Waller**,* b. 1395, England; d. England, m. Sylvia **Gulby**,* b. England; d. England[2]

William **De Haute**, b. 1390, England; d. October 4, 1462, England, m. Joan **Wydville**, b. 1410, England; d. England[2]

Henry **Horne**,* b. 1411, England; d. England[2]

Henry **De Frowick**, b. 1380, England; d. England, m. Isabel (Last Name Unknown),* b. 1399 or 1400, England; d. 1464, England[2]

Richard **Sturgeon**,* b. England; d. England, m. Joan **Cotton**, b. England; d. England[2]

Richard **Worsley**, b. 1380, England; d. England, m. Katherine **Clark**,* b. England; d. England[2]

Edward ap Daydd, b. Wales; d. Wales, m. Anharad **Puleston**[2]

John **Cornish**, b. England; d. England[2, 4]

Thomas **Poley**,* b. England; d. England, m. Maud **Gislingham**,* b. England; d. England[2, 5]

Simon **Blyant**,* b. England; d. England, m. Agnes **De Bresworth**,* b. England; d. England[2, 5]

Henry **De Frowick**, b. 1345, London, England; d. 1385, England, m. Alice **De Cornwall**, b. 1350, Willesden, England; d. England[2]

Walter **Cotton**,* b. England; d. England, m. Joan **Reade**,* b. England; d. England[2]

John **Dudley**,* b. 1341, Sutton, England; d. September 16, 1411, Dudlery Castle, England, m. Mathilda (Last Name Unknown),* b. England; d. England[3]

Sir Walter **Blount**, b. 1350, England; d. July 21, 1403, Shrewsbury, England, m. Sacha **De Ayala**, b. 1360, Toledo, Spain; d. 1418, Newark, England[3]

Thomas **De Berkeley**, b. 1298, Berkeley, England; d. October 27, 1368, Berkeley, England, m. Katherine **Cliveden**,* b. England; d. England[3]

William **Dacre**,* b. England; d. England, m. Joan **Douglas**,* b. England; d. England[3]

Ralph **De Neville**,* b. England; d. England, m. Margaret **Stafford**,* b. England; d. England[3]

G-13

John **Isaac**,* b. 1350, Canterbury, England; d. 1419, Patrickbourne, England, m. 1370, Agnes **Grubbe**, b. England; d. England[2]

William **Guilford**, b. England; d. England, m. Joan **De Halden**, b. England; d. England[2]

Nicholas **De Haute**,* b. September 21, 1358, Kent, England; d. England, m. Alice **De Coven**, b. 1365, Kent, England; d. March 11, 1400, England[3]

Richard **De Wydville**, b. 1386, England; d. England, m. Elizabeth **Bedelgate**, b. 1390, England; d. England[3]

Robert **Worsley**, b. 1345, England; d. 1402, England, m. Isabel **De Trafford**,* b. England; d. England[2]

Dafydd ap Aednyfed Gam, b. Wales; d. Wales, m. Gwenlwyfan (Last Name Unknown), b. Wales; d. Wales[2]

Robert **Puleston**, m. Lowri (Last Name Unknown),* b. Wales; d. Wales[2]

Thomas **Cornish**,* b. England; d. England, m. Iodena **Hunt**, b. England; d. England[4]

Thomas **De Frowick**, b. 1320, Essex, England; d. November 20, 1374, England, m. Maud **De Durham**, b. 1327, England; d. England[2]

John **De Cornwall**, b. England; d. England[2]

Sir John **Blount**, b. 1298, Soddington, England; d. 1316, England, m. Eleanor **De Beauchamp**, b. Hocke, England; d. June 13, 1391, England[3]

Diego **De Ayala**, b. Toledo, Spain; d. Spain, m. Inez Alfron **De Ayala**, b. 1338, Toledo, Spain; d. Spain[3]

Maurice **De Berkeley**, b. 1271, Berkeley, England; d. May 31, 1326, England, m. Evela **La Zouche***[3]

G-14

Robert **Grubbe**,* b. England; d. England, m. Margaret **Conley**,* b. England; d. England[2]

Edward **Guilford**, b. England; d. England, m. Alice **Sambourne**, b. England; d. England[2]

John **De Halden**, b. England; d. England[2]

Sir Thomas **De Croven II**, b. England; d. England, m. Lora **Maurant**, b. England; d. England[2]

John **De Wydville**, b. England; d. England, m. Isabel **Lyons**,* b. England; d. England[2]

John **Bedelgate**,* b. England; d. England, m. Mary **De Beauchamp**, b. England; d. England[2]

William **De Worsley**, b. 1325, England; d. England, m. Ellen **De Hulton**,* b. England; d. England[2]

Ednyfed Gam ap Iorweth,* b. Wales; d. Wales, m. Gladys (Last Name Unknown),* b. Wales; d. Wales[2]

Adda Gooch ap Isuaf,* b. Wales; d. Wales, m. Angharad (Last Name Unknown),* b. Wales; d. Wales[2]

Richard **Puleston**, m. Lleucir (Last Name Unknown),* b. Wales; d. Wales[2]

Gruffydd **Fychan**, b. Wales; d. Wales, m. Ellen (Last Name Unknown), b. Wales; d. Wales[2]

John **Hunt**,* b. England; d. England, m. Margaret **Pecche**, b. England; d. England[4]

Henry **De Frowick**, b. 1295, London, England; d. ca. 1377,

England, m. Margaret **De Poyns,*** b. 1300, London, England; d. England[2]

John **De Durham,*** b. 1300, London, England; d. England, m. Joan (Last Name Unknown),* b. England; d. England[2]

Richard **De Cornwall,*** b. England; d. England, m. Joan **De Gloucester** ,* b. Gloucester, England; d. England[2]

Sir Walter **Blount**, b. 1270, Worcester, England; d. 1316, England, m. Johanna **De Soddington,*** b. 1274, Soddington, England; d. England[3]

Sir John **De Beauchamp**, b. 1304, Warwick, England; d. England, m. Margaret **St. John,*** b. England; d. England[3]

Pero Lopez **De Ayala,*** b. 1278, Toledo, Spain; d. Spain, m. Sancha **De Barroso,*** b. 1282, Toledo, Spain; d. Spain[3]

Ferman Perez **De Ayala,*** b. 1306, Toledo, Spain; d. Spain, m. Elvira **De Tavallos,*** b. 1310, Toledo, Spain; d. Spain[3]

Thomas **De Berkeley,*** b. England; d. England, m. Lady Joan **De Ferriers,*** b. England; d. England[3]

G-15

John **Guilford**, b. England; d. England[2]

William **Sambourne,*** b. England; d. England[2]

William **De Halden,*** b. England; d. England[2]

Thomas **De Croven I,*** b. England; d. England[2]

Sir Thomas **Maurant,*** b. England; d. England[2]

Robert **De Worsley**, b. England; d. England, m. Cecily **De Broomhall,*** b. England; d. England[2]

Sir Roger **Puleston*** b. England; d. England, m. Angharad verch Llwelyn,* b. Wales; d. Wales[2]

Madoc Foel ap Iefou ap Llewelyn,* b. Wales; d. Wales, m. Anharad verch Dafydd Hen,* b. Wales; d. Wales[2]

Gruffydd ap Madoc,* b. Wales; d. Wales, m. Elizabeth **Le Strange***[2]

Thomas ap Llewelyn ap Owen,* b. Wales; d. Wales, m. Eleanor Goch verch Philin,* b. Wales; d. Wales[2]

Sir Simon **Pecche**, b. England; d. England, m. Agnes **Holme**, b. England; d. England[3]

Renald **De Frowick**, b. 1260, England; d. 1300, England, m. Agnes (Last Name Unknown),* b. England; d. England[2]

Sir William **Blount**, b. 1245, Worchester, England; d. England, m. Isabel **De Beauchamp**, b. 1249, Worcester, England; d. England[3]

John **De Beauchamp**, b. 1224, Warwick, England; d. England, m. Joan **Chenduit,*** b. May 9, 1227, Devon, England; d. England[3]

G-16

Richard **Guilford**, b. England; d. England[2]

Henry **De Worsley**, b. England; d. England, m. Joan (Last Name Unknown),* b. England; d. England[2]

Gilbert **Pecche**, b. England; d. England, m. Iseult (Last Name Unknown)*[3]

Henry **De Frowick**, b. 1230, Essex, England; d. England, m. Isabel **Durham**, b. 1235, London, England; d. 1300, England[2]

Robert **Blount**, b. 1198, Worcester, England; d. England, m. Isabel **Odinsels**,* b. England; d. England[2]

William **De Beauchamp**,* b. 1197, Elmsley Castle, England; d. England, m. Isabel **De Mauduit**,* b. England; d. England[2]

G-17

Thomas **Guilford**,* b. England; d. England, m. Jane (Last Name Unknown),* b. England; d. England[2]

Richard **De Worsley**, b. England; d. England, m. Maude **De Wardley**, b. England; d. England[2]

Gilbert **Pecche**, b. England; d. May 25, 1291, Bourn, England, m. Joan **De Creye**, b. England; d. England[2]

Lawrence **De Frowick**,* b. 1200, Essex, England; d. 1277, Essex, England, m. Alice (Last Name Unknown),* b. 1204, Essex, England; d. Essex, England[2]

Thomas **Durham**,* b. London, England; d. England[2]

Sir Stephen **Blount**,* b. 1166, Worcester, England; d. England, m. Maria **Blount**, b. England; d. England[3]

G-18

Geoffrey **De Worsley**, b. 1210, England; d. England, m. Agnes (Last Name Unknown),* b. England; d. England[2]

Hamon **Pecche**, b. 1185, England; d. 1241, England[3]

Simon **De Creye**,* b. England; d. England[3]

Sir Gilbert **Blount**,* b. England; d. England, m. Agnes **Le Isle***[3]

Sir William **Blount**,* b. England; d. England[3]

G-19

Richard **De Worsley**,* b. England; d. England, m. Maud **De Singleton*** b.England; d. England[2]

Gilbert **Pecche**, b. 1150, England; d. England, m. Alice **Fitz Walter**, b. 1150, England; d. England[3]

G-20

Hamon **Pecche**,* b. England; d. England, m. Alice **Peverel**,* b. England; d. England[3]

Walter **Fitz Robert**, b. 1110, Dunmow, England; d. 1198, Dunmow Castle, England, m. Maud **De Lacy**,* b. England; d. England[2]

Robert **De Clare**, b. England; d. England, m. Mathilda **De Lis**.[3]

G-21

Richard **De Clare**,* b. 1035, Brionne, England; d. 1090, Tunbridge, England, m. Rohese **Gifford**,* b. England; d. England[3]

Simon **De Lis**, b. 1068, Normandy, France; d. 1111[3]

G-22

Ranulph The Rich **De Lis***[3]

Waltheof II of Huntingdon, b. England; d. England, m. Judith **De Lens**[3]

G-23

Siward **Bjornsson**,* m. Elfleda of Northumberland,* b. England; d. England[3]

Lambert **De Lens**, m. Adelaide **De Gand***[3]

G-24

Eustache I, b. 984, m. Mahaut **De Mahaut**[3]

G-25

Baldwin II,* m. Adela of Holland[3]

Lambert **De Louwain**,* m. Gerberge **De Lorraine***[3]

G-26

Charles, Prince of France, b. 953; d. May 21, 992, m. Adelaide, Duchess of Lorraine,* b. France; d. France[3]

G-27

King Louis IV, b. September 10, 921, France; d. September 10, 954, France, m. Gerberge of Saxony,* b. Germany[3]

G-28

King Charles III "The Simple," b. September 17, 879, France; d. October 7, 929, France, m. Eadgifu*[3]

G-29

King Louis II "The Stammerer," b. France; d. France, m. Adelaide*[3]

G-30

King Charles II "The Bald," b. June 13, 823, France; d. October 6, 877, France, m. Ermentrude,* b. September 27, 830; d. October 6, 869[3]

G-31

King Louis I "The Pious," b. April 16, 778; d. June 20, 840, m. Judith, Princess of Bavaria,* b. 800, Germany; d. April 19, 843[3]

G-32

Charlemagne, b. April 2, 742, France, m. Hildegarde **De Vinzzau***[3]

G-33

King Pepin "The Short,"* b. 714, France; d. France, m. Bertha, Countess De Laon,* b. France; d. France[3]

Sarah Polk

G+1

Sarah **Polk** had no children.

Sarah Childress, b. September 4, 1803, Murfreesboro, Tennessee; d. August 14, 1891, Nashville, Tennessee, m. January 1, 1824, James Knox Polk, b. November 2, 1795; d. January 15, 1849, Tennessee[1, 2]

G-1

Joel **Childress**, m. Elizabeth **Whitsitt**[1]

G-2

Joel **Childress**, m. Mary **Sevier**[*1]
John **Whitsitt**[1]

G-3

William **Whitsitt**, m. Ellen **Meness**[*1]

G-4

William **Whitsitt**, m. Elizabeth **Dawson**[1]

Jane Reagan (Wyman)

G+2

Children of Maureen Reagan and Dennis Revell:

Rita **Revell** (Adopted)[1]

Children of Michael and Colleen (Sterns) Reagan:

Cameron **Reagan**[1]
Ashley **Reagan**[1]

G+1

Maureen **Reagan**, b. January 4, 1941; d. August 8, 2001, m. Dennis **Revell**[1, 2]

Michael **Reagan** (Adopted), b. March 18, 1945, m. Colleen **Sterns**[1, 2]

Sarah Jane Mayfield aka Jane Wyman, b. January 4, 1914, St. Joseph, Missouri, m. January 26, 1940, Ronald Reagan (Refer to Nancy Reagan for information on Ronald Reagan)[1, 4]

G-1

Manning J. **Mayfield**,* b. 1891, Tarkio, Missouri; d. January 21, 1922, St. Joseph, Missouri, m. Gladdys Hope **Christian**, b. June 8, 1895, Tarkio, Missouri; d. 1960[2]

G-2

Christopher Columbus **Christian**,* b. 1858; d. 1921, m. Flora Diana **Bennett**, b. 1857; d. 1917[2]

G-3

Thomas Ford **Bennett**, b. 1815; d. 1904, m. Diana **Howard***[2]

G-4

Walter **Bennett**, b. May 2, 1786, Newtown, Connecticut d. 1843, Livingston, New York, m. Huldah **Coe,** b. 1793; d. 1866[2]

G-5

Thomas **Bennett**, b. November 9, 1752, Newtown, Connecticut; d. 1836, m. Molly **Ford,** b. 1756; d. 1824[2]

Joel **Coe**, b. 1761; d. 1846, m. Huldah **Horton,** b. 1762; d. 1803[2]

G-6

Ephraim **Bennett,*** b. 1714, Newtown, Connecticut; d. 1779, m. Ann **Baldwin**, b. 1727, Newtown, Connecticut; d. 1772

Ebenezer **Ford***m. Sarah **Tousey***[2]

Joseph **Coe,** b. 1713; d. 1794, m. Abigail **Curtiss,** b. 1719; d. 1776[2]

Nathaniel **Horton**, b. 1741; d. 1824, m. Rebecca **Robinson,*** b. 1742[2]

G-7

Caleb **Baldwin**, b. 1702; d. 1772, m. Mehitable (Last Name Unknown)*[2]

Joseph **Coe**, b. 1687; d. 1754, m. Abigail **Robinson**, b. 1690; d. 1775[2]

John **Curtiss,*** b. 1681; d. 1745, m. Hannah **Johnson***[2]

Nathaniel **Horton**, b. 1719; d. 1804, m. Mehitable **Wells**, b. 1724; d. 1801[2]

G-8

Daniel **Baldwin**, b. 1667; d. 1725, m. Sarah **Camp**, b. 1662; d. 1710[2]

John **Coe**, b. 1658; d. 1741, m. Mary **Hawley**, b. 1663; d. 1731[2]

David **Robinson,*** b. 1660; d. 1747, m. Abigail **Kirby,*** b. 1666; d. 1694[2]

Caleb **Horton,*** m. Phebe **Terry*** (Refer to G-3 Anna **Harrison** to continue their lines.)[2]

William **Wells,*** m. Esther **Homan***[2]

G-9

Daniel **Baldwin**, m. Elizabeth **Botsford**[2]

Nicholas **Camp,*** b. 1630; d. 1706, m. Sarah **Beard***[2]

Robert **Coe,*** m. Hannah **Mitchell**[2]

Joseph **Hawley,*** m. Catherine **Birdsey***[2]

G-10

Nathaniel **Baldwin**, b. 1610, England; d. 1658, m. Abigail **Camp**, b. England[2]

Henry **Botsford**,* b. 1608, England; d. 1685, m. Elizabeth **Wolhead*** England[2]

Matthew **Mitchell**,* b. England, m. Sarah **Butterfield**,* b. England[2]

G-11

Richard **Baldwin**, b. June 3, 1576, England; d. November 2, 1632, m. Isabel **Harding***[2]

G-12

Richard **Baldwin**, b. 1540, England; d. 1631, m. Isabel **Chase**,* b. England[(2)]

G-13

Richard **Baldwin**, b. 1503, England; d. 1552, England, m. Ellen **Apuke**,* b. 1507, England; d. 1565, England[2]

G-14

Robert **Baldwin**, b. August 11, 1475, England; d. October 25, 1553, England, m. Agnes **Dormer**,* b. 1482, England; d. England[2]

G-15

William **Baldwin**,* b. 1441, England; d. England, m. Jane **Aylesbury**, b. 1443, England; d. England[2]

G-16

Richard **Aylesbury**,* b. 1414, England; d. England[2]

Nancy Reagan

G+2

Nancy **Reagan** has no grandchildren.

G+1

Patricia Ann **Reagan**, b. October 22, 1952, m. Paul **Grilley**[1]
Ronald Prescott **Reagan**, b. May 20, 1958[1]

Anne Frances (Nancy) Robbins, b. July 6, 1921, New York, New York, m. March 6, 1952, Ronald Wilson Reagan, b. February 6, 1911, Tampico, Illinois[2, 10]

G-1

Kenneth Seymour **Robbins**, b. 1890, Pittsfield, Mass.; d. New Jersey, m. Edith **Luckett**, b. Petersburg, Va.[2]

G-2

John Newell **Robbins**,* m. Anne **Francis**[3]

Charles Edward **Luckett**, b. 1860, Jefferson Co., Kentucky, m. Sarah Frances **Whitlock**, b. 1849, Russeville, Alabama[2]

G-3

Frederick Augustus **Francis**, m. Jessie Anne **Stevens***[3]

Dr. Edward Hobbs **Luckett**, b. January 3, 1833, Jefferson Co., Kentucky; d. Owensbow, Kentucky, m. Ann Hartley **Murry**, b. September 6, 1837, Johnson Co., Kentucky; d. December 18, 1920, Washington, D.C.[2]

Benjamin Franklin **Whitlock**,* m. Elizabeth (Last Name Unknown)*[2]

G-4

Manning **Francis**, m. Elizabeth **Root**[3]

Alfred Peyton **Luckett**, b. May 12, 1800, Loudon Co., Kentucky; d. Barren Co., Kentucky, m. February 1, 1827, Susan Eveline **Hobbs**, b. June 3, 1809, Charles Co., Maryland; d. February 14, 1881, Galveston, Texas[2]

G-5

Luke **Francis**,* m. Mehitable **Sackett**, b. December 4, 1779, Westfield, Mass.

George **Root**, m. Honor **Robbins***[5]

Levi **Luckett**, b. December 20, 1762, Frederick Co., Virginia; d. 1829, Loudon Co., Kentucky, m. Letitia **Peyton**; d. December 26, 1821, Loudon Co., Kentucky[2]

Basil **Hobbs**, b. 1786, Maryland; d. 1839, m. Mary Ann **Dorsey**, b. September 13, 1791, Maryland[3, 4, 9]

G-6

Daniel **Sackett**, b. March 6, 1734, Westfield, Mass.; d. 1824, m. Mehitable **Caldwell**,* b. 1736, Mass.[1]

Ezekiel **Root**, m. Ruth **Noble**[5]

William **Luckett**, b. 1717, Frederick Co., Maryland; d. 1829, Loudon Co., Kentucky, m. Charity **Middleton**, b. 1717, Charles Co., Maryland[2]

Francis **Peyton**, b. 1734, Va.; d. ca. 1814, Va., m. Frances **Dade**, b. 1734[2, 6]

Nicholas **Hobbs**,* b. 1759, Maryland, m. Elizabeth **Cummings**,* b. 1761, Maryland[3, 4, 9]

G-7

Daniel **Sackett**,* m. Mary **Weller**, b. 1707, Westfield, Mass. (1)(5)

John **Root**,* m. Anna **Loomis**[5]

Asa **Noble**, m. Bethia (Last Name Unknown)*[5]

Samuel **Luckett**, b. October 10, 1685, Port Tobacco, Maryland, m. Ann **Smoot***[2]

John **Middleton**, b. Charles Co., Maryland; d. 1783, Montgomery Co., Maryland, m. Mary (Last Name Unknown),* b. 1695, Prince George Co., Maryland; d. Montgomery Co., Maryland[6]

Valentine **Peyton**, b. 1686; d. 1751, m. Frances **Harrison**[2, 6]

Henry **Dade**, m. Elizabeth **Massey**[2, 6, 7]

G-8

Eleazer **Weller**,* b. October 8, 1675, Westfield, Mass.; d. 1744, m. Mary **Moseley**, b. May 3, 1673, Windsor, Conn.; d. September 21, 1746, Westfield, Mass.[5]

William **Loomis**, b. 1672, Windsor, Conn.; d. 1738, Westfield, Mass., m. Martha **Morley**,* b. 1682, Springfield, Mass.; d. 1752, Westfield, Mass.[5]

Luke **Noble**,* m. Ruth **Wright***[5]

Samuel **Luckett**,* m. Elizabeth **Hussey**,* b. 1667, Charles Co., Maryland; d. 1748, Charles Co., Maryland[2]

Robert **Middleton**,* m. Mary **Wheeler***[6]

Henry **Harrison**[2]

Robert **Dade**, b. 1684; d. 1714, m. Mary **Burkett***[2, 6, 7]

Benjamin **Massey**,* m. Elizabeth (Last Name Unknown)*[6, 7]

G-9

John **Moseley**, b. 1638, Dorcester, England; d. August 18, 1690, Windsor, Conn., m. December 14, 1664, Mary **Newberry**, b. March 10, 1648, Windsor, Conn.; d. December 14, 1703, Windsor, Conn.[5, 7, 8]

Samuel **Loomis**, m. Elizabeth **Judd***[5]

Henry **Harrison**[2]

Francis **Dade**, b. 1659; d. 1698, m. Frances **Townsend**[2, 3, 5]

G-10

John **Moseley**, b. 1614, Lancastershire, England; d. October 8. 1661, Norwich, Conn., m. Elizabeth (Last Name Unknown),* b. Lancastershire, England; d. December 3, 1661, Norwich, Conn.[5, 7, 8]

Benjamin **Newberry**, m. Mary **Allyn**[5, 8]

Joseph **Loomis**, b. England; d. Windsor, Conn., m. Mary **White**, b. England; d. Windsor, Conn.[5]

John **Harrison***[2]

Francis **Dade**, b. 1621, Tannington, England; d. May 1, 1662, at sea, m. Beheathland **Bernard**[7]

Robert **Townsend**, b. England[2]

G-11

John **Moseley**,* b. 1588, Lancstershire, England[5]

Thomas **Newberry**, b. November 10, 1594, Yarcombe, England; d. December 1, 1636, Windsor, Conn., m. Jane **Dabinot**, b. 1615, Yarcombe, England; d. April 23, 1645, Norwich, Conn.[5, 8]

Matthew **Allyn**, b. England, m. Margaret **Wyatt**, b. England[1]

John **Loomis**,* b. England, m. Agnes **Linwood**,* b. England[5]

Robert **White**,* b. England, m. Bridget **Allgar**, b. March 11, 1562, Shalford, England[5]

William **Dade**, b. 1579, England; d. February 22, 1659, m. Mary **Wingfield**, b. 1583, England; d. February 3, 1624[7]

Thomas **Bernard**, b. England, m. Mary **Beheathland**, b. England[7]

Richard **Townsend***[2]

G-12

Richard **Newberry**, b. 1557, England; d. 1629, England, m. Grace **Matthews**, b. England; d. England[5, 8]

John Christopher **Dabinot**,* m. Johanna (Last Name Unknown)*[5, 8]

Richard **Allyn**,* b. England[1]

John **Wyatt**, b. England, m. Frances **Chichester**, b. England[1]

William **Allgar**,* b. 1536, England Shalford, England; d. August 25, 1575, Shalford, England, m. Margaret **Parye**,* b. 1540, Shalford, England; d. August 25, 1612, Shalford, England[5]

Thomas **Dade**,* b. 1556, England; d. April 13, 1619, England, m. Anne **Cornwallis**, b. 1558, England; d. May 2, 1622, England[7]

Henry **Wingfield**,* b. 1560, England, m. Elizabeth **Risby**,* b. 1560, England; d. February 3, 1624, England[7]

Thomas **Bernard**,* b. 1555, England; d. 1640, m. Sharon (Last Name Unknown),* b. England[7]

Robert **Beheathland**,* b. 1586, England, m. Mary **Nicholson**,* b. 1590, England[7]

G-13

Richard **Newberry (Newburgh)**, b. Yarcombe, England; d. England, m. Elizabeth **Horsey**, b. England; d. England[5, 8]

Amyas **Chichester**, b. March 28, 1527, Devonshire, England; d. July 4, 1577, Devonshire, England, m. Jane **Giffard**, b. England; d. England[5]

Richard **Cornwallis**, b. England; d. England, m. Margaret **Louthe**, b. England; d. England[7]

G-14

Walter **Newberry (Newburgh)**, b. England; d. England, m. Elizabeth **Birport**,* b. England; d. England[5, 8]

John **Chichester**,* b. 1475, England; d. 1537, England, m. Joan **Brett**,* b. 1480, England; d. England[5]

John **Cornwallis**, b. 1496, England; d. April 23, 1544, England, m. Mary **Sulyard**,* b. England; d. England[7]

Lionel **Louthe**,* b. England; d. England, m. Elizabeth **Blennerhasset**,* b. England; d. England[7]

G-15

Thomas **Newberry (Newburgh)**, b. England; d. England[5, 8]

William **Cornwallis**, b. 1447, England; d. 1519, England, m. Elizabeth **Stanford**, b. England; d. England[7]

G-16

John **Newberry(Newburgh)**, b. England; d. England, m. Alice **Carent**,* b. England; d. England[5, 8]

Thomas **Cornwallis**, b. 1410, England; d. May 26, 1484, England, m. Philippa **Tyrrel**,* b. England; d. England[7]

G-17

John **Newberry (Newburgh)**, b. England; d. England, m. Joan **Delamere**,* b. England; d. England[5, 8]

John **Cornwallis**, b. 1373, England; d. 1436, England, m. Philippa **Burton**, b. England; d. England[7]

G-18

John **Newberry (Newburgh)**,* b. England; d. England, m. Margaret **Poyntz**, b. England; d. England[5, 8]

Thomas **Cornwallis**,* b. England; d. England, m. Jane **Hansard**,* b. England; d. England[7]

G-19

Nicholas **Poyntz**, b. England; d. England, m. Eleanor **Erleigh**,* b. England; d. England[5, 8]

G-20

Hugh **Poyntz**, b. England; d. England, m. Margaret **Paveley**,* b. England; d. England[5, 8]

G-21

Nicholas **Poyntz**,* b. England; d. England, m. Elizabeth **La Zouche**, b. England; d. England[5, 8]

G-22

Eudes **La Zouche**,* m. Millicient **De Cantelupe*** (Refer to Eudes **La Zouche** G-15 Martha **Jefferson** to continue his line.)[5, 8]

Alice Roosevelt

G+2

Paulina **Longworth**, b. February 14, 1925, in Chicago, Illinois[1]

G+1

Alice Lee **Roosevelt**, b. February 12, 1884, New York, New York; d. February 20, 1980, Washington, D.C., m. February 17, 1906, in the White House Nicholas **Longworth**, b. November 5, 1869, Cincinnati, Ohio[1]

Alice Hathaway Lee, b. July 29, 1861, Boston, Massachusetts; d. February 14, 1884, New York, New York, m. October 27, 1880, Brookline, Massachusetts, Theodore Roosevelt (Refer to Edith Roosevelt for information on Theodore Roosevelt)[1, 2]

G-1

George Cabot **Lee**, b. March 21, 1830, Boston, Massachusetts; d. March 21, 1910, Brookline, Massachusetts, m. December 10, 1857, Boston, Massachusetts Caroline Watts **Haskell**, b. January 4, 1834, Worcester, Massachusetts[1, 2, 3]

G-2

John Clarke **Lee**, b. April 9, 1804, Boston, Massachusetts; d. November 19, 1877, Salem, Massachusetts, m. July 29, 1826, Harriet Paine **Rose**[1, 2, 3]

Elias **Haskell**,* b. Boston, Massachusetts, m. Alice **Hathaway**[*3]

G-3

Nathaniel Cabot **Lee**, b. May 30, 1772, Beverly, Massachusetts; d. January 14, 1806, Barbados, m. April 11, 1803, Mary Ann **Cabot**, b. 1784, Salem, Massachusetts[1, 2, 3]

Joseph Warner **Rose**,* m. Harriet **Paine***[3]

G-4

Joseph **Lee**, b. May 24, 1744, Salem, Massachusetts; d. February 6, 1831, Salem, Massachusetts, m. June 9, 1769, Salem, Massachusetts Elizabeth **Cabot**, b. February 24, 1746, Salem, Massachusetts[1, 2, 3]

Francis **Cabot**, b. June 14, 1757; d. 1832, m. Ann **Clarke**[3, 4]

G-5

Thomas **Lee**, b. December 17, 1702, Boston, Massachusetts; d. July 14, 1747, Salem, Massachusetts, m. December 29, 1737, Salem, Massachusetts Lois **Orne**, b. March 16, 1711, Boston, Massachusetts[1, 2, 3]

Joseph **Cabot**, m. Elizabeth **Higginson**, b. March 22, 1722, Salem, Massachusetts; d. October 25, 1781, Beverly, Massachusetts[3, 4]

Joseph **Cabot**,* m. Elizabeth **Higginson*** (Refer to previous Joseph **Cabot** to continue Joseph's line.)[3, 4]

John **Clarke**, b. 1719, Salem, Mass.; d. 1801, m. Sarah **Pickering**[3]

G-6

Thomas **Lee**, b. 1673, Boston, Massachusetts; d. July 16, 1766, Boston, Massachusetts, m. 1700, Boston, Massachusetts Deborah **Flint**, b. 1672, Salem, Massachusetts[1, 2, 3]

Timothy **Orne**, m. Lois **Pickering***[3]

John **Cabot**, b. January 25, 1670, Massachusetts d. June 7, 1742, Massachusetts, m. Anne **Orne**, b. April 14, 1678, Salem, Massachusetts[3, 4]

John **Higginson**, b. January 10, 1698, Salem, Massachusetts; d. July 15, 1744, Salem, Massachusetts, m. December 4, 1719, Ruth **Boardman**, b. November 15, 1698, Cambridge, Massachusetts[3, 4]

Josiah **Clarke**,* m. Mary **Wingate***[3]

G-7

Thomas **Lee**,* b. 1650, Boston, Massachusetts, m. Martha **Mellowes**, b. February 8, 1654, Boston, Massachusetts; d. 1675[1, 2]

Edward **Flint**, m. Elizabeth **Hart***[3]

Joseph **Orne**, m. Anne **Thompson***[3]

Francis **Cabot**, b. Isle of Jersey, m. Susanna **Gruchy**, b. Isle of Jersey[2,3]

Joseph **Orne**,* m. Anne **Thompson*** (Refer to previous Joseph Orne to continue his line.)[3]

John **Higginson**, m. Hannah **Gardner**, b. April 4, 1676, Salem, Massachusetts; d. June 20, 1718, Salem, Massachusetts[3]

Andrew **Boardman**,* m. Elizabeth **Truesdale***[3]

G-8

John **Mellowes**, b. June 6, 1622, Sutterton, England, m. Martha **Cotton**,* b. 1630, Sutterton, England[1, 2]

William **Flint**,* b. 1603, England; d. April 2, 1673, Salem, Massachusetts, m. Alice **Williams**,* b. 1608, England; d. October 5, 1700, Salem, Massachusetts[3]

John **Orne**,* b. 1602, England; d. 1684, m. Frances **Stone**, b. England[3]

John **Cabot**, b. Isle of Jersey, b. ca. 1587, Isle of Jersey; d. 1650, Isle of Jersey, m. Catherine **Gifford***[3]

Peter **Gruchy**, m. Ellen **Le Sueur***[3]

John **Higginson**, m. Sarah **Savage**[3]

Samuel **Gardiner**,* m. Elizabeth **Brown***[3]

G-9

Oliver **Mellowes**, b. 1595, England; d. 1638, Braintree, Massachusetts, m. Mary **James**, b. October 13, 1597, England[1, 2]

Simon **Stone**, b. England, m. Joana **Clark***[3]

Nicholas **Cabot**,* b. ca. 1555, Isle of Jersey, m. Collette **Hamon***[3]

John **Gruchy**,* m. Elizabeth **Hamon***[3]

John **Higginson**, b. Claybrooke, England, m. Sarah **Whitfield**[3]

Thomas **Savage**,* b. England, m. Mary **Symmes**, b. Claybrooke, England[3]

G-10

Abraham **Mellowes**,* b. England, m. Martha **Bulkeley**, b. 1572, England; d. 1639[1, 2]

David **Stone**, b. ca. 1540, Essex, England, m. Ursula (Last Name Unknown)*[3]

Francis **Higginson**,* b. England, m. Anne (Last Name Unknown)*[3]

Henry **Whitfield**,* b. Surry, England[3]

Zachariah **Symmes**,* m. Sarah **Baker*** (Refer to G-5 Anna Harrison to continue their lines.)[3]

G-11

Edward **Bulkeley**,* m. Olive **Irby*** (Refer to G-9 Mary **Lincoln** to continue their lines.)[1, 2]

Simon **Stone**,* b. Essex, England; d. England, m. Agnes (Last Name Unknown),* b. England d. England*[3]

Edith Roosevelt

G+2

Children of Theodore and Eleanor (Alexander) Roosevelt:

Grace **Roosevelt**, b. 1911; d. 1994, m. William **McMillan**[1]

Theodore **Roosevelt**, m. Anne **Babcock**[1]

Cornelius **Roosevelt**, b. October 23, 1915, New York, New York; d. 1992, m. Frances **Webb**[1]

Quentin **Roosevelt**, b. November 4, 1919; d. December 21, 1948[1]

Children of Kermit and Belle (Willard) Roosevelt:

Kermit **Roosevelt**, m. Mary **Lowe**[1]

Joseph Willard **Roosevelt**, m(1) Nancy **Cummings**, m(2) Carol Adele **Russell**[1]

Belle **Roosevelt**, b. November 8, 1919, New York, New York; d. 1985, m. John Gorham **Palfrey**[1]

Dinah **Roosevelt**, b. January 11, 1925, New York, New York; d. January 6, 1953, New York[1]

Children of Richard and Ethel (Roosevelt) Derby:

Richard **Derby**, b. March 7, 1914, New York, New York; d. October 2, 1922, Sagamore Hill, Oyster Bay, New York[1]

Edith **Derby**, m. Andrew Murray **Andrews**[1]

Sarah **Derby**, m. Robert T. **Gannett**[1]

Judith **Derby**, b. 1973; d. September 26, 1973, Concord, Mass., m. Adelbert **Ames**[1]

Children of Archibald Bullock and Grace (Lockwood) Roosevelt:

Archibald Bullock **Roosevelt**, b. February 18, 1918, Boston; d. May 31,1990, m(1) Katherine **Tweed**, m(2) Sellva **Showke**[1]

Theodora **Roosevelt**, m(1) Thomas **Keough**, m(1) Thomas **O'Toole**[1]

Nancy **Roosevelt**, m. William Aldred **Jackson**[1]

Edith **Roosevelt**, m. Alexander Gregory **Barmine**[1]

G+1

Theodore **Roosevelt**, b. September 13, 1887, Oyster Bay, New York; d. July 12, 1944, Normandy, France, m. June 29, 1910, New York, New York Eleanor **Alexander**, b. 1889, New York, New York; d. May 29, 1960, Oyster Bay, New York[2]

Kermit **Roosevelt**, b. October 10, 1889, Oyster Bay, New York; d. June 4, 1943, Alaska, m. June 10, 1914, Madrid, Spain Belle **Willard**, b. July 1, 1892, Baltimore, Maryland; d. March 30, 1968, Manhattan, New York[1]

Ethel **Roosevelt**, b. August 13, 1891, Oyster Bay, New York; d. 1977, Oyster Bay, New York, m. April 4, 1913, Oyster Bay, New York Richard **Derby**, b. April 7, 1881, New York, New York; d. July 21, 1963, Brattleboro, Vermont[1]

Archibald Bullock **Roosevelt**, b. April 9, 1894, Washington, D.C.; d. 1979, Palm Springs, Florida, m. April 14, 1917, Boston, Mass. Grace Stackpole **Lockwood**[1]

Quentin **Roosevelt**, b. November 19, 1897, Washington, D.C.; d. July 14, 1919, Cambrai, France[1]

Edith Carow, b. August 6, 1861, Norwich, Conn.; d. September 30, 1948, Sangamore, Long Island, New York, m. December 2, 1886, Theodore Roosevelt, b. October 27, 1858, New York, New York; d. January 6, 1919, New York, New York[3, 12]

G-1

Charles **Carow**, b. October 4, 1825, New York, New York; d. March 17, 1883, New York, New York, m. Gertrude Elizabeth **Tyler**, b. 1836, Norwich, Conn.; d. April 27, 1895, Turin, Italy[3, 4]

G-2

Isaac **Carow**, b. March 29, 1778; d. 1850, m. Eliza **Mowatt,*** b. 1785; d. 1837[3, 4]

Daniel **Tyler**, b. January 7, 1799, Booklyn, Conn.; d. November 28, 1882, New York, New York, m. Emily **Lee**, b. 1804, Cambridge, Mass.; d. March 9, 1864, New York, New York[3, 4]

G-3

Isaac **Carow**, b. 1741; d. 1783, m. Anne **Cooper***[3]

Daniel **Tyler**, b. May 21, 1750, Canterbury, Conn.; d. April 29, 1832, Brooklyn, Conn., m. Sarah **Edwards**, b. 1761; d. 1841[3,4]

Mr. **Lee**,* m. Elizabeth **Gorham**[5]

G-4

Joshua **Carow**, m. Judith **Quentin***[3]

Daniel **Tyler**, b. February 22, 1701, Groton, Conn.; d. February 20, 1802, Brooklyn, Conn., m. Mehitable **Shurtleff**, b. 1716; d. 1769[4]

Timothy **Edwards**, b. July 25, 1738, Mass.; d. October 27, 1813, m. 1760, Rhoda **Ogden**[3,6]

Stephen **Gorham**, b. June 23, 1683, Barnstable, Mass.; d. 1743, Nantucket, Mass., m. 1683, Elizabeth **Gardner**[5,7]

G-5

Elias **Carow***[3]

Daniel **Tyler**, b. 1676, Mass.; d. 1735, Groton, Conn., m. Anna **Geer**[4]

Thomas **Shurtleff**, b. March 16, 1686, Plymouth, Mass.; d. 1730, Plymouth, Mass., m. Phebe **Shaw**, b. May 10, 1690, Plymouth, Mass.; d. 1736, Plymouth, Mass.[6]

Jonathan **Edwards**, b. 1703; d. 1758, m. 1727, Sarah **Pierrepont**[6]

John **Gorham**,* m. Mary **Otis**, b. England; d. England[5]

James **Gardner**, b. May 19, 1664, Salem, Mass.; d. April 1, 1723, Nantucket, Mass., m. Mary **Starbuck**, b. March 30, 1663, Nantucket, Mass.; d. March 30, 1696, Nantucket, Mass.[7]

G-6

Hopestill **Tyler**, b. 1646, Roxbury, Mass.; d. January 20, 1734, Preston, Conn., m. Mary **Lovett**[4]

George **Geer**, b. 1621, England; d. Preston, Conn., m. Sarah **Allyn**, b. England[9]

William **Shurtleff**, b. 1657, Plymouth, Mass., m. Susanna **Lathrop**, b. February 28, 1662, Barnstable, Mass.; d. August 9, 1726, Plympton, Mass.[8]

Jonathan **Shaw**, b. 1663, Plymouth, Mass., m. Mehitable **Pratt**[10]

Timothy **Edwards**, b. 1669; d. 1758, m. Esther **Stoddard**, b. June 2, 1672, Northampton, Mass.; d. January 19, 1771, East Windsor, Conn.[3,6]

John **Gorham**, b. England; d. England, m. Desire **Howland**, b. 1625, England; d. 1683, Plymouth, Mass.[5]

John **Otis**, b. England; d. England, m. Mary **Jacob**, b. England; d. England[5]

Rev. James **Pierrepont**, b. 1659; d. 1698, m. 1682, Mary **Hooker**, b. 1673; d. 1740[6]

John **Howland** (Mayflower **Pilgrim**), b. 1592, England; d. February 23, 1672, Plymouth, Mass., m. Elizabeth **Tilley**, b. 1607, England; d. December 21, 1687, Plymouth, Mass.[5]

Nathaniel **Starbuck**, b. 1635; d. August 6, 1719, Nantucket, Mass.[7]

Richard **Gardner**, b. 1632; d. 1714, Nantucket, Mass., m. Sarah **Coffin**, b. February 20, 1646, Haverhill, Mass.; d. March 13, 1717, Nantucket, Mass.[7]

G-7

Job **Tyler**, b. 1619, Cranbrook, England; d. 1700, Mendon, Mass., m. Mary **Horton**, b. 1619, England; d. May 28, 1665, Rawley, Mass.[4]

Daniel **Lovett**, b. 1620, Buckingham, England; d. 1691, Milton, Mass., m. Joanna **Blott**, b. October 1, 1620, England; d. June 18, 1670[4]

Jonathan **Geer**, b. England[9]

Robert **Allyn**, b. 1608, England; d. 1683, New Haven, Conn., m. Sarah **Gager**, b. England[9]

William **Shurtleff**, b. May 16, 1624, Yorkshire, England; d. June 23, 1666, Plymouth, Mass., m. Elizabeth **Lettice**, b. 1636, England; d. October 31, 1693, Swansea, Mass.[8]

Barnabas **Lathrop**, b. June 6, 1636, Scituate, Mass.; d. October 26, 1715, Barnstable, Mass., m. Susanna **Clark**, b. 1650, Plymouth, Mass.[8]

Jonathan **Shaw**, b. 1629, England; d. July 30, 1701, Plympton, Mass., m. Phebe **Watson**, b. 1638, Plymouth, Mass.; d. 1672, Plymouth, Mass.[10]

Benajah **Pratt**, b. 1641, Plymouth, Mass., m. Persis **Dunham**, b. Plymouth, Mass.; d. July 30, 1701[7]

Richard **Edwards**, m. Elizabeth **Tuttle**, b. 1649[3, 6]

Solomon **Stoddard**, b. September 27, 1643, Boston, Mass.; d. July 11, 1728, Northampton, Mass., m. Esther **Warham**, b. 1644, Windsor, Conn.; d. July 10, 1735, Northampton, Mass.[6]

John **Pierrepont**, b. 1617, England; d. 1682, m. Thankful **Snow**[*6]

Samuel **Hooker**, b. 1633, Cambridge, Conn.; d. November 6, 1697, Farmington, Conn., m. Mary **Willet**, b. November 10, 1637, Plymouth, Mass.; d. June 24, 1712, Norwalk, Conn.[6]

Henry **Howland**,* b. 1564, England; d. May 19, 1635, England, m. Margaret (Last Name Unknown)[*5]

John **Tilley** (Mayflower Pilgrim), b. 1573, England; d. 1621, Plymouth, Mass., m. 1596, Joan **Hurst**, b. England; d. Plymouth, Mass.[5]

G-8

Lawrence **Tyler,*** b. England, m. Dorothy (Last Name Unknown),* b. England[4]

Thomas **Horton**, b. 1596, England; d. 1640, m. Mary **Eddy**, b. England; d. September 19, 1683[4]

Robert **Blott,*** b. 1582, England; d. Boston, Mass., m. March 1, 1664, Susan **Selbee,*** b. 1586, England; d. January 20, 1658, Boston, Mass.[4]

George **Geer**, b. England[9]

Edward **Allyn,*** b. 1581, Manchester, England; d. London, England[9]

William **Gager,*** b. England[9]

Thomas **Lettice,*** b. 1604, England; d. October 25, 1681, Plymouth, Mass., m. Ann (Last Name Unknown),* b. England[8]

Rev. John **Lathrop,*** b. December 20, 1584, England; d. November 8, 1653, m. Hannah **Howse,*** b. England[8]

Thomas **Clark,*** b. England, m. Susanna **Ring,*** b. England[8]

George **Watson,*** b. 1602, England, m. Phoebe **Hicks**, b. England[10]

Joshua **Pratt,*** b. England, m. Bathsheba **Fay,*** b. England[7]

John **Durham,*** b. England, m. Abigail **Barlow***[7]

William **Edwards,*** b. 1620, England, m. Agnes **Spencer,*** b. England[3, 6]

William **Tuttle**, b. 1609, England; d. 1673, m. Elizabeth (Last Name Unknown),* b. England[3, 6]

Anthony **Stoddard,*** b. 1614, England; d. March 16, 1686, Boston, Mass., m. Mary **Downing,*** b. 1620, England; d. June 16, 1647, Boston, Mass.[6]

John **Warham,*** b. England, m. Jane (Last Name Unknown),* b. England[6]

James **Pierrepont,*** b. England, m. Margaret (Last Name Unknown),* b. England[3, 6]

Thomas **Hooker,*** b. 1586, England; d. 1647, Hartford, Conn., m. Susanna **Harkes,*** b. 1593, England; d. May 17, 1676, Farmington, Conn.[3, 6]

Thomas **Willet,*** b. England, m. Sarah **Cornell,*** b. England[3, 6]

Robert **Tilley**, b. 1540, England; d. 1612, England, m. Elizabeth (Last Name Unknown),* b. England[5]

William **Hurst,*** b. England; d. England, m. Rose **Fisher,*** b. England; d. England[5]

G-9

Joseph **Horton**,* b. England; d. England, m. Mary **Schuyler**, b. England; d. England[4]

John **Eddy**, b. March 27, 1597, Cranbrook, England; d. October 12, 1684, Watertown, Mass., m. Amy **Doggett**, b. England; d. England[4]

John **Geer**, b. England; d. England, m. Beatrice **Jermyn*** b. England; d. England[9]

Robert **Hicks**, b. 1578, London, England; d. May 24, 1647, Plymouth, Mass., m. Margaret **Winslow**,* b. England; d. England[10]

Henry **Tuttle**,* b. England; d. England[3, 6]

William **Tilley**,* b. 1575, England; d. 1578, England, m. Agnes (Last Name Unknown),* b. England; d. England[5]

G-10

William **Eddy**,* b. England; d. England, m. Mary **Foster**, b. England; d. England[4]

John **Geer**, b. England; d. England, m. Alice **Trowbridge**, b. England; d. England[9]

James **Hicks**, b. 1550, Southwark, England; d. England, m. Phebe **Allyne**, b. England; d. England[10]

Edward **Winslow**, b. October 19, 1595; d. April 18, 1655, m. Eleanor **Pelham**,* b. England; d. England[10]

Thomas **Tilley**, b. 1490, England; d. 1556, England, m. Margaret (Last Name Unknown),* b. England; d. England[5]

G-11

John **Foster**, b. England; d. England, m. Elizabeth Ellen **Mann**,* b. England; d. England[4]

Walter **Geer**,* b. England; d. England, m. Alice **Somaster**, b. England; d. England[9]

Baptist **Hicks**, b. ca. 1525, Gloucester, England; d. 1565, England, m. Mary **Everard**,* b. 1528; d. England[10]

Edward **Winslow**, b. England; d. England, m. Magdelen **Ollyer**,* b. England; d. England[10]

Henry **Tilley**,* b. 1465, England; d. 1520, England, m. Joan (Last Name Unknown),* b. England; d. England[5]

G-12

John **Foster**,* b. 1511, England; d. England[4]

John **Somaster,*** b. England; d. England[9]

Thomas **Hicks,*** b. 1487, Gloucester, England; d. Gloucester, England, m. Margaret **Atwood,*** b. England; d. England[10]

Kenelin **Winslow,*** b. England; d. England, m. Elizabeth **Follitt,*** b. England; d. England[10]

Eleanor Roosevelt

G+2

Children of Anna Eleanor Roosevelt and Curtis Bean Dall:

Anna Eleanor (Sistie) **Dall**, b. March 25, 1927[1]
Curtis Roosevelt (Buzzie) **Dall**, b. April 19, 1930[1]

Children of Anna Eleanor Roosevelt and Clarence John Boettiger:

John Roosevelt **Boettiger**, b. March 30, 1939[1]

Children of James and Betsey (Cushing) Roosevelt:

Sara **Roosevelt**, b. March 13, 1932[1]
Kate **Roosevelt**, b. February 16, 1936[1]

Children of James and Romelle Theresa Schneider:

James **Roosevelt**[1]
Michael Anthony **Roosevelt**[1]
Anna Eleanor **Roosevelt**[1]

Children of Elliott and Elizabeth (Donner) Roosevelt:

William Donner **Roosevelt**[1]

Children of Elliott and Ruth Josephine (Googins) Roosevelt:

Ruth Chandler **Roosevelt**[1]
Elliott **Roosevelt**[1]
David Boynton **Roosevelt**

Children of Franklin Delano and Ethel (Du Pont) Roosevelt:

Franklin Delano **Roosevelt**[1]
Christopher Du Pont **Roosevelt**[1]

Children of John Aspinwall and Anne Lindsay (Clark) Roosevelt:

Haven Clark **Roosevelt**[1]
Anne Sturgis **Roosevelt**[1]
Joan **Roosevelt**[1]

G+1

Anna Eleanor **Roosevelt**, b. May 3, 1906, Hyde Park, New York;

d. December 1, 1975, New York, New York, m(1) June 5, 1926, Charles **Dall**, m(2) January 8, 1935, New York, New York John **Boettiger**, m(3) November 11, 1952, Mailbu, Calif. James Addison **Halstead**[1]

James **Roosevelt**, b. December 23, 1907, New York, New York; d. August 31, 1991, Orange Co., Calif., m(1) June 4, 1930, Brookline, Mass. Betsey **Cushing**, m(2) April 14, 1941, Beverly Hills Romelle Theresa **Schneider**, m(3) July 2, 1956, Los Angeles, Calif. Gladys Irene **Owens**, m(4) October 3, 1969, Hyde Park, New York Mary Lena **Winskill**[1]

Franklin Delano **Roosevelt**, b. March 18. 1909, New York, New York; d. November 8, 1909, New York, New York[1]

Elliott **Roosevelt**, b. September 23, 1910, New York, New York; d. October 27, 1990, Scottsdale, Arizona, m(1) July 22, 1933, Burlington, Iowa Ruth Josephine **Googins**, m(2) December 3, 1944, Colorado Faye Margaret **Emerson**, m(3) March 15, 1951, Miami Beach, Florida Minerva **Bell**, m(4) 1960, British Columbia, Canada Patricia **Whitehead**, m(5) Elizabeth **Donner**[1]

Franklin Delano **Roosevelt**, b. August 17, 1914, Campobello, New Brunswick, Canada; d. August 17, 1988, Poughkeepsie, New York, m(1) June 30, 1937, Wilmington, Delaware Ethel **Du Pont**, m(2) August 31, 1949, Suzanne **Perrin**, m(3) July 1, 1970, New York, New York Felicia **Schiff**, m(4) May 6, 1977, Dutchess Co., New York Patricia Louise **Oakes**, m(5) Lynda **Stevenson**[1]

James Aspinwall **Roosevelt**, b. May 13, 1916, Washington, D.C.; d. April 27, 1981, m(1) June 18, 1938, Mass. Anne Lindsay **Clark**, m(2) October 28, 1965, New York, New York Irene **Boyd**[1]

Anna Eleanor Roosevelt, b. October 11, 1884, New York, New York; d. November 7, 1962, New York, New York, m. March 20, 1905, Franklin Delano Roosevelt, b. January 30, 1882, Hyde Park, New York; d. April 12, 1945, Warm Springs, Georgia[2,4]

G-1

Elliott **Roosevelt**, b. February 28, 1860, New York, New York; d. August 15, 1894, New York, New York, m. December 1, 1883, Anna Rebecca **Hall**, b. March 17, 1863; d. December 7, 1892, New York, New York[2]

G-2

Theodore **Roosevelt**, b. September 22, 1837, New York, New York;

d. February 9, 1878, New York, New York, m. December 22, 1853, Martha **Bullock**, b. July 8, 1834, Hartford, Conn.; d. February 12, 1884, New York, New York[2]

Valentine Gill **Hall**, b. March 27, 1834, New York, New York; d. July 17, 1880, New York, m. Mary **Ludlow**, b. April 24, 1843, Trivoli, New York; d. New York, New York[2]

G-3

Cornelius **Roosevelt**, b. January 39, 1794, New York, New York; d. July 17, 1871, New York, New York, m. 1821, Margaret **Barnhill**, b. December 13, 1799, New York, New York; d. January 23, 1861[2]

Stephen **Bullock**, b. 1793, Roswell, Georgia; d. February 18, 1849, m. January 6, 1818, Martha **Stewart**, b. 1799, Newport, Ga.; d. 1862[2]

Valentine **Hall**,* b. 1797; d. 1880, m. Susan **Tonneli***[2]

Dr. Edward **Ludlow**, b. August 3, 1810; d. November 27, 1884, m. Elizabeth **Livingston**, b. October 10, 1813, Clermont, New York; d. 1833, New York, New York[2]

G-4

Jacobus **Roosevelt**, b. 1759, New York, New York; d. August 13, 1840, New York, New York, m. 1793, Mary Helen **Van Schaack**, b. December 23, 1773, New York, New York; d. February 3, 1845, New York, New York[2]

Robert **Barnhill**, b. June 30, 1754, Bucks Co., Pa.; d. August 12, 1814, m. September 22, 1778, Elizabeth **Potts**, b. January 20, 1750, Philadelphia, Pa.; d. August 20, 1807[2]

James **Bullock**, b. 1765, Savannah, Georgia; d. February 9, 1806, m. April 13, 1786, Anne **Irvine**, b. January 14, 1770, Georgia; d. 1810[2]

Gen. Daniel **Stewart**, b. December 20, 1760, Liberty Co., Georgia; d. 1830, m. Susannah **Oswald**,* b. November 2, 1770, Newport, Georgia[2]

Gabriel Ver Plank **Ludlow**, b. 1768; d. April 30, 1825, m. Elizabeth **Hunter***[2]

Edward Philip **Livingston**, b. November 24, 1779, Kingston, Jamaica; d. November 3, 1843, m. Elizabeth **Livingston**, b. May 5, 1780, Hunterdon Co., New Jersey; d. November 3, 1843, Clermont, New York[2]

G-5

Jacobus **Roosevelt**, b. August 9, 1724, Kingston, New York; d. October 6, 1777, New York, m. December 2, 1746, Annetje **Bogart**, b. 1728, New York, New York[2]

Cornelius **Van Schaack**, b. 1734, New York, New York; d. March 18, 1797, New York, New York, m. Angeltje **Yates**[2]

John **Barnhill**, b. 1729, Bucks Co., Pa.; d. February 27, 1797, m. 1749, Sarah **Craig**, b. 1725[2]

Thomas **Potts**, b. ca. 1729, Philadelphia, Pa.; d. July 26, 1776, New Jersey, m. January 16, 1753, m. January 16, 1753, Elizabeth **Lukens**[2]

Gov. Archibald **Bullock**, b. ca. 1729, Charleston, South Carolina; d. February 22, 1777, Georgia, m. Mary **De Veaux**, b. June 26, 1748; d. May 26, 1818[2]

Dr. John **Irvine**, b. September 15, 1742; d. October 15, 1808, m. Anne Elizabeth **Baillie**, b. September 27, 1749; d. July 23, 1807[2]

John **Stewart**, b. February 23, 1726, South Carolina; d. September 4, 1776, Liberty Co., Georgia, m. Susannah **Bacon**,* b. 1729, South Carolina; d. October 21, 1766[2]

Gabriel George **Ludlow**, b. April 16, 1736, New York, New York; d. February 12, 1808, Hyde Park, New York, m. September 3, 1760, Ann **Ver Planck**, b. October 11, 1745, New York, New York; d. December 31, 1822, Carlton, New Brunswick, Canada[2]

Philip **Livingston**, b. May 28, 1741, Albany, New York; d. November 2, 1787, New York, m. Sarah **Johnson**[2]

Robert R. **Livingston**, b. November 27, 1746, New York; d. February 26, 1813, Clermont, New York, m. Mary **Stevens**, b. 1752; d. March 22, 1814[2]

G-6

Johannes **Roosevelt**, b. ca. 1688, Kingston, New York, m. September 25, 1708, Heyltje **Sjoerts**, b. February 27, 1689[2]

John **Bogart**, b. 1697, m. Hannah **Peeck**[2]

Cornelius **Van Schaack**, b. October 17, 1705; d. October 13, 1776, m. Lydia **Van Dyck**, b. July 16, 1704; d. May 17, 1786[2]

Johannes **Yates; d.** June 4, 1776, m. November 28, 1737, Rebecca **Waldron**, b. 1719[2]

Robert **Barnhill**,* b. 1700, Ireland, m. Sarah (Last Name Unknown),* b. 1707, Ireland[2]

Daniel **Craig**,* b. 1700, Paisley, Scotland; d. 1776, m. Margaret (Last Name Unknown)[2]

John **Potts**, b. August 8, 1696, Philadelphia, Pa., m. Elizabeth **McVaugh**, b. 1699; d. January 5, 1791[2]

William **Lukens**, m. Elizabeth **Tyson**[2]

James **Bullock**,* b. Baldernock, Scotland; d. October 25, 1780, m. Jean **Stobo**[2]

James **De Veaux**, b. 1704, m. Anne **Fairchild**; d. March 8, 1765[2]

Charles **Irvine**,* b. 1696; d. May 28, 1779, m. Euphemia **Douglas**, b. 1733; d. December 21, 1766[2]

Kenneth **Baillie**, b. July 10, 1766, m. Elizabeth **Mackey**[*2]

John **Stewart**,* b. 1696; d. 1765, m. Jerusha (Last Name Unknown)*

Gabriel **Ludlow**,* m. Frances **Duncan**[*2]

Geleyn **Ver Planck**, b. May 31, 1698, New York, New York; d. November 11, 1751, m. September 1, 1737, Mary **Crommelin**, b. 1690, New York, New York[2]

Philip **Livingston**, b. January 15, 1716, Albany, New York; d. June 12, 1778, m. April 14, 1740, Christina **Ten Broeck**, b. December 30, 1718[2]

Robert R. **Livingston**, b. 1718; d. December 9, 1775, Clermont, New York, m. December 8, 1742, Margaret **Beekman**, b. ca. 1723; d. 1800, Kingston, New York[2]

John **Stevens**,* m. Elizabeth **Alexander**[*2]

G-7

Nicholas **Roosevelt**, b. 1658, Amsterdam, Holland; d. July 30, 1742, m. 1682, Heyltje Jans **Kunst**, b. January 24, 1664[2]

Olfert **Sjoerts**, b. 1661; d. 1710, m. Margaret **Clopper**[2]

Claes **Bogart**, b. 1668; d. January 5, 1727, m. June 28, 1695, Beeltje **Van Schaack**[2]

Jan **Peeck**, b. 1653, m. July 18, 1683, Elizabeth **Van Imbruck**[2]

Emmanuel **Van Schaack**, b. 1680; d. November 19, 1706, m. June 11, 1703, Margaret Lucasse **Wyndgard**[2]

Hendrick **Van Dyck**, b. 1660; d. April 11, 1707, m. February 3, 1689, Maria **Schuyler**, b. September 29, 1666[2]

Cristojel **Yates**, m. Angeltse (Last Name Unknown)[*2]

William **Waldron**,* m. Engeltje **Stoutenburgh**[*2]

David **Potts**, b. 1670; d. November 16, 1730, m. 1694, Alice **Croasdale**, b. August 3, 1673[2]

Edmund **McVaugh**,* m. Alice **Dickinson**[*2]

Jan **Lukens***; d. January 24, 1744, m. 1683, Mary **Teisen**[*2]

Reynier **Tyson**,* b. 1659; d. July 27, 1745, m. Mary (Last Name Unknown)[*2]

Rev. Archibald **Stobo**,* b. 1674; d. 1737, m. 1700, Elizabeth **Park**[2]

Andre **De Veaux**[*2]

Richard **Fairchild**,* m. Anne **Bellinger**[2]

John **Douglas**, m. Agnes **Horn**[2]

John **Baillie**[2]

Samuel **Ver Planck**, b. Deacember 16, 1669, New York, New York; d. November 20, 1698, Jamaica, New York, m. October 26, 1691, Ariantje **Baird**, b. November 18, 1667, New York, New York[2]

Charles **Crommelin**,* b. 1675, m. Anna **Sinclair**, b. 1675[2]

Philip **Livingston**, b. July 9, 1686, Albany, New York; d. February 4, 1749, New York, New York, m. Catrina **Van Brugh**, b. 1689, Albany, New York; d. February 20, 1756[2]

Dirck **Ten Broeck**,* m. Marjarita **Cuyler***[2]

Robert **Livingston**, b. July 24, 1688; d. June 27, 1775, Clermont, New York, m. November 11, 1717, Margaret **Howarden**,* b. 1690, New York, New York[2]

Henry **Beekman**,* b. 1688, Kingston, New York, m. Janet **Livingston**[2]

G-8

Claes **Van Roosevelt**,* b. 1626; d. 1659, m. August 6, 1655, Jannetje Samuels **Thomas***[2]

Jan Berentsen **Kunst**,* b. 1663, m. Jacomyntje **Cornelis***[2]

Joert **Olfertsen**,* m. Itje **Roelofs***[2]

Cornelius Jansen **Clopper**,* m. Heyltje **Pieters***[2]

Jan Louwe **Bogart**,* m. Cornelia **Evarts***[2]

Heidrick **Van Schaack**, m. Weeltse Hendricks **Stiles**[2]

John **Peeck**,* m. Maria **Truax**, b. 1617, Holland[2]

Gysbert **Van Imbruck**,* m. Rachel **De La Montague**[2]

Claes **Van Schaack**,* m. Jannetje (Last Name Unknown)*[2]

Lucas **Wyndgard**,* m. Anna **Van Hoesen***[2]

Cornelius **Van Dyck**,* m. Elizabeth **Lukens***[2]

David Pieterse **Schuyler**,* b. 1636, m. Catalyntje **Ver Planck**,* b. 1636[2]

Joseph **Yates**,* m. Hubertse **Marselis***[2]

Thomas **Potts**,* b. 1632, in Wales[2]

Thomas **Croasdale***; d. September 2, 1684, m. Agnes **Hathernthwaite***[2]

James **Park**,* m. Jean **Scofield***[2]

Edmund **Bellinger**,* m. Sarah **Cartwright***[2]

John **Douglas**, m. Grizel **Forbes**[2]

Rev. James **Horn**,* m. Isabel Leslie **Ramsey***[2]

Alexander **Baillie**,* m. Jean **MacKenzie**[2]

Geleyn **Ver Planck**, b. January 1, 1637, Albany, New York; d. April

23, 1684, Albany, New York, m. Henrica **Wessels**,* b. 1644, New York, New York[2]

Balchazar **Baird**, b. 1631, m. Marritje **Loockermans**, b. November 3, 1641, Holland[2]

Robert **Sinclair**,* m. Maria **Duyckinck***[2]

Robert **Livingston**, b. December 13, 1654, Scotland; d. October 1, 1728, m. July 7, 1674, Alida **Schuyler**, b. February 28, 1656; d. March 27, 1729[2]

Pieter **Van Brugh**,* m. Sarah **Cuyler***[2]

Robert **Livingston**,* m. Alida **Schuyler***[2]

G-9

Cornelius **Van Schaack**,* m. Belitje **Hendricks***[2]

Cornelius Jacobsen **Stiles**,* m. Claesje **Theunis***[2]

Philip **Truax**,* m. Jacqueline **Noirett***[2]

Jean **De La Montague**,* b. 1595, m. Rachel **De Forest**, b. 1609[2]

James **Douglas**[2]

Thomas **Forbes**, m. Jean **Ramsay***[2]

Sir Kenneth **MacKenzie**, m. Jean **Chisholm***[2]

Abram Isaacse **Ver Planck**, b. 1608; d. 1690, Albany, New York, m. 1630, Maria **Vigne**, b. 1612; d. 1670, Albany, New York[2]

Samuel **Baird** b.* 1609, Breda, Netherlands, m. October 21, 1638, Anna **Stuyvesant***[2]

Govert **Loockermans**,* b. 1616, Holland; d. New York, m. Marie Ariantze **Jans***[2]

Rev. John **Livingston**, b. June 21, 1603, England; d. June 13, 1635, m. Janet **Fleming**, b. 1613, England; d. 1691, Rotterdam, Holland[2]

Philip Peterse **Schuyler**,* m. Margerita **Van Schlicten***[2]

G-10

Jesse **De Forest**, b. 1580, England; d. October 22, 1624, m. September 23, 1601, Marie **Du Cloux***[2]

John **Douglas**[2]

William **Forbes**,* m. Janet **Ogilvy**, b. England[2]

Alexander **MacKenzie**, m. Christian **Munro***[2]

Lazare **Baird**,* b. 1577, Norwich, England; d. 1643, m. Judith **De Vos***[2]

Isaac **Ver Planck***[2]

Geleyn **Vigne**,* b. 1586; d. 1632, m. Adriana **Cuvilje***[2]

William **Livingston**, b. 1576, England; d. 1641, m. January 6, 1601, m. Agnes **Livingston**, b. England[2]

Bartholomew **Fleming**, b. England; d. England, m. Marion **Hamilton**,* b. England; d. England[2]

G-11

Jean **De Forest**, b. 1543, England; d. England, m. Ann **Maillard**,* b. England; d. England[2]

John **Douglas**[2]

George **Ogilvy**,* b. England; d. England, m. Beatrix **Seton**, b. England; d. England[2]

Colin **MacKenzie**[2]

Alexander **Livingston**, b. 1550, England; d. 1598, England, m. 1570, Barbara **Livingston**, b. England; d. England[2]

Alexander **Livingston**, b. England; d. England, m. Marion **Bryson***[2]

Thomas **Fleming**, m. Isabel of Wigtown*[2]

G-12

Melchor **De Forest**,* b. 1538, England; d. England, m. Catherine **De Forest**,* b. England; d. England[2]

Arthur **Douglas**[2]

George **Seton**, b. England; d. England, m. Elizabeth **Hay**,* b. England; d. England[2]

Sir Kenneth **MacKenzie**,* m. Elizabeth **Stewart**[2]

James **Livingston**, b. England; d. England[2]

Alexander **Livingston**, b. England; d. England, m. Barbara **Forrester**,* b. England; d. England[2]

Thomas **Livingston**, b. England; d. England, m. Agnes **Monieth***[2]

George **Fleming**[2]

G-13

James **Douglas**[2]

Lord George **Seton**,* b. England; d. England, m. Lady Janet **Hepburn**, b. England; d. England[2]

John **Stewart**, m. Mary **Campbell**[2]

Sir William **Livingston**, b. England; d. England, m. Agnes **Hepburn**, b. England; d. England[2]

Sir William **Livingston**,* m. Agnes **Hepburn*** (Refer to Sir William **Livingston** G-13 Eleanor **Roosevelt** to continue their lines.)[2]

Alexander **Livingston**, b. England; d. England, m. Elizabeth **Hepburn**, b. England; d. England[2]

Patrick **Fleming***[2]

G-14

David **Douglas**[2]

Sir Patrick **Hepburn**, b. England; d. England, m. Lady Janet **Douglas**[2]

John **Stewart**, m. Eleanor **Sinclair**[2]

Archibald **Campbell**, m. Elizabeth **Stewart***[3]

Sir James **Livingston**, b. England; d. 1472, England, m. Beatrice Elizabeth **Fleming**[2]

Alexander **Hepburn**, b. England; d. England, m. Janet **Napier**[2]

Alexander **Livingston**, b. England; d. England, m. Alison **Gourlay***[2]

Sir Adam **Hepburn**, b. England; d. England, m. Elizabeth **Ogstoun**[2]

G-15

John **Douglas**[2]

Adam **Hepburn**, b. England; d. England, m. Helen **Home**, b. England; d. England[2]

James **Douglas**,* m. Joan **Stewart**[2]

Sir James **Stewart**, m. Joan **Beaufort**, b. England; d. England[2]

William **Sinclair**, m. Margaret **Sutherland***[2]

Colin **Campbell**, m. Isabel **Stewart***[3]

Sir Alexander **Livingston**, b. England; d. January 21, ca. 1449, executed for high treason[2]

Robert **Fleming**,* m. Lady Janet **Douglas**[2]

Sir Patrick **Hepburn**, b. England; d. England, m. Elene **Wallace***[2]

Sir Alexander **Napier**,* m. Elizabeth **Lauder***[2]

Adam **Hepburn**,* m. Helen **Home** (Refer to Adam **Hepburn** G-14 Eleanor **Roosevelt** to continue her line.)[2]

Walter **Ogstoun***[2]

G-16

James **Douglas**, m. Elizabeth **Gifford***[2]

Patrick **Hepburn**,* b. England; d. England[2]

Lord Alexander **Home**, b. England; d. England, m. Elizabeth **Lauder***[2]

King Robert III,* m. Annabelle **Drummond*** (Refer to King Robert III G-13 Dolley **Madison** to continue their lines.)[2]

John **Beaufort**, b. England; d. England, m. Margaret **De Holland**[2]

Henry **Sinclair**,* m. Egidia **Douglas*** (Refer to Henry **Sinclair** G-13 Dolley **Madison** to continue their lines.)[2]

Archibald **Campbell**, m. Elizabeth **Somerville***[3]

Sir James **Douglas**,* m. Lady Beatrix **Sinclair*** (Refer to Sir James **Douglas** G-12 Dolley **Madison** to continue their lines.)[2]

Sir Adam **Hepburn**, b. England; d. England, m. Janet **Barthwick**, b. England; d. England[2]

Sir James **Douglas**,* m. Lady Beatrix **Sinclair*** (Refer to Sir James **Douglas** G-12 to continue their lines)[2]

Sir Alexander **Home**, b. England; d. England, m. Jean **De Haya**[2]

John of Gaunt,* m. Catherine **Roet*** (Refer to John of Gaunt G-14 Abigail **Adams** to continue their lines.)[2]

Duncan **Campbell**,* m. Margery **Stewart***[3]

Sir Patrick **Hepburn**,* b. England; d. England[2]

William **Barthwick**,* m. Beatrice **Sinclair***[2]

G-17

Sir Thomas **Home**,* b. England; d. England, m. Nicola **Papedy***[2]

Sir William **De Haya**, b. England; d. England, m. Alice **De Haya**, b. England; d. England[2]

G-18

Sir Thomas **De Haya**, b. England; d. England, m. Lady Joanna **Gifford**,* b. England; d. England[2]

Sir Thomas **De Haya**, b. England; d. England, m. Elizabeth of Scotland*[2]

G-19

Sir William **De Haya**, b. England; d. England[2]

Sir David **De Haya**, b. England; d. England[2]

G-20

Sir Thomas **De Haya**, b. England; d. England, m. Lora **De Cunningsburg**, b. England; d. England[2]

Sir Nicholas **De Haya**, b. England; d. England[2]

G-21

Sir Gilbert **De Haya**,* b. England; d. England, m. Mary **Fraser**,* b. England; d. England[2]

Sir William **De Cunningsburg**,* b. England; d. England[2]

Sir Gilbert **De Haya**,* b. England; d. England[2]

Helen Taft

G+2

Children of Robert Alphonso and Martha Wheaton (Bowers) Taft:

William Howard **Taft**, b. August 7, 1915, Bar Harbor, Maine; d. February 23, 1991, Washington, D.C., m. Barbara Holt **Bradfield**[1]

Robert AlphonsoTaft, m(1) Blanca **Noel**, m(2) Katherine **Whitch**, m(3) Joan **Warner**[1]

Lloyd Bowers **Taft**, b. January 1, 1923; d. October 25, 1985, m. Virginia Ann **Stone**[1]

Horace Dwight **Taft**, b. April 2, 1925, Cincinnati, Ohio, m. Mary Jane **Badger**[1]

Children of Frederick Johnson and Helen (Taft) Manning:

Helen **Manning**, m. Holland **Hunter**[1]

Caroline **Manning**, m. Frederick **Cunningham**[1]

Children of Charles Phelps and Eleanor (Chase) Taft:

Eleanor **Taft**, m. Donald Thornton **Hall**[1]

Sylvia **Taft**, m. William Douglas **Lotsperch**[1]

Seth Chase **Taft**, m. Frances **Prindle**[1]

Lucia **Taft**, b. June 9, 1924, Waterbury, Conn.; d. October 29, 1955, Cincinnati, Ohio[1]

Cynthia **Taft**, m. Donald Richard **Morris**[1]

Rosalyn **Taft**, b. June 6, 1930; d. 1941[1]

Peter **Taft**[1]

G+1

Robert Alphonso **Taft**, b. September 8, 1889, Cincinnati, Ohio; d. July 31, 1953, New York, New York, m. October 17, 1914, Washington, D.C. Martha Wheaton **Bowers**, b. December 17, 1891, Winona, Minnesota; d. October 2, 1958, Cincinnati, Ohio[2]

Helen **Taft**, b. August 1, 1891, Cincinnati, Ohio, m. July 15, 1920, Fredrick Johnson **Manning**, b. 1894, Braintree, Mass.; d. December 15, 1966, Nevis, British West Indies[2]

Charles Phelps **Taft**, b. September 20, 1897, Cincinnati, Ohio; d. June 24, 1983, Cincinnati, Ohio, m. October 6, 1917, Westbury, Conn. Eleanor Kellogg **Chase**, b. October 9, 1891, Waterbury, Conn.; d. August 28, 1961, Cincinnati, Ohio[2]

Helen Herron, b. June 2, 1861, Cincinnati Ohio; d. May 23, 1943, Washington, D.C., m. June 19, 1886, William Howard Taft, b. September 15, 1857, Cincinnati, Ohio; d. March 8, 1930, Washington, D.C.[3, 10]

G-1

John Williamson **Herron**, b. May 10, 1827, Shippensburg, Pa.; d. August 6, 1912, Cincinnati, Ohio, m. Harriet Ann **Collins**, b. September 15, 1833, Lowville, New York; d. January 20, 1902[3, 4]

G-2

Francis **Herron**, b. Shippensburg, Pa.; d. 1841, Pa., m. Jane **Wills**, b. 1800, Cumberland, Pa.; d. December 19, 1877, Middle Spring, Pa.[4]

Eli **Collins**, b. February 14, 1786, Meridon, Conn.; d. November 23, 1848, Lowville, New York, m. July 11, 1811, Marie **Clinton**, b. May 4, 1791, Southwick, Mass.; d. September 5, 1871, Lowville, New York[3]

G-3

William **Herron**, b. 1750, Pequea, Pa.; d. November 21, 1828, Shippensburg, Pa., m. Nancy **Reynolds***[4]

James **Wills**, b. 1767, Pa., m. Hannah **Jack**, b. 1768, Pa.; d. 1815, Pa.[4]

Gen. Oliver **Collins**, b. August 25, 1762, Wallingford, Conn.; d. August 14, 1838, New Hartford, Conn., m. January 25, 1784, Lois **Cowles**[3]

Isaac **Clinton**, b. January 21, 1759, Woodbury, Conn.; d. March 18, 1840, m. 1787, Charity **Wells**[2]

G-4

Francis **Herron**,* b. 1720, Antrim, Ireland; d. 1753, Pa., m. Mary **McNutt***[4]

David **Wills**,* m. Mary **Strihan***[4]

James **Jack**, b. October 1, 1728, Cumberland Co., Pa.; d. September 3, 1776, Cumberland Co., Pa., m. Mary Jane **Carnahan**,* b. 1722, Ireland[4]

Jonathan **Collins**, b. April 28, 1698, Meridon, Conn., m. Agnes **Lynn**,* b. 1723; d. May 30, 1765[3]

Ebenezer **Cowles**, b. December 18, 1710, Hatfield, Mass.; d. October 28, 1800, Hatfield, Mass., m. Kezziah **Cowles**, b. September 6, 1708, Hatfield, Mass.; d. December 2, 1796, Hafield, Mass.[5]

Lawrence **Clinton**, b. 1719, Woodbury, Conn.; d. December 9, 1794, Woodbury, Conn., m. Sarah (Last Name Unknown),* b. 1728[3]

David **Wells**,* m. Joanna **Wilcoxson***[3]

G-5

James **Jack**,* b. May 2, 1705, Londonderry, Ireland; d. Ireland, m. Elizabeth **McNulty**,* b. 1705, Ireland[4]

Robert **Collins**, b. March 15, 1650, Ipswich, Mass., m. Lois **Burnett***[3]

Samuel **Cowles**, b. May 27, 1673; d. 1750, m. 1698, Sarah **Hubbard**, b. 1672; d. 1754[5]

Jonathan **Cowles**, b. January 26, 1671, Hatfield, Mass.; d. November 13, 1756, Hatfield, Mass., m. Prudence **Frary**, b. May 7, 1677, Hatfield, Conn.; d. July 1, 1756, Hatfield, Mass.[5]

Thomas **Clinton**, b. 1693, New Haven, Conn.; d. 1761, Wallingford, Conn., m. August 7, 1718, Hope **Downs**, b. March 11, 1698, New Haven, Conn.; d. 1729, Wallingford, Conn.[3, 6]

Timothy **Wilcoxson**,* m. Abigail **Platt**[3]

G-6

Robert **Collins**, b. 1618, England; d. June 17, 1688, Haverhill, Mass., m. Hester **Fowler**, b. 1622, Marlborough, England[3]

John **Cowles; d.** 1711, m. 1668, Deborah **Bartlett**[5]

John **Hubbard**, m. Mary **Merriam***

John **Cowles**, m. Deborah **Bartlett** (Refer to John **Cowles** G-6 Helen **Taft** to continue their lines.)[5]

Eleazer **Frary**, b. February 14, 1640, Dedham, Mass.; d. December 19, 1709, Hatfield, Mass., m. Mary **Graves**, b. July 5, 1647, Hartford, Conn.; d. Hartford, Conn.[5]

Lawrence **Clinton**, b. 1642, England; d. 1707, Ipswich, Mass.m. Margaret **Painter**[6]

Ebenezer **Downs**, b. April 3, 1667, New Haven, Conn.; d. March 20, 1711, New Haven, Conn., m. Mary **Humbreville**, b. 1667, New Haven, Conn.; d. New Haven, Conn.[6]

John **Platt**,* m. Phebe **Bressie**[3]

G-7

John **Collins**,* m. Mary **Kingsworth***[2]

Philip **Fowler**, b. 1594, Marlborough, England; d. June 24, 1679, Ipswich, Mass., m. Mary **Winslow**, b. 1592, Essex, England; d. August 30, 1659, Ipswich, Mass.[7]

John **Cowles**,* b. 1598, Glouchestershire, England; d. Hatfield, Mass., m. Hannah **Hart**, b. 1613, Gloucestershire, England; d. March 17, 1683, Hartford, Conn.[5]

Robert **Bartlett**,* b. England; d. March 14, 1676, Northampton, Mass., m. Mary **Warren**, b. England[5]

George **Hubbard**,* b. 1591, England; d. 1683, Guilford, Conn., m. Mary (Last Name Unknown),* b. England[5]

John **Frary**, b. 1600, England; d. June 14, 1675, Medfield, Mass., m. Prudence **Townsend**, b. 1601, Norwich, England; d. February 24, 1691, Boston, Mass.[5]

Isaac **Graves**, b. 1620, England; d. September 19, 1677, Hatfield, Mass., m. Mary **Church**, b. England; d. June 9, 1695, Hatfield, Mass.[5]

Shubael **Painter**, b. 1635, Westerly, Rhode Island; d. 1661, Westerly, Rhode Island, m. Mercy **Lamberton**, b. June 17, 1641, New Haven, Conn.; d. 1677, New Haven, Conn.[6]

John **Downs**,* b. 1630, Kent, England; d. New Haven, Conn., m. 1684, Mary (Last Name Unknown),* b. 1634, Kent, England; d. New Haven, Conn.[6]

John **Humbreville**,* b. 1641, England; d. New Haven, Conn.[6]

Thomas **Bressie**, b. England, m. Mary **Osborn**,* b. England[3]

G-8

Philip **Fowler**,* b. 1565, England; d. England[7]

John **Winslow**,* b. 1569, Colchester, England; d. Mass. Elizabeth **Paddy**, b. 1573, Colchester, England; d. Mass.[7]

Richard **Warren*** (Mayflower Pilgrim), b. 1580, London, England; d. 1628, Plymouth, Mass., m. Elizabeth (Last Name Unknown),* b. 1583, England; d. October 22, 1673, Plymouth, Mass.[5]

Henry **Frary**,* b. 1578, England[5]

Edmund **Townsend**,* b. 1552, England; d. England, m. Amy **Gallawaye**,* b. 1560, Brunswick, England[5]

Thomas **Graves**,* b. 1585, England; d. 1662, Hadley, Mass., m. Sarah **Whiting**,* b. England; d. December 17, 1666, Hadley, Mass.[5]

Richard **Church**,* b. England; d. December 16, 1667, Hadley, Mass., m. Anne (Last Name Unknown),* b. England[5]

Thomas **Painter**,* b. 1610, England; d. 1706, Westerly, Rhode Island, m. Katherine (Last Name Unknown),* b. 1612, England; d. 1661[6]

George **Lamberton**,* b. 1604, London, England; d. 1646, London, England, m. Margaret (Last Name Unknown),* b. 1614, London, England; d. July 21, 1655, New Haven, Conn.[6]

Thomas **Bressie**, b. England; d. England, m. Phebe **Bisby**,* b. England; d. England[3]

G-9

Edmund **Bressie**,* b. England; d. England, m. Constance **Shepherd**, b. England; d. England[8]

G-10

Thomas **Shepherd**, b. England; d. England, m. Amphyllis **Chamberlain**,* b. England; d. England[8]

G-11

Thomas **Shepherd**, b. England; d. England[8]

G-12

Thomas **Shepherd**,* b. England; d. England, m. Constance **Hawes**, b. England; d. England[8]

G-13

Thomas **Hawes**,* b. England; d. England, m. Elizabeth **Brome**, b. England; d. England[8]

G-14

Nicholas **Brome**, b. England; d. England, m. Katherine **Lampick**,* b. England; d. England[8]

G-15

John **Brome**, b. England; d. England, m. Beatrix **Shirley**, b. England; d. England[8]

G-16

John **Brome**, b. England; d. England, m. Joan **Rodge,*** b. England; d. England[8]

Ralph **Shirley**, b. England; d. England, m. Joan **Basset**, b. England; d. England[8]

G-17

Robert **Brome**, b. England; d. England[8]

Hugh **Shirley**, b. 1351; d. July 22, 1403, m. Beatrice **Broose,*** b. England; d. England[8]

Thomas **Basset**, b. England; d. England, m. Margaret **Meringe,*** b. England; d. England[8]

G-18

Robert **Brome**, b. England; d. England, m. Margery **Brooke**, b. England; d. England[8]

Thomas **Shirley,*** b. England 1315; d. 1363, England, m. Isabella **Basset**, b. England; d. England[8]

John **Basset**, b. England; d. England, m. Joan **Brailsford,*** b. England; d. England[8]

G-19

William **Brome**, b. England; d. England, m. Hawise (Last Name Unknown),* b. England; d. England[8]

William **Brooke,*** b. England; d. England[8]

Ralph **Basset**, b. 1305; d. 1335, m. Alice **Audley,*** b. England; d. England[8]

John **Basset,*** b. England; d. England[8]

G-20

Robert **Brome**, b. England; d. England, m. Parnell **Storeton,*** b. England; d. England[8]

Ralph **Basset**, b. 1279, England; d. 1343, England, m. Joan **De Grey,*** b. England; d. England[8]

G-21

John **Brome,*** b. England; d. England[8]

Ralph **Basset**, b. 1247, Drayton, England; d. December 21, 1299, Drayton, England, m. Helvisa **Grey***b. 1250, England; d. England

John **De Grey**, b. 1268, Wilton, England; d. October 28, 1323,

England, m. Anne **De Ferriers,*** b. 1264, Griby, England; d. 1324, England[8]

G-22

Ralph **Basset**, b. 1215, Drayton, England; d. August 4, 1265, England, m. Margaret **De Somery**, b. 1229, Dudley, England; d. June 18, 1293, England[8, 9]

Reginald **De Grey**, b. 1242, Ruthin, Wales; d. April 5, 1308, m. Maud **De Longcamp,*** b. 1240, Wilton Castle, England; d. November 21, 1302, England[8, 9]

G-23

Ralph **Basset**, b. 1162, Drayton, England; d. 1254, England, m. Egelina **De Courtenay***[8, 9]

Roger **De Somery,*** b. England; d. England, m. Nicole **De Albini**[8, 9]

John **De Grey** (Sheriff of Buckingham),* b. 1214, Shirland, England; d. March 18, 1266, m. Emma **De Glanville,*** b. England; d. England[8, 9]

G-24

Ralph **Basset**, b. 1141, England; d. 1211, England[8, 9]

William **De Albini,*** m. Mabel **De Meschines**, b. England; d. England[8 9]

G-25

Ralph **Basset**, b. 1111, England; d. 1160, England[8, 9]

Hugh **De Meschines**, b. England; d. England, m. Bertrade **De Montfort***

G-26

Richard **Basset**, b. 1081, England; d. 1146, m. Maud **Ridel,*** b. 1090, England; d. England[8, 9]

Ranulph **De Meschines**, b. England; d. England, m. Maud **Fitz Robert,*** b. England; d. England[8, 9]

G-27

Ralph **Basset**, b. 1050, England; d. 1120, England[8, 9]

Ranulph **De Meschines,*** b. England; d. England, m. Lucy **Taillebois**, b. England; d. England[8, 9]

G-28

Thurston "The Norman" **Bassett,*** b. 1030, Normandy, France; d. 1080[8, 9]

Lucy of Mercia, b. 1040, Mercia, England; d. England, m. Ivo **De Taillebois,*** b. England; d. England[8, 9]

G-29

Alfgar III of Mercia, b. Mercia, England; d. England, m. Elfgifu (Last Name Unknown),* b. England; d. England[8, 9]

G-30

Leofric III,* b. May 14, 968, England; d. August 31, 1057, Bromley, England, m. Lady Godiva,* b. 980, England; d. September 10, 1067, England[7, 8]

Margaret Taylor

G+2

Children of Robert and Ann Margaret (Taylor) Wood:

John Taylor **Wood**, b. August 13, 1830; d. July 19, 1904, Halifax, Nova Scotia[1]

Robert Crook **Wood**, b. April 4, 1832, Fort Snelling, Minn.; d. September 7, 1892[1]

Blandina **Wood**, b. January 9, 1835, Fort Crawford, Wisconsin[1]

Sarah **Wood**, b. November 21, 1839, Wisconsin[1]

Children of Richard and Louise Marie (Bringier) Taylor:

Louise Margaret **Taylor**, b. 1852; d. 1901[1]

Betty **Taylor**, b. 1854, m. Walter Robinson **Stauffer**[1]

Zachory **Taylor**, b. 1857[1]

Richard **Taylor**, b. 1860[1]

Myrtle Bianca **Taylor**, b. 1864, Nachtoches, Louisiana; d. 1942, New Orleans, Louisiana, m. Isaac Hull **Stauffer**[1]

G+1

Ann Margaret **Taylor**, b. April 9, 1811, Jefferson Co., Kentucky; d. December 2, 1875, Freilburg, Germany, m. September 20, 1829, Fort Crawford, Wisconsin Robert **Wood**, b. September 23, 1801, Rhode Island; d. March 28, 1869, Fort Snelling, Minn.[2]

Sarah **Taylor**, b. March 6, 1814, Vincennes, Indiana; d. September 15, 1835, Locust Grove, Louisiana, m. March 17, 1835, Louisville, Kentucky Jeffrey Finis **Davis**[2]

Octavia Pannill **Taylor**, b. August 16, 1816, Jefferson Co., Kentucky; d. July 8, 1820, Bayou Sara, Louisiana[2]

Margaret **Taylor**, b. July 27, 1819, Jefferson Co., Kentucky; d. October 22, 1820, Bayou Sara, Louisiana[2]

Mary Elizabeth **Taylor**, b. April 20, 1824, Jefferson Co., Kentucky; d. July 25, 1909, Winchester, Virginia, m(1) December 5, 1848, William Smith **Bliss**, b. August 17, 1815; d. August 4, 1853, m(2) February 11, 1858, Philip Pendleton **Dandridge**[2]

Richard **Taylor**, b. January 27, 1826, Louisville, Kentucky; d. April 12, 1879, New York, New York, m. February 10, 1851, Louise Marie **Bringier**, b. Louisiana; d. 1875[2]

Margaret Smith, b. September 21, 1788, Calvert Co., Maryland; d. August 18, 1852, m. June 18, 1810, Zachory Taylor, b. November 24, 1784; d. July 8, 1850, Washington, D.C.[3, 12]

G-1

Walter **Smith**, b. August 12, 1747, Calvert Co., Maryland; d. 1804, Calvert Co., Maryland, m. Ann **Mackall**, b. March 12, 1753, Calvert Co., Maryland; d. Calvert Co., Maryland[3]

G-2

Walter **Smith**, b. 1715, Calvert Co., Maryland; d. Calvert Co., Maryland, m. Elizabeth **Chew**, b. November 29, 1722, Calvert Co., Maryland; d. Calvert Co., Maryland[3]

James John **Mackall**, b. 1717, Maryland; d. 1770, Maryland, m. Mary **Hance**[3]

G-3

Walter **Smith**, b. Calver Co., Maryland; d. Calvert Co., Maryland, m. Susanna **Brooke**[3]

Dr. Samuel **Chew**, b. August 30, 1693, Calvert Co., Maryland; d. June 16, 1744, Dover, Delaware, m. October 22, 1715, Mary **Galloway**, b. 1694, Philadelphia, Pa.; d. May 26, 1734, Philadelphia, Pa.[3]

John **Mackall**, b. 1669, Maryland; d. 1739, Maryland, m. 1713, Susanna **Parrott**, b. 1675; d. 1763[3]

Benjamin **Hance**, b. 1692; d. 1773, m. Mary **Hutchins**, b. 1694; d. 1751[4, 5, 6]

G-4

Walter **Smith**, b. 1667, Calvert Co., Maryland; d. June 4, 1711, Calvert Co., Maryland, m. Rachel **Hall**, b. 1671, Calvert Co., Maryland; d. October 28, 1730, Calvert Co., Maryland[3]

Clement **Brooke**, b. 1674, m. Jane **Sewall**, b. 1674, St. Mary's Co., Maryland; d. February 20, 1761, Prince George Co., Maryland[3]

Benjamin **Chew**, b. April 13, 1671, Ann Arundel Co., Maryland; d. March 3, 1700, m. Elizabeth **Benson**, b. 1677, Calvert Co., Maryland; d. 1725[3]

Samuel **Galloway**, m. Ann **Webb**[3]

James **Mackall*** 1630, Scotland; d. 1693, Scotland, m. Mary **Grahame***[3]

Gabriel **Parrott**,* m. Elizabeth **Parran***[3]

John **Hance**, b. 1645; d. 1709, m. Mary Ann **Sewell***[4, 5, 6]

Francis **Hutchins**; d. 1698, m. Elizabeth **Burrage**, b. 1660; d. 1740, Calvert Co., Maryland[4]

G-5

Richard **Smith**,* b. ca. 1640, England; d. 1714, Maryland, m. Barbara **Morgan**[3]

Richard **Hall**,* b. 1635, England; d. 1688, Calvert Co., Maryland, m. Elizabeth (Last Name Unknown),* b. England[3]

Thomas **Brooke**,* m. Eleanor **Hatton*** (Refer to Thomas **Brooke** G-7 Julia **Grant** to continue their lines.)[3]

Nicholas **Sewall**,* b. 1651; d. Ann Arundel Co., Maryland, m. Susanna **Burgess**,* b. 1655, Ann Arundel Co., Maryland[3]

Samuel **Chew**, b. 1627, Jamestown, Virginia; d. March 15, 1677, m. Ann **Ayres**, b. 1635, Nausemond Co., Virginia; d. April 13, 1695, Maryland[3]

John **Benson**,* m. Elizabeth **Smith***[3]

Richard **Galloway***; d. 1663, m. Hannah (Last Name Unknown)*[3]

Borrington **Webb***[3]

John **Hance**,* b. 1622; d. 1662, m. Sarah **Hall***[4, 5, 6]

John **Burrage**,* m. Margaraet **Maudelin**[4, 5]

G-6

John **Chew**, b. 1590, Chewton, England; d. 1655, Maryland, m. Sarah **Bond**,* b. 1600 England; d. 1650, Jamestown, Virginia[3]

G-7

Joseph **Chew**,* b. 1570, Bewdly, England, m. Elizabeth **Gott***[3]

ELIZABETH (BESS) TRUMAN

G+2

Children of Clifton and Margaret (Truman) Daniel:

Clifton Truman **Daniel**, b. June 5, 1957[1]
William Wallace **Daniel**, b. May 19, 1959[1]
Harrison Gates **Daniel**[1]
Thomas Washington **Daniel**[1]

G+1

Margaret **Truman**, b. February 17, 1924, Independence, Missouri, m. April 21, 1956, Independence, Missouri Clifton **Daniel**, Jr., b. September 19, 1912, Zebulon, North Carolina[1]

Elizabeth Virginia (Bess) Wallace, b. February 13, 1885, Independence, Missouri; d. October 20, 1982, Independence, Missouri, m. June 28, 1919, Harry S. Truman, b. May 8, 1884, Independence, Missouri; d. December 26, 1972, Kansas City, Missouri[2, 12]

G-1

David Willock **Wallace**, b. June 15, 1860, Independence, Missouri; d. June 17, 1903, Independence, Missouri, m. Margaret **Gates** b. 1855, Independence, Missouri; d. December 5, 1952, Washington, D.C.[2, 3]

G-2

Benjamin Franklin **Wallace**, b. April 26, 1817, Kentucky; d. June 2, 1877, m. Virginia **Willock**, b. May 20, 1824, Green, Kentucky; d. May 18, 1908, Independence, Missouri[2, 3]

George Porterfield **Gates**, b. April 2, 1835, Lundenburg, Vermont;

d. June 25, 1918, Independence, Missouri, m. Elizabeth **Emery**, b. February 21, 1841; d. June 19, 1924, Independence, Missouri[2, 3]

G-3

Thomas **Wallace**, b. May 18, 1775, Kent Co., Delaware; d. December 21, 1803, Bath Co., Virginia, m. Mary Jane **Percy**, b. February 1, 1775, Bath Co., Virginia[2]

Maj. Gen. David **Willock**, b. August 1, 1802, Green Co., Kentucky; d. Palmyra, Missouri, m. April 17, 1823, Dorothy, m. **Johnston**, b. August 8, 1804, Caroline Co., Virginia; d. June 13, 1833, Palmyra, Missouri[3, 4]

George William **Gates**, b. 1807, Kentucky, m. Sarah **Todd***[2, 3]

G-4

Thomas **Wallace**, b. 1745, Murderkill, Delaware; d. January 9, 1800, Bath Co., Viriginia, m. 1770, Elizabeth **Wardle***[2]

Thomas **Percy**,* m. Sarah (Last Name Unknown)*[2]

David **Willock**,* b. 1765, Scotland; d. 1830, Green Co., Kentucky, m. Rachel **McFarland**,* b. 1770, Scotland; d. June 5, 1825, Green Co., Kentucky[2]

William **Johnston**,* m. Ann **Buckner**[2, 4]

Samuel **Gates**, b. 1782, Hartford, Conn.; d. 1870, m. Jerusha **Clark**[2]

G-5

Matthew **Wallace**, b. 1705, Murderkill, Delaware; d. December 25, 1762, Kent Co., Delaware, m. 1739, Agnes **Wallace**, b. 1714, Kent Co., Delaware; d. May 14, 1770[2]

William **Buckner**, m. Mary **Madison***[4]

Samuel **Gates**, b. August 16, 1760, Marlborough, Mass.; d. September 5, 1854, Hartford, Conn., m. February 25, 1781, Lucretia **Williams***[2]

Ebenezer **Clark**, b. October 3, 1747, Mass.; d. July 7, 1834, Vermont, m. Eunice **Pomeroy**[2]

G-6

David **Wallace**, b. 1680, Murderkill, Delaware; d. Kent Co., Delaware; d. April 19, 1751, Kent Co., Delaware, m. Barbara **Fleming**,* b. 1684, Murderkill, Delaware; d. Kent Co., Delaware[2, 5]

Thomas **Wallace**, b. 1680[5]

John **Buckner**, b. 1700, Virginia; d. 1752, Virginia, m. Elizabeth (Last Name Unknown)*

Silas **Gates**, b. February 3, 1727, Marlborough, Mass.; d. August 25, 1793, Marlborough, Mass., m. Elizabeth **Bragg**, b. January 10, 1731, Shrewsbury, Mass.; d. March 20, 1706, Marlborough, Mass.[5,6]

Ebenezer **Clark**, m. Jerusha **Russell***[2]

Ebenezer **Pomeroy**, b. May 1, 1723, Hockamum, Mass.; d. 1801, Mass., m. Mindwell **Lyman**[2,7]

G-7

Matthew **Wallace**,* b. Raphoe, Ireland; d. New Castle, Delaware, m. 1675, Elizabeth **Alexander**[5]

Matthew **Wallace**,* m. Elizabeth **Alexander** (Refer to Matthew **Wallace** G-6 Bess **Truman** to continue their lines.)[5]

John **Buckner**, m. Ann **Ballard**[4]

Simon **Gates**, b. January 5, 1676, Marlborough, Mass.; d. March 10, 1735, Marlborough, Mass., m. March 29, 1710, Sarah **Woods**, b. April 23, 1685, Marlborough, Mass.; d. 1751, Marlborough, Mass.[2,6]

Ebenezer **Bragg**, b. November 13, 1699, Ipswich, Mass.; d. September 4, 1766, Shrewsbury, Mass., m. Zerviah **Brigham**, b. October 9, 1698, Marlborough, Mass.; d. June 1, 1736, Shrewsbury, Mass.[5]

Ebenezer **Clark**, m. Abigail **Parsons**[2]

Ebenezer **Pomeroy**, b. September 18, 1697, Northampton, Mass.; d. April 22, 1774, m. Elizabeth **Hunt**, b. March 2, 1701, Northampton, Mass.; d. June 10, 1782[7]

John **Lyman**, m. Abigail **Moseley**[2]

G-8

James **Alexander**,* b. 1634, Bughall, Scotland; d. 1704, Raphoe, Ireland, m. Mary **Maxwell**,* b. 1836[5]

John **Buckner**, b. 1630, Oxford, England; d. 1694, Essex, England, m. Deborah **Ferriers**,* b. England[4]

Simon **Gates**, b. 1645; d. April 21, 1692, m. Margaret **Bartsow***[2,6]

John **Woods**,* m. Lydia (Last Name Unknown)*[2]

Timothy **Bragg**,* m. Lydia **Gott**[5]

Jonathan **Brigham**, m. Mary **Fay***[5]

John **Clark**,* m. Mary **Strong***[2]

Joseph **Parsons**,* m. Elizabeth **Strong***[2]

Ebenezer **Pomeroy**, b. May 30, 1669, Northampton, Mass.; d. January 27, 1754, Northampton, Mass., m. Sarah **King**, b. May 3, 1671, Northampton, Mass.; d. November 5, 1747, Northampton, Mass.[2,7]

Jonathan **Hunt**,* b. January 26, 1665, Northampton, Mass.; d. July

1, 1738, Northampton, Mass., m. Martha **Williams**,* b. May 19, 1671, Roxbury, Mass.; d. March 21, 1751, Northampton, Mass.[2,7]

John **Lyman**, m. Mindwell **Sheldon**[2]

John **Moseley**, m. Abigail **Root***[2]

G-9

Thomas **Buckner**, b. February 20, 1590, Oxford, England; d. May 6, 1645, Cummor, England, m. Jane Alice **Page***[4]

Stephen **Gates**,* b. 1600, Hingham, Mass.; d. 1662, Cambridge, Mass., m. May 5, 1623, Ann **Veare**,* b. 1603; d. February 5, 1682, Stowe, Mass.[2,6]

Charles **Gott**, b. June 1, 1639, Salem, Mass.; d. February 11, 1707, Wenham, Mass., m. Lydia **Clark**,* b. October 31, 1642, Lynn, Mass.; d. 1717, Wenham, Mass.[5]

Thomas **Brigham**,* b. March 9, 1641, Cambridge, Mass.; d. November 25, 1717, Marlborough, Mass., m. Mary **Rice**, b. September 19, 1646, Sudbury, Mass.; d. May 30, 1695, Marlborough, Mass.[5]

Medad **Pomeroy**, b. August 19, 1638, Northampton, Mass.; d. December 30, 1716, Northampton, Mass., m. Experience **Woodward**, b. November 10, 1643, Dorcester, Mass.; d. July 8, 1686, Northampton, Mass.[7]

John **King**, m. Sarah **Holton**[8]

John **Lyman**, b. September 16, 1623, England; d. August 20, 1690, Northampton, England, m. Dorcas **Plumbe**, b. 1635, Hartford, Conn.; d. November 21, 1725, Northampton, Mass.[5]

Isaac **Sheldon**, m. Mary **Woodford**[2]

John **Moseley**,* m. Mary **Newberry**[2]

G-10

Hugh **Buckner**, b. England; d. England, m. Martha **Crackpole**,* b. England; d. England[4]

Charles **Gott**,* b. March 12, 1598, Brokenbury, England; d. October 3, 1667, Wenham, Mass., m. Gift **Palmer**, b. England; d. August 8, 1665, Wenham, Mass.[5]

Thomas **Rice**, b. 1620, England; d. February 10, 1710, Franingham, Mass., m. Elizabeth **Moore**,* b. 1622; d. August 23, 1705, Sudbury, Mass.[5]

Eltweed **Pomeroy**, b. 1585, Dorset, England; d. 1673, Northampton, Mass., m. Mary **Rocket**, b. England[7]

Henry **Woodward**, b. March 22, 1607, Much Worton, England; d.

April 7, 1683, Northampton, Mass., m. Elizabeth **Mather**, b. 1618, England; d. August 30, 1690, Northampton, Mass.[7]

John **King**,* b. England, m. Catherine **Drury**,* b. England[8]

William **Holton**,* b. England, m. Mary **Winche**,* b. England[8]

Richard **Lyman**,* b. 1580, England; d. 1640, m. Sarah **Osborne**,* b. England[5]

John **Plumbe**,* b. 1594, Essex, England; d. 1648, New Haven, Conn., m. Dorothy **Wood**,* b. 1595, Essex, England[5]

Ralph **Sheldon**,* b. England, m. Barbara **Stone**,* b. England[9]

Thomas **Woodward**,* b. England, m. Mary **Blott**,* b. England[9]

Benjamin **Newberry**, b. England, m. Mary **Allyn**, b. England[10, 11]

G-11

William **Buckner**, b. England; d. England, m. Martha **Hord**,* b. England; d. England[4]

Edmund **Rice**,* b. 1594, Stanstead, England; d. May 3, 1663, Marlborough, Mass., m. Thomasine **Frost*** v. August 10, 1600, Stanstead, England; d. June 13, 1654, Sudbury, England[5]

Richard **Pomeroy**,* b. 1556, England; d. 1601, England, m. Eleanor (Last Name Unknown),* b. England; d. England[7]

Thomas **Rocket**,* b. England; d.England[7]

Thomas **Woodward**,* b. 1567, Lancaster, England; d. 1612, England, m. Elizabeth **Tyler**,* b. England; d. England[7]

Thomas **Mather**,* b. 1575, Winwick, England; d. England, m. Margarite **Abram**,* b. Winwick, England[7]

Thomas **Newberry**, b. November 10, 1594, Yarcombe, England; d. December 1, 1656, Windsor, Conn., m. Jane **Dabinot**,* b. 1615, Yarcombe, England; d. April 23, 1645, Norwich, Conn.[10, 11]

Matthew **Allyn**, b. 1604, England; d. 1671, m. Margaret **Wyatt**, b. England[1]

G-12

Richard **Buckner**,* b. 1451, Cummor, England; d. September 4, 1548, Cummor, England, m. Mary **Fabian**, b. 1453, Compton, England; d. 1485, Cummor, England[4]

Richard **Newberry*** b.1557, England; d. 1629, England, m. Grace **Matthews**,* b. England; d. England[10, 11]

Richard **Allyn**,* b. England; d. England[1]

John **Wyatt*** b. England; d. England, m. Frances **Chichester**, b. England; d. England[1]

G-13

Thomas **Fabian**,* b. England; d. England, m. Katherine **Hungerford**,* b. 1412 England; d. England[4]

Amyas **Chichester**, b. England; d. England, m. Jane **Giffard**, b. England; d. England[1]

G-14

John **Chichester**,* b. 1475, England; d. 1537, England, m. Joan **Brett**,* b. 1480, England; d. England[1]

Sir Roger **Giffard**,* b. England; d. England, m. Margaret **Cobleigh**, b. England; d. England[1]

G-15

John **Coberleigh**,* b. England; d. England Jane **Fortescue**, b. England; d. England[1]

G-16

William **Fortescue**, b. England; d. England, m. Elizabeth **Champernowne**, b. England; d. England[1]

G-17

John **Fortescue**, b. England; d. England, m. Jane **Preston**,* b. England; d. England[1]

Richard **Champernowne**, b. England; d. England[1]

G-18

William **Fortescue**, b. England; d. England, m. Isabelle **Falwell**, b. England; d. England[1]

John **Champernowne**, b. 1370, England; d. England[1]

G-19

William **Fortescue**, b. England; d. England, m. Elizabeth **De Beauchamp**, b. England; d. England[1]

Richard **Champernowne**, b. England.; d. England[1]

G-20

William **Fortescue**, b. England; d. England, m. Alice **Strechleigh**,* b. England; d. England[1]

Sir John **De Beauchamp**,* b. England; d. England, m. Margaret **Whalesburgh**,* b. England; d. England[1]

Thomas **Champernowne,*** b. England; d. England[1]

G-21

Adam **Fortescue,** b. England; d. England, m. Anna **De La Port,*** b. England; d. England[1]

G-22

Adam **Fortescue,** b. England; d. England[1]

G-23

Sir Adam **Fortescue,** b. Eng; d. England[1]

G-24

Richard **Fortescue,*** b. England; d. England[1]

Julia Tyler

G+2

Children of David Gardiner and Mary (Jones) Tyler:

Mary **Tyler**, b. March 31, 1895, Washington, D.C.[1]

Margaret **Tyler**, b. February 3, 1897, Washington, D.C.

David **Tyler**, b. 1899, Sherwood Forest, Virginia

James Alfred **Tyler**, b. August 16, 1902, Sherwood Forest, Virginia[1]

Children of John Alexander and Sarah (Gardiner) Tyler:

Unnamed **Tyler**

Gardiner **Tyler**, b. January 5, 1878; d. March 11, 1892[1]

Lillian **Tyler**, b. January 9, 1879; d. May 9, 1918, m. Alben **Maigrab**[1]

Children of Lion Gardiner and Annie (Tucker) Tyler:

Julia **Tyler**, b. December 7, 1881, Memphis, Tennessee, m. James Southall **Wilson**[1]

Elizabeth **Tyler**, b. March 13, 1885, Richmond, Virginia, m. Alfred Hart **Miles**[1]

John **Tyler**, b. February 1, 1887 Richmond, Virginia, m. Elizabeth **Parker**[1]

G+1

Gardiner **Tyler**, b. July 17, 1846, East Hampton, New York; d. September 1, 1927, Charles City Co., Virginia, m. June 6, 1894, Richmond, Virginia Mary **Jones**, b. June 1, 1865; d. August 30, 1931, Sherwood Forest, Virginia[1]

John Alexander **Tyler**, b. April 7, 1848, Sherwood Forest, Virginia; d. September 1, 1883, m. Sarah **Gardiner**[1]

Julia **Tyler**, b. December 25, 1849, Sherwood Forest, Virginia; d. May 8, 1871, m. June 26, 1869, New York, New York William H. **Spencer**[1]

Lachlan **Tyler**, b. December 2, 1851, Sherwood Forest, Virginia, m. 1876, Georgia **Powell**[1]

Lion Gardiner **Tyler**, b. August 24, 1852, Sherwood Forest, Virginia; d. February 12, 1935, m(1) November 14, 1878, Annie **Tucker**, b. April 8, 1855, Charlottesville, Virginia; d. November 2, 1921, Richmond, Virginia, m(2) September 12, 1973, Sue **Ruffin**, b. May 5, 1889, Charles City Co., Virginia; d. May 2, 1953[1]

Robert Fitz Walter **Tyler**, b. March 12, 1856, Sherwood Forest, Virginia; d. 1927, m. Fannie **Glinn**[1]

Pearl **Tyler**, b. June 13, 1860, Sherwood Forest; d. 1947, m. 1894, William Mumford **Ellis**[1]

Julia Gardiner, b. May 4, 1820, New York, New York; d. July 10, 1889, Richmond, Virginia, m. June 26, 1855, John Tyler, b. March 29, 1790, Virginia; d. January 18, 1862, Virginia[2, 5]

G-1

David **Gardiner**, b. 1784, Long Island, New York; d. 1844, New York, m. Julia **McLachlin**[2]

G-2

Abraham **Gardiner**, b. January 25, 1763, Long Island, New York; d. 1797, Long Island, New York, m. May 31, 1781, Phoebe **Dayton**, b. Long Island, New York[3, 4]

Michael **McLachlin**[2]

G-3

Abraham **Gardiner**, b. February 19, 1721, Long Island, New York; d. August 21, 1782, Long Island, New York, m. Mary **Smith**,* b. 1722, Long Island, New York[2, 3, 4]

John **Dayton**, m. Mary **Mulford**[4]

G-4

David **Gardiner**, b. January 3, 1691, Long Island, New York; d. July 4, 1751, Long Island, New York, m. April 15, 1713, Rachel **Schellinger**[2, 3, 4]

John **Dayton**, m. Joanna **Parsons**[4]

John **Mulford**,* m. Anna **Chatfield**[4]

G-5

John **Gardiner**, b. April 19, 1661, Hartford, Conn.; d. January 25, 1738, Hartford, Conn., m. Mary **King**, b. August 7, 1669, Southold, New York[3, 4]

Abraham **Schellinger**, m. Joanna **Hedges**, b. 1658, East Hampton, New York; d. November 11, 1708, East Hampton, New York[4]

Benah **Dayton**, b. 1674; d. April 30, 1746, m. Jane **Miller**, b. 1679; d. March 22, 1750[4]

John **Parsons**, b. 1660, East Hampton, New York; d. March 19, 1702, East Hampton, New York, m. Sarah **Hand***[4]

Thomas **Chatfield**, b. 1680; d. January 12, 1754, m. Hannah **Stratton***[4]

G-6

David **Gardiner**, b. April 22, 1636, Saybrook, Conn.; d. July 10, 1689, Hartford, Conn., m. 1657, Mary **Leringman***[2, 3, 4]

Samuel **King**, m. Frances **Ludlam**[4]

Jacob **Schellinger***[4]

Isaac **Hedge**,* m. Johanna **Barnes***[4]

Robert **Dayton**, m. Elizabeth **Woodruff**[4]

John **Miller**, m. Elizabeth **Dimon**[4]

Samuel **Parsons**, m. Hannah **Talmage***[4]

Thomas **Chatfield**[4]

G-7

Lion **Gardiner**, b. 1599, Holland; d. 1663, m. Mary **Deureant***[4]

William **King**, b. England, m. Dorothy **Hayne**,* b. England[4]

William **Ludlam**, b. England, m. Clemence **Fordham**, b. England[4]

Ralph **Dayton**,* b. 1588, Ashford, England; d. East Hampton, New York, m. Alice **Goldhatch**, b. Ashford, England; d. 1655, Suffolk Co., New York[4]

John **Woodruff**,* b. England, m. Ann **Gosmer**,* b. England[4]

George **Miller**,* b. England, m. Hester **Conkling***[4]

Thomas **Dimon**,* b. England, m. Mary **Sheaffe**,* b. England[4]

Samuel **Parsons**,* b. England, m. Hannah **Hand**,* b. England[4]

Thomas **Chatfield**,* b. England, m. Ann **Higginson**,* b. England[4]

G-8

Lionel **Gardiner**, b. 1573, m. Elizabeth **Woodhouse***[3, 4]

William **King**,* b. 1574, Weymouth, Mass.; d. 1625, Hawkchurch,

England, m. Ann **Bowdiege,*** b. 1574, Weymouth, England; d. England[4]

William **Ludlam,*** b. England; d. England, m. Mary (Last Name Unknown),* b. England; d. England[4]

Philip **Fordham,*** b. England; d. England, m. Elizabeth **Gourney,*** b. England; d. England[4]

Robert **Goldhatch,*** b. England; d. England, m. Bennett **Meade,*** b. England; d. England[4]

G-9

George **Gardiner**, b. 1535, England; d. 1589, England, m. Dorothy **Constable,*** b. England; d. England[3, 4]

G-10

George **Gardiner,*** b. 1510, England; d. England, m. Margaret **Neville,*** b. England; d. England[3, 4]

Letitia Tyler

G+2

Children of Henry Lightfoot and Mary (Tyler) Jones:

John **Jones**[1]
Henry **Jones**[1]
Robert **Jones**[1]

Children of Robert and Elizabeth Priscilla (Cooper) Tyler:

Letitia **Tyler**[1]
Grace **Tyler**, m. John **Scott**[1]
Lizzie **Tyler**, m. Thomas G. **Foster**[1]
Priscilla **Tyler**, m. Albert G. **Goodwin**[1]
Julia **Tyler**, m(1) Henry **Tyson**, m(2) Robert (Last Name Unknown)[1]

Children of John and Martha (Rockellen) Tyler:

Letitia **Tyler**, m. William, b. **Shands**[1]
Martha **Tyler**[1]
James **Tyler**[1]

Children of William Newsom and Elizabeth (Tyler) Waller:

Mary **Waller**[1]
William **Waller**[1]
John **Waller**[1]
Robert **Waller**[1]

Children of Rev. Henry Mandeville and Alice (Tyler) Denison:

Bessie **Dennison**[1]

Children of Tazewell and Nannie (Brydges) Tyler:

Martha **Tyler**[1]
James **Tyler**[1]

G+1

Mary **Tyler**, b. April 15, 1815, Charles City Co., Virginia d. June

17, 1848, New Kent Co., Virginia, m. December 14, 1835, Henry Lightfoot **Jones**, b. 1813, North Carolina[1]

Robert **Tyler**, b. September 9, 1816, Charles City Co., Virginia; d. December 3, 1877, Montgomery, Alabama, m. September 12, 1839, Bristol, Pa. Elizabeth Priscilla **Cooper**, b. June 14, 1816, New York, New York; d. December 29, 1889, Montgomery, Alabama[1]

John **Tyler**, b. April 27, 1819; d. 1896, m. October 25, 1838, Martha **Rockellen**, b. January 23, 1820; d. January 11, 1867[1]

Letitia **Tyler**, b. May 11, 1821; d. December 28, 1907, m. 1839, James **Semple**[1]

Elizabeth **Tyler**, b. July 11, 1823; d. June 1, 1850, m. January 31, 1842, White House William Newsom **Waller**[1]

Ann **Tyler**, b. April 5, 1825; d. 1825[1]

Alice **Tyler**, b. March 23, 1827; d. August 8, 1854, m. July 11, 1850, Charles City Co., Virginia Rev. Henry Mandeville **Denison**[1]

Tazewell **Tyler**, b. December 6, 1830; d. January 8, 1874, Calif., m. 1857, Nannie **Brydges**[1]

Letitia Christian, b. November 12, 1790, Cedar Grove, Virginia; d. September 10, 1842, Richmond, Virginia, m. March 29, 1813, John Tyler, b. March 29, 1790, Charles City Co., Virginia; d. January 18, 1862, Richmond, Virginia[2,4]

G-1

Robert **Christian**, b. May 5, 1760, Cedar Grove, Virginia, m. Mary **Brown**, b. 1764, James City Co., Virginia[2]

G-2

William **Christian**, b. 1726, Charles City Co., Virginia d. 1814, Virginia, m. Elizabeth **Collier**, b. 1736, Charles City Co., Virginia[2]

William **Brown**,* m. Alice **Eaton***[2]

G-3

William **Christian**, b. 1700, Charles City Co., Virginia d. 1771, m. Mary **Collier**, b. 1704, New Kent Co., Virginia[2]

Robert **Collier**,* m. Elizabeth **Tazewell***[2]

G-4

James **Christian**, b. 1674; d. June 12, 1754, m. Amy **Macon**, b. 1678, New Kent Co., Virginia[2]

Benjamin **Collier**[2]

G-5

Thomas **Christian**,* b. 1630, Isle of Man; d. March 15, 1716, m. Eleanor **Kowley**,* b. 1648, Isle of Man[2]

Gideon **Macon**, b. 1654, Saone, France d. 1702, New Kent Co., Virginia, m. Martha **Woodward**[*3]

John **Collier***; d. York Co., Virginia[2]

G-6

Louis **De Macon**, b. 1609, Clermont, France d. France, m. Catherine **De Prades**,* b. Clermont, France; d. France[3]

G-7

Jean **De Macon**,* b. France; d. France, m. Madeline **Bacaine**,* b. France; d. France[3]

Hannah Van Buren

G+2

Children of Abraham and Angelica (Singleton) Van Buren:

Rebecca **Van Buren**, b. 1840, White House; d. 1840, White House[1]

Singleton **Van Buren**, b. 1840, White House; d. 1879, New York, New York[1]

Travis **Van Buren**, b. 1843[1]

Martin **Van Buren**, b. 1845[1]

Children of John and Elizabeth (Vanderpool) Van Buren:

Sarah Anna **Van Buren** July 30, 1842; d. 1923, m. Edward Alexander **Duer**[1]

Children of Smith Thompson and Ellen (James) Van Buren:

Ellen **Van Buren**, b. June 10, 1844; d. 1929, m. Stuyvesant **Morris**[1]

Hannah **Van Buren**, b. 1846; d. 1846[1]

Edward **Van Buren**, b. 1848; d. 1873[1]

Katherine **Van Buren**, b. 1849; d. 1942, m(1) Peyton F. **Miller**, m(2) **Wilson**[1]

Children of Smith Thompson and Henrietta (Irving) Van Buren:

Martin **Van Buren**, b. March 4, 1856; d. December 28, 1942, New York, New York[1]

Eliza **Van Buren**, b. 1858; d. 1942[1]

Marion **Van Buren**, b. 1860; d. 1927, m. Hamilton **Emmons**[1]

G+1

Abraham **Van Buren**, b. November 27, 1807, Kinderhook, New York; d. March 15, 1873, New York, New York, m. 1838, Angelica **Singleton**, b. 1816, South Carolina; d. December 29, 1878, New York, New York[2]

John **Van Buren**, b. February 10, 1810, Columbia Co., New York; d. October 13, 1866, m. June 22, 1841, Elizabeth **Vanderpool**, b. May 22, 1810; d. November 19, 1844[2]

Martin **Van Buren**, b. December 20, 1812; d. March 19, 1855, Paris, France[2]

Winfield Scott **Van Buren**, b. 1814, Hudson, New York; d. 1814, Hudson, New York[2]

Smith Thompson **Van Buren**, b. January 6, 1817; d. 1876, m(1) June 18, 1842, Ellen **James**, b. January 20, 1813; d. October 3, 1849, m(2) February 1, 1855, Henrietta **Irving**, b. April 13, 1821, Bournemouth, England[2]

Hannah Hoes, b. March 8, 1783, Kinderhook, New York; d. July 24, 1819, Albany, New York, m. February 21, 1804, Martin Van Buren, b. December 5, 1782, Kinderhook, New York; d. July 24, 1862, Kinderhook, New York[3, 4]

G-1

Johannes Dircksen **Hoes**, b. May 25, 1753, Kinderhook, New York, m. February 4, 1776, Maria **Quackenbush**, b. January 26, 1754; d. December 5, 1852[3]

G-2

Dirck **Hoes**, b. 1724, Kinderhook, New York; d. January 31, 1773, m. 1746, Christina **Van Alen**, b. ca. 1722, Kinderhook, New York; d. May 5, 1776[3]

Pieter **Quackenbush**,* m. Martie (Last Name Unknown)*[3]

G-3

Johannes **Hoes**, b. 1700, Kinderhook, New York, m. Janneyie **Van Schaick**[3]

Pieter **Van Alen**,* m. Jastina **Dingman***[3]

G-4

Dirk Janse **Hoes**, b. 1625, m. Elizabeth **Wyngaard**[3]

Laurens **Van Schaick**, m. Jannetje **Van Voothout**[3]

G-5

Jan Tyssen **Hoes***; d. May 31, 1705, m. Christyntje **Van Hoesen**[3]

Luykas Gerritsen **Wyndgard,*** m. Anna **Van Hoesen***[3]

Claes Gerritse **Van Schaick,*** m. Jannetje (Last Name Unknown)*[3]

Jan Janse **Van Voothout**, b. Greenbush, New York; d. 1696, m. Hendrickje Cornelisse **Van Ness**[3]

G-6

Jan Franssen **Van Hoesen,*** m. Valkestje **Jurriaens***[3]

Claes Cornlisz **Van Voothout,*** m. Brecktje **Manus***[3]

Cornelis **Van Ness,*** m. Marijgen **Van Den Burchgraeff***[3]

MARTHA WASHINGTON

G+2

Children of John "Jacky" Custis and Eleanor "Nelly" Calvert:

Elizabeth **Custis**, b. 1776
Martha **Custis**, b. December 31, 1777, Mount Vernon, Virginia
Eleanor **Custis**, b. 1779
George Washington Parke **Custis**, b. April 20, 1781

G+1

Children of Martha Dandridge and Daniel Park Custis:

Daniel **Custis**[2]
John "Jacky" **Custis**[2]
Martha **Custis**[2]
Frances **Custis**[2]

Martha Dandridge, b. June 2, 1731, New Kent Co., Virginia; d. May 22, 1802, Mount Vernon, Virginia, m(1) Daniel Park Custis, m(2) January 6, 1759 George Washington, b. February 12, 1732, Virginia; d. December 14, 1799, Mount Vernon, Virginia[2,4]

G-1

John **Dandridge**, b. July 14, 1700, New Kent Co., Virginia; d. August 31, 1756, New Kent Co., Virginia, m. July 22, 1730, Frances **Jones**, b. August 6, 1710, Williamsburg, Virginia; d. April 9, 1785[2]

G-2

John **Dandridge**, b. April 29, 1655, London, England; d. 1731, Virginia, m. Ann **Matthews**[2]

Orlando **Jones**, b. December 31, 1681; d. June 12, 1719, New Kent

Co., Virginia, m. January 31, 1703, Martha **Macon**, b. 1687, New Kent Co., Virginia; d. May 4, 1719, Williamsburg, Virginia[2]

G-3

John **Dandridge**, b. England[2]

Samuel **Matthews***[2]

Rowland **Jones**, b. 1644, England; d. 1688, m. Jane **Champion***[1]

Gideon **Macon**, m. Martha **Woodward** (Refer to Gideon **Macon** G-5 Letitia **Tyler** to continue their lines.)[2]

G-4

Bartholomew **Dandridge**,* b. England; d. England, m. Agnes **Wilder**,* b. 1580, Oxford, England[2]

Rowland **Jones**, b. England, m. Ann **Lane**,* b. England[2, 3]

G-5

Rowland **Jones**, b. 1608, England; d. September 6, 1665, m. Alice **Collier***[3]

G-6

Thomas **Jones**, b. 1570, England; d. 1624, England[3]

G-7

John **Jones**, b. 1520, England; d. England, m. Eliza **Vaughn**,* b. England; d. England[3]

G-8

Thomas **Jones**,* b. 1477, England; d. England, m. Mary **Berkeley**, b. 1480, England; d. England[3]

G-9

James **Berkeley**, b. England; d. England, m. Susan **Fitz Alan**, b. England; d. England[3]

G-10

Maurice **Berkeley**, b. England; d. England, m. Isabel **Meade***[3]

G-11

James **De Berkeley**, b. England; d. England, m. Isabel **De Mowbray**, b. England; d. England[3]

G-12

James **De Berkeley**, b. England; d. England, m. Elizabeth **Bluett**,* b. England; d. England[3]

Thomas **De Mowbray**,* b. England; d. England, m. Elizabeth **De Alan**,* b. England; d. England[3]

G-13

Maurice **De Berkeley**,* b. England; d. England, m. Elizabeth **Le De Spencer**, b. England; d. England[3]

G-14

Hugh **Le De Spencer**,* b. England; d. England, m. Alianore **De Clare**, b. England; d. England[3]

G-15

Gilbert "The Red" **De Clare**, b. England; d. England, m. Joan **Plantagenet**, b. England; d. England[3]

G-16

Richard **De Clare**,* m. Maud **De Lacy*** (Refer to Richard **De Clare** G-18 Abigail **Adams** to continue his line.)

King Edward I,* m. Eleanor **De Castille*** (Refer to King Edward I G-17 Abigail **Adams** to continue their lines.)

Edith Wilson

G+1

Edith **Wilson** did not have any children.

Edith Bolling, b. October 15, 1872, Wytheville, Virginia; d. December 28, 1961, Washington, D.C., m(1) Norman Galt, m(2) December 18, 1915, Thomas Woodrow Wilson, b. December 28, 1856, Staunton, Virginia; d. February 3, 1924, Washington, D.C.[1,2,4]

G-1

William Holcombe **Bolling**, b. May 29, 1837, Virginia; d. July 6, 1899, Virginia, m. September 18, 1860, Sallie **White**, b. January 5, 1843; d. November 21, 1925, Virginia[1,2]

G-2

Archibald **Bolling**, b. Virginia; d. 1860, Virginia, m. Ann E. **Wigginton**[1,2]

William Allen **White**, b. 1798; d. 1844, m. Lucy **McDaniel***[1]

G-3

Archibald **Bolling**, b. Virginia; d. Virginia, m. Catherine **Payne**[1,2]

Benjamin **Wigginton**, b. 1780; d. 1864, Lynchburg, Virginia, m. Harriett, b. **Scott**, b. October 24, 1791, Campbell Co., Virginia[1]

Jacob **White; d.** June 2, 1832, Bedford Co., Virginia, m. Hannah **Spiers***[1]

G-4

John **Bolling**, b. June 24, 1737, Virginia; d. 1800, Virginia, m. June 19, 1760, Martha **Jefferson** (Sister of President Thomas **Jefferson**), b. October 1, 1741[1,2]

Archibald **Payne**, b. 1748, m. Martha **Dandridge**, b. September 20, 1748, Virginia; d. September 28, 1791, Virginia[1]

John **Wigginton**, b. 1741, Stafford Co., Virginia; d. April 22, 1825, Culpeper Co., Virginia, m. Elizabeth **Botts**, b. 1741; d. 1824[3]

William **Scott**, b. December 15, 1756, Campbell Co., Virginia; d. October 6, 1818, Lynchburg, Virginia, m. Ann **Jones**[3]

Henry **White**, b. April 24, 1724; d. June 17, 1802, Bedford Co., Virginia, m. Celia **Page***[3]

G-5

John **Bolling**, b. January 20, 1700; d. September 6, 1757, Virginia, m. Elizabeth **Blair**, b. April 4, 1712, Virginia; d. April 22, 1775, Virginia[1, 2]

Peter **Jefferson**, b. February 29, 1708, Osborne, Virginia, m. October 3, 1739, Jane **Randolph**, b. February 20, 1720, London, England; d. March 31, 1776, Monticello, Charlottesville, Virginia[1]

John **Payne**, b. December 4, 1713, Goochland, Virginia; d. July 28, 1784, Campbell Co., Virginia, m. Hannah **Harris**[3]

Nathaniel **Dandridge**, b. September 7, 1729, King William Co., Virginia; d. January 16, 1786, m. Dorothea **Spotswood**, b. 1747, Virginia[1]

Seth **Botts**, b. 1713; d. 1776, m. 1735, Sabrina **Birdwell**[3]

Thomas **Scott**, b. June 12, 1718, Caroline Co., Virginia, m. Martha **Williams**[3]

Gabriel **Jones**,* m. Martha **Waller**[3]

Daniel **White**[3]

G-6

John **Bolling**, b. January 27, 1676; d. April 20, 1729, Virginia, m. December 29, 1697, Mary **Kennon**, b. June 29, 1679; d. 1735[1, 2]

Archibald **Blair**,* b. 1675, Scotland; d. 1736, Virginia, m. Mary **Wilson***[1]

Thomas **Jefferson**, b. 1680, Chesterfield Co., Virginia, m. November 20, 1697, Mary **Field**, b. February 3, 1679, Henrico Co., Virginia[1]

Isham **Randolph**, b. February 24, 1685, Henrico Co., Virginia, m. Jane **Rogers**, b. 1696, London, England; d. 1761[1]

George **Payne**, m. Mary **Woodson** (Refer to George Payne G-3 Dolley **Madison** to continue their lines.)[3]

William **Dandridge**, b. England; d. 1743, Virginia, m. 1719, Unity **West**[1, 2]

Alexander **Spotswood**, b. 1706, Tangiers, m. Anne **Bryan**[1, 2]

Thomas **Botts**,* b. 1674; d. 1742, m. 1699, Elizabeth (Last Name Unknown),* b. 1681; d. 1751[3]

Samuel **Birdwell**, b. 1700; d. 1796, m. Sarah (Last Name Unknown)*[3]

William **Waller**, b. 1714; d. October 22, 1756, m. Ann **Stenard***[3]

G-7

Robert **Bolling**, b. December 26, 1646, Virginia; d. 1709, Virginia, m. 1675, Jane **Rolfe**, b. 1655, Virginia; d. 1676[1, 2]

Richard **Kennon**, b. Bristol, England; d. 1695, Henrico Co., England, m. Elizabeth **Warsham**[1, 2]

Thomas **Jefferson**,* b. 1656, Henrico Co., Virginia; d. 1697, m. Mary **Branch**, b. 1660, Charles City Co., Virginia; d. 1715, Chesterfield Co., Virginia[1, 2]

Peter **Field**, b. 1635, Charles City Co., Virginia, m. October 21, 1678, Judith **Soane**, b. 1648, James City Co., Virginia[1, 2]

William **Randolph**, b. 1651, Yorks, England; d. April 11, 1711, m. 1680, Mary **Isham**, b. 1658, Henrico Co., Virginia[1, 2]

Charles **Rogers**,* b. London, England, m. Jane **Lilburne***[1, 2]

John **Dandridge**, b. April 29, 1655, London, England; d. 1731, Virginia, m. Ann **Matthews** (Refer to John **Dandridge** G-2 Martha **Washington** to continue their lines.)[1]

Nathaniel **West**, m. Martha **Woodward**[2]

Robert **Spotswood**, m. Katherine **Mercer** or **Maxwell***[1]

Richard **Bryan***[1]

Abraham **Birdwell**, b. 1650[1]

John **Waller**, b. February 23, 1673, England; d. August 2, 1753, Newport, Virginia, m. Dorothy **King**, b. 1675, Spotswood, Virginia; d. 1759, Newport, Virginia[3]

G-8

John **Bolling**, b. ca. 1610; d. 1648, m. Mary **Carrie***[1, 2]

Thomas **Rolfe**, b. 1615, England, m. Jane **Poythress**, b. England[1]

William **Warsham**,* b. England, m. Elizabeth (Last Name Unknown)*[1]

Christopher **Branch**, m. Sarah **Almond***[3]

James **Field**, b. 1604, Herefordshire, England[1]

Henry **Soane**,* b. England[1]

Richard **Randolph**, b. February 21, 1621, Warrick, England; d. 1671, England, m. Elizabeth **Rayland**,* b. 1625, England; d. 1675, England[3]

Henry **Isham**, m. Katherine **Banks** (Refer to Henry Isham G-4 Martha **Jefferson*** to continue his line.)[1]

John **West**, b. June 6, 1632, York Co., Virginia; d. New Kent Co., Virginia, m. Unity **Croshaw***[1]

William **Woodward***[1]

Robert **Spotswood**, b. 1596, Scotland, m. Bethia **Morrison**[1]

Thomas **Birdwell***[3]

John **Waller,*** b. 1645; d. 1723, m. Mary **Key,*** b. 1648[3]

G-9

Robert **Bolling**, b. 1575, England; d. 1639, England, m. Anne **Clark**, b. England; d. England[1, 2]

John **Rolfe**, b. May 6, 1585, Heachun. England; d. March 22, 1621, Virginia, m. Pocahantas, b. September 17, 1595; d. 1617, Gravesend, England[4]

Christopher **Branch**, b. 1602, London, England; d. 1681, Henrico Co., Virginia, m. Mary **Addie**, b. England[3]

Bishop Theophilus **Field,*** b. 1573, England; d. June 2, 1636, m. Alice (Last Name Unknown)*[1]

William **Randolph**, b. 1604, England; d. 1634, m. Dorothy **Lane**, b. England[3]

John **West**, b. 1590, England[1]

John **Spotswood**[1]

Alexander **Morrison,*** b. England, m. Eleanor **Maule**, b. England[1]

G-10

Edward **Bolling**, b. 1540, England; d. 1592, England, m. Maud or Magdeline **Greene,*** b. England; d. England[1, 2]

John **Rolfe**, b. England; d. England, m. Dorothea **Mason,*** b. England; d. England[4]

Lionel **Branch**, b. August 18, 1566, Abington, England; d. July 7, 1596, England, m. Valentia **Sparke,*** b. England; d. England[3]

William **Randolph**, b. England; d. England, m. Elizabeth **Smith**, b. England; d. England[3]

Richard **Lane,*** b. England; d. England, m. Elizabeth **Vincent**, b. England; d. England[3]

Thomas **West**, b. 1555, Halnaker, England; d. March 24, 1603, Wherwell, England, m. Anne **Knollys**, b. England; d. England[1]

John **Spotswood,*** b. England; d. England, m. Rachel **Lindsay**, b. England; d. England[1]

William **Maule**, b. England; d. England, m. Bethia **Guthrie**,* b. England; d. England[1]

G-11

Tristram **Bolling**, b. 1510, England; d. 1561, England, m. Ann **Rookes**,* b. England[1, 2]

Eustache **Rolfe**, b. England; d. England, m. Joanna **Jenner**,* b. England; d. England[4]

William **Branch**, b. 1524, Abington, England; d. England, m. Katherine **Jennings**, b. England; d. England[1]

Robert **Randolph**,* b. England; d. England, m. Rose **Roberts**,* b. England; d. England[3]

Thomas **Smith**,* b. England; d. England[3]

Clement **Vincent**,* b. England; d. England, m. Anne **Tanfield**, b. England; d. England[3]

William **West**, b. England; d. England, m. Elizabeth **Strange**, b. England; d. England[1]

Francis **Knollys**,* b. England; d. England, m. Mary **Cary**, b. England; d. England[1]

Alexander **Lindsay**, b. England; d. England, m. Mariota **Dunbar**, b. England; d. England[1]

Robert **Maule**,* b. England; d. England, m. Isabel **Arbuthnott**, b. England; d. England[1]

G-12

Edward **Bolling**, b. 1480, England; d. 1543, England[1, 2]

Robert **Rolfe**,* b. England; d. England[4]

Richard **Branch**,* b. 1496, England; d. England, m. Elizabeth **Blackforest**[*1, 3]

Thomas **Jennings**, b. England; d. England, m. Alice **Bright**,* b. England; d. England[3]

Francis **Tanfield**, b. England; d. England, m. Bridget **Cave**,* b. England; d. England[3]

George **West***b. England; d. England, m. Elizabeth **Norton**,* b. England; d. England[1]

Thomas **Strange**,* b. England; d. England[1]

William **Cary**, b. England; d. England, m. Mary **Boleyn*** (Sister of Anne **Boleyn**, wife of King Henry VIII)[1]

David **Lindsay**,* b. England; d. England, m. Catherine **Stewart**[1]

James **Arbuthnott**,* b. England; d. England, m. Jean **Stewart**[1]

G-13

Tristram **Bolling**, b. 1438, England; d. 1502, England, m. Ellen (Last Name Unknown),* b. England; d. England[1]

William **Jennings**,* b. England; d. England, m. Joan **Bostock**, b. England; d. England[3]

William **Tanfield**, b. England; d. England, m. Isabel **Stavely**,* b. England; d. England[1, 3]

Thomas **Cary**,* b. England; d. England, m. Margaret **Spencer**, b. England; d. England[1]

King Robert II* of Scotland, m. Elizabaeth **Mure*** (Refer to King Robert II G-14 Dolley **Madison** to continue their lines.)[1, 3]

John **Stewart**, m. Janet **Campbell***[1]

G-14

Robert **Bolling**, b. England; d. England, m. Isabel (Last Name Unknown),* b. England; d. England[1, 2]

George **Bostock**, b. England; d. England, m. Joan **Horne**,* b. England; d. England[3]

Richard **Tanfield**,* b. England; d. England, m. Catherine **De Neville**, b. England; d. England[1]

Sir Robert **Spencer**, b. England; d. England, m. Eleanor **Beaufort**, b. England; d. England[1]

John **Stewart**[1]

G-15

John **Bolling**, b. 1364, England; d. 1408, England, m. Grace **Popely**,* b. England; d. England[1, 2]

Hugh **Bostock**, b. England; d. England, m. Joan **De Heath**,* b. England; d. England[3]

Edward **De Neville**, b. England; d. England, m. Catherine **Howard**,* b. England; d. England[1]

Edmund **Beaufort**, b. England; d. England, m. Eleanor **De Beauchamp**,* b. England; d. England[1]

Sir James **Stewart**,* m. Joan **Beaufort**, b. England; d. England[1]

G-16

Robert **Bolling**,* b. 1325, England; d. 1398, England[1, 2]

Nicholas **Bostock**,* b. England; d. England, m. Catherine **Mobberly**,* b. England; d. England[3]

Ralph **De Neville**,* b. England; d. England, m. Joan **Beaufort**, b. England; d. England[1]

John **Beaufort**,* b. 1371, England; d. March 16, 1410, England, m. Margaret **De Holland*** (Refer to John **Beaufort** G-16 Edith **Wilson** to continue their lines.)[1]

G-17

John of Gaunt,* m. Catherine **Roet*** (Refer to John of Gaunt G-14 Abigail **Adams** to continue their lines.)[1]

Ellen Wilson

G+2

Children of Francis Bowes and Jessie (Wilson) Sayre:

Francis Bowes **Sayre**, b. April 30, 1885, South Bethlehem, Pa.; d. March 29, 1972, Washington, D.C.[1]

Eleanor **Sayre**[1]

Woodrow Wilson **Sayre**, m. Edith **Chase**[1]

G+1

Margaret **Wilson**, b. August 6, 1886, Gainesville, Georgia; d. February 12, 1944, Pondicherry, India[2]

Jessie **Wilson**, b. August 28, 1887, Gainesville, Georgia; d. January 15, 1933, Cambridge, Mass., m. November 25, 1913, White House Francis Bowes **Sayre**, b. April 30, 1885, South Bethlehem, Pa.; d. March 29, 1972, Washington, D.C.[2]

Eleanor **Wilson**, b. October 5, 1889, Middletown, Conn.; d. April 5, 1967, Calif., m. May 7, 1914, White House William Gibbs **McAdoo**[2]

Ellen Louise Axson, b. May 13, 1860, Savannah, Georgia; d. August 6, 1914, Washington, D.C., m. June 22, 1885, Thomas Woodrow Wilson, b. December 28, 1856, Staunton, Virginia; d. February 3, 1924, Washington, D.C.[3, 10]

G-1

Rev. Samuel Edward **Axson**, b. December 23, 1838, Walthowville, Georgia, m. November 23, 1858, Margaret Jane **Hoyt**, b. September 8, 1838, Rome, Georgia; d. November 4, 1881[3]

G-2

Isaac **Axson**,* b. 1805, Walthowville, Georgia; d. March 31, 1891, m. October 28, 1834, Rebecca Longstreet **Fitz Randolph**, b. 1810, Columbia, South Carolina; d. 1887, Savannah, Georgia[3]

Rev. Nathan **Hoyt**, m. Margaret **Bliss**[3]

G-3

Isaac **Fitz Randolph**, b. November 13, 1766, Monmouth Co., New Jersey, m. 1790, Eleanor **Hunter**, b. 1771, Charleston, South Carolina; d. 1847, Liberty Co., Georgia[3]

Edward **Hoyt**,* b. 1775, Savannah, Georgia, m. Margaret (Last Name Unknown)*[3]

Alexander **Bliss**, b. 1753, Springfield, Mass.; d. 1843, Springfield, Mass., m. 1790, Abigail **Williams**, b. 1760, Savannah, Georgia[3]

G-4

James **Fitz Randolph**, b. October 1, 1730, Monmouth Co., New Jersey; d. 1781, m. Deliverance **Coward**, b. November 24, 1734, Freehold, New Jersey; d. February 13, 1787, Monmouth Co., New Jersey[1, 2, 4]

David **Hunter**, b. 1740, Scotland[3, 5]

Jedediah **Bliss**, b. 1709; d. 1777, m. 1749, Miriam **Hitchcock**[3, 6]

Thomas **Williams**, m. Abigail **Williams**[3]

G-5

Isaac **Fitz Randolph**, b. April 10, 1701, Stony Brook, New Jersey; d. May 13, 1750, Upper Freehold, New Jersey, m. Rebecca **Seabrook**, b. June 8, 1708; d. March 25, 1744[4]

John **Coward**, b. 1704, Burlington Co., New Jersey; d. July 30, 1760, Red Valley, New Jersey, m. Alice **Brittain***[2, 9]

James **Hunter**, b. April 25, 1696, Clackmanan, Scotland, m. Margaret **Hunter**, b. January 1, 1696, Scotland[5]

Ebenezer **Bliss**, m. Mary **Gaylord**[6]

Ebenezer **Williams**, b. 1695, m. Sarah **Tileston***[7]

Elijah **Williams**, m. Lydia **Dwight***[7]

G-6

Benjamin **Fitz Randolph**, b. October 5, 1663, Barnstable, Mass.; d. October 5, 1746, Stoney Brook, New Jersey, m. Sarah **Dennis**[4]

Hugh **Coward**,* b. 1678, Bristol, England, m. Patience **Throckmorton**[2, 9]

Robert **Hunter**, b. September 13, 1671, Scotland, m. Janet **Patterson**, b. December 26, 1674[5]

William **Hunter**, b. 1674, Scotland, m. Margaret **Snedon**, b. 1676, Scotland[5]

Samuel **Bliss**, b. 1624, Devonshire, England; d. March 23, 1720, Springfield, Mass., m. Mary **Leonard**, b. September 14, 1647, Springfield, Mass.; d. March 11, 1724, Springfield, Mass.[6]

John **Gaylord**, b. January 27, 1649, Windsor, Conn.; d. 1699, Windsor, Conn., m. Mary **Clark** September 22, 1658, Windsor, Conn.; d. 1738, Windsor, Conn.[6]

Samuel **Williams**, b. April 27, 1656; d. August 8, 1735, m. Sarah **May**[7]

John **Williams**, m. Abigail **Allyn**[7]

G-7

Edward **Fitz Randolph**, b. July 5, 1607, Nottinghamshire, England; d. 1676, Piscataway, New Jersey, m. May 10, 1637, Scituate, Mass. Elizabeth **Blossom**, b. 1620, Leyden, Holland; d. 1713, Piscataway, New Jersey[4]

John **Dennis**, b. 1643, Yarmouth, Mass.; d. May 8, 1689, Woodbridge, New Jersey, m. Sarah **Bloomfield**, b. December 30, 1643, Newbury, Mass.; d. May 15, 1689, Woodbridge, New Jersey[4]

John **Throckmorton**, m. Alice **Stout**[2]

James **Hunter**,* b. Scotland, m. Janet **Paterson***[5]

James **Patterson**,* m. Agnes **Atkin***[5]

William **Hunter**,* m. Margaret (Last Name Unknown)*[5]

Thomas **Bliss**, b. England, m. Margaret **Hulings**,* b. England[6]

John **Leonard**, b. 1615, Pontpool, Wales; d. March 20, 1675, Springfield, Mass., m. Sarah **Heath**, b. England[6]

William **Gaylord**,* b. England, m. Anna **Porter**, b. England[6]

Daniel **Clark**,* b. 1644, England, m. Mary **Newberry**, b. England[6]

Samuel **Williams**,* b. 1632; d. September 30, 1698, m. Theoda **Parke**, b. July 26, 1637; d. August 2, 1718[7]

John **May**, b. 1631; d. September 11, 1671, m. Sarah **Brewer**, b. March 8, 1638; d. January 8, 1708[7]

Samuel **Williams**,* m. Theoda **Parke*** (Refer to Samuel **Williams** G-7 Ellen **Wilson** to continue their lines.)[7]

Thomas **Allyn**, m. Abigail **Warham***[7]

G-8

Edward **Fitz Randolph**,* b. England, m. Frances **Howis**, b. England[4]

Thomas **Blossom,*** b. 1580, Cambridge, England; d. 1632, Plymouth, Mass., m. Anna **Neilson,*** b. 1584, Cambridge, Mass.[4]

Robert **Dennis,*** b. England, m. Mary (Last Name Unknown),* b. England[4]

Thomas **Bloomfield,*** b. England, m. Mary (Last Name Unknown)*[4]

John **Throckmorton**, b. England, m. Rebecca (Last Name Unknown)*[2]

Richard **Stout,*** b. England, m. Penelope **Van Princis***[2]

Thomas **Bliss,*** b. England, m. Margaret **Lawrence,*** b. England[6]

Thomas **Leonard,*** b. England, m. Lydia **White,*** b. England[6]

John **Heath,*** b. England, m. Dorothy **Royle,*** b. England[6]

John **Porter,*** b. England, m. Anna **White,*** b. England[6]

Thomas **Newberry,*** m. Jane **Dabinot*** (Refer to Thomas **Newberry** G-11 Bess **Truman** to continue his line.)[6]

Robert **Williams,*** b. 1607, England; d. September 1, 1693, m. Elizabeth **Stallan,*** b. England; d. July 28, 1674[7]

William **Parke,*** b. 1607, England; d. May 11, 1685, m. Martha **Holgrave,*** b. 1615, England; d. August 25, 1708[7]

John **May,*** b. 1590, England; d. April 28, 1670[7]

Daniel **Brewer,*** b. 1596, England; d. March 28, 1646, m. Joanna **Morrill,*** b. 1602; d. February 7, 1688[7]

Matthew **Allyn**, m. Margaret **Wyatt** (Refer to Richard **Allyn** G-11 Nancy **Reagan** to continue their lines.)[7]

G-9

Bassingbourne **Throckmorton**, b. 1564, England; d. 1638, m. Mary **Hill,*** b. England[2]

G-10

Lionel **Throckmorton**, b. England; d. 1599, England, m. Elizabeth **Blennerhasset**, b. England; d. England[2]

G-11

Simon **Throckmorton**, b. England; d. England, m. Ann **Loweth**, b. England; d. England[2]

John **Blennerhasset**, b. England; d. England, m. Elizabeth **Cornwallis**, b. England; d. England[2]

G-12

John **Throckmorton,*** b. 1460, England; d. 1507, England, m. Jane **Baynard,*** b. England; d. England[2]

Edmund **Loweth*** b. England; d. England, m. Edith **Stukeley,*** b. England; d. England[2]

Thomas **Blennerhasset,*** b. England; d. England, m. Margaret **Braham,*** b. England; d. England[2]

John **Cornwallis,** b. England; d. England, m. Mary **Sulyard,*** b. England; d. England[2]

G-13

William **Cornwallis,** b. England; d. England, m. Elizabeth **Stafford,** b. England; d. England[2]

G-14

Thomas **Cornwallis,*** b. England; d. England, m. Philippa **Tyrell,*** b. England; d. England[2]

G-15

Edward **Tyrell***b. England; d. England, m. Anne **Pashley,** b. England; d. England[2]

G-16

Sir Robert **Pashley,*** b. England; d. England, m. Philippa **Sergeaux**[2]

G-17

Richard **Sergeaux,*** m. Philippa **Fitz Alan,** b. England; d. England[2]

G-18

Sir Edmund **Fitz Alan,** b. England; d. England, m. Sybil **Montague,** b. England; d. England[2]

G-19

Richard **Fitz Alan,*** b. England; d. England, m. Isabella **De Spencer,** b. England; d. England[2]

William **De Montague,*** b. England; d. England, m. Catherine **De Grandison,*** b. England; d. England[2]

G-20

Hugh **De Spencer,*** b. England; d. England, m. Eleanor **De Clare,** b. England; d. England[2]

G-21

Gilbert **De Clare,*** b. England; d. England, m. Joan **Plantagenet**, b. England; d. England[2]

G-22

King Edward I,* m. Eleanor **De Castille*** (Refer to King Edward I G-17 Abigail **Adams** to continue their lines.)[2]

Sources

Many individuals provided valuable information for this book. I am grateful for their willingness to share this information. Some have agreed to the inclusion of their e-mail addresses here to facilitate communication with others interested in genealogy.

Abigail Adams

1. Sheila Stratton-Peel, Niagara Falls, New York.
2. Ronald Vern Jackson and Altha Polson, *American Patriots.* Salt Lake City, Utah: A.G.E.S., 1982. Courtesy of Scott Thomas Genealogical Services, Inc., West Jordan, Utah.
3. Rev. Darrell and Sallyann Joiner, Lincoln, Maine.
4. Hans A.M. Weebers: E-Mail weebers@t-online.de, Website legacy familytree.com/uspresidents.
5. John De Land, Cedar City, Utah.
6. Ryan Pemble, Belen, New Mexico.
7. Mitch Draper, Lexington, South, Carolina.
8. Jim Beecroft, Roy, Utah.
9. Donna J. Baker, Wolcott, Vermont.
10. Michael and Mare Blewett, Tucker, Georgia.
11. David Hunter Brown, Fort Meyers, Florida.
12. Jeff Harper, San Diego, California.
13. The National First Ladies Library, 205 Market Avenue South, Canton, Ohio 44702.

Louisa Adams

1. Sheila Stratton-Peel, Niagara Falls, New York.
2. Ronald Vern Jackson and Altha Polson *American Patriots.* Salt Lake City, Utah: A.G.E.S., 1982. Courtesy of Scott Thomas Genealogical Services, Inc., West Jordan, Utah.
3. The National First Ladies Library, 205 Market Avenue South, Canton, Ohio 44702.

Ellen Arthur

1. Irv Mitchell, Sun City, Arizona.
2. Ronald Vern Jackson and Altha Polson *American Patriots.* Salt Lake City, Utah: A.G.E.S., 1982. Courtesy of Scott Thomas Genealogical Services, Inc., West Jordan, Utah.
3. Hans A.M. Weebers: E-Mail weebers@t-online.de, Website legacyfamilytree.com/uspresidents.
4. Mark Willis Ballard, Chicago, Illinois.
5. Jim Culver, Austin, Texas.
6. Rick Lewis, Harker Heights, Texas.
7. Cathy Babbs, Charleston, Illinois.

8. Vickie Kaufman, Callaway, Nebraska.

9. Kaye Steele, Medford, Oregon.

10. Michael and Marie Blewett, Tucker, Georgia.

11. David Hunter Brown, Fort Meyers, Florida.

12. Donna J. Baker, Wolcott, Vermont.

13. The National First Ladies Library, 205 Market Avenue South, Canton, Ohio 44702.

Barbara Bush

1. George Bush Presidential Library, 1000 George Bush Drive West, College Station, Texas 77845.

2. Ronald Vern Jackson and Altha Polson *American Patriots*. Salt Lake City, Utah: A.G.E.S., 1982. Courtesy of Scott Thomas Genealogical Services, Inc., West Jordan, Utah.

3. Fred Milligan. *The Moravian Ancestors of George W. Bush*. Courtesy of Laird Towle. Bowie, Maryland: Heritage Books, Inc.

4. Richard Pierce, Dedham, Massachusetts.

5. Matthew D. Friend. California: E: Mail: friends1995@yahoo.com, Website: "An American Portrait—The Friend Family," freepages. genealogy.rootsweb.com/~friends 1995/.

6. Norman Schofield.

7. Don and Jeanine Hartman, Bountiful, Utah.

8. Linda Dill, Greensburg, Pennsylvania.

9. Hans A.M. Weebers: E: Mail weebers@t-online.de, Website legacyfamilytree.com/uspresidents.

10. Patrick Harrington, Palatine, Illinois.

11. Ross Johnson, Hansville, Washington.

12. The National First Ladies Library, 205 Market Avenue South, Canton, Ohio 44702.

Laura Bush

1. George Bush Presidential Library, National Archives and Records Administration, Washington, D.C.

2. Jennifer J. Zuker, Lawson, Missouri.

3. Robert Suddath, Little, Colorado.

4. Juanita Alexander, Lawrenceville, Georgia.

5. Pam Hamlin Crabb, Corinth, Mississippi.

6. Tom Johnston, Millstadt, Illinois.

7. Pam Crain, Lamont, Oklahoma.

8. Susan Mills, Whiteville, North Carolina.

9. The National First Ladies Library, 205 Market Avenue South, Canton, Ohio 44702.

Rosalynn Carter

1. President Jimmy Carter "The Family of Wiley Carter."

2. Ken Thomas, Decatur, Georgia.

3. Susan Rockford Bradley, Brundidge, Alabama.

4. Kevin Singer, Tulsa, Oklahoma.

5. Joyce Kersey Karr, Houston, Texas.

6. Brian Brooks, Columbia, Missouri.

7. The National First Ladies Library, 205 Market Avenue South, Canton, Ohio 44702.

Frances Cleveland

1. Charles J. Ernst.

2. Ronald Vern Jackson and Altha Polson *American Patriots*. Salt Lake City, Utah: A.G.E.S., 1982. Courtesy of Scott Thomas Genealogical Services, Inc., West Jordan, Utah.

3. Robert Haack, Houston, Texas: "The Haack Family and Related Lines."

4. John De Land, Cedar City, Utah.

5. Susan Dennis Winters, West Palm Beach, Florida.
6. David B. Robinson, Davis, California.
7. Tanya Babcock, West Carthage, New York.
8. Raymond B. Howard, Oakland, California.
9. Darryl Boyd, Concord, California.
10. Herbert Davis, Salem, Utah.
11. Matt and Deb Gunther, Glendale, Wisconsin.
12. Rick Ingersoll, Barrow, Alaska.
13. Robby Robinson, Talladega, Alabama.
14. Richard Burns, Canoga Park, California.
15. Terry Frank, Tampa Bay, Florida.
16. Quinta Scott, St. Louis, Missouri.
17. Bonnie Hamilton, Lewisberry, Pennsylvania.
18. Earl Peckham, Tampa Bay, Florida.
19. David Buchroder, Edgewood, British Columbia, Canada.
20. Skip Nunweiler, Indianapolis, Indiana.
21. The National First Ladies Library, 205 Market Avenue South, Canton, Ohio 44702.

Hillary Rodham Clinton

1. Hans A.M. Weebers, E-Mail: weebers@t-online.de. Website: legacyfamilytree.com/uspresidents.
2. David Buchroder, Edgewood, British Columbia, Canada.
3. The National First Ladies Library, 205 Market Avenue South, Canton, Ohio 44702.

Grace Coolidge

1. Rick Ingersoll, Barrow, Alaska.
2. Ronald Vern Jackson and Altha Polson *American Patriots*. Salt Lake City, Utah: A.G.E.S., 1982. Courtesy of Scott Thomas Genealogical Services, Inc., West Jordan, Utah.
3. William Whipple, Orem, Utah.
4. David B. Robinson, Davis, California.
5. John De Land, Cedar City, Utah.
6. Matthew Misbach, Orem, Utah.
7. Sean Duffie: E-Mail sean_duffie@hotmail.com.
8. Jill McLeester, Spokane, Missouri.
9. Mike Lewis, Papillion, Nebraska.
10. Rhea McAllister Beck.
11. Herbert Davis, Salem, Utah.
12. The National First Ladies Library, 205 Market Avenue South, Canton, Ohio 44702.

Mary Geneva (Mamie) Eisenhower

1. Dwight Eisenhower Presidential Library, Abilene, Kansas.
2. Mamie Eisenhower Birthplace Library, Boone, Iowa.

Abigail Fillmore

1. Hans A.M. Weebers: E-Mail weebers@t-online.de, Website legacyfamilytree.com/uspresidents.
2. Ronald Vern Jackson and Altha Polson *American Patriots*. Salt Lake City, Utah: A.G.E.S., 1982. Courtesy of Scott Thomas Genealogical Services, Inc., West Jordan, Utah.
3. Roberta Barnes: E-Mail rb_barnes2@hotmail.com.
4. William Whipple, Orem, Utah.
5. David B. Robinson, Davis, California.
6. Susan Selks, Michigan State University, East Lansing, Michigan.
7. Cory Stimpson.

8. The National First Ladies Library, 205 Market Avenue South, Canton, Ohio 44702.

Caroline Fillmore

1. David Buchroder-Edgewood, British Columbia, Canada.
2. John De Land-Cedar City, Utah.
3. Larry Cheseboro, O'Fallon, Missouri.

Elizabeth (Betty) Ford

1. Gerald Ford Presidential Library, 1000 Beal Avenue, Ann Arbor, Michigan 48109.
2. Ronald Vern Jackson, Ronald Vern Jackson and Altha Polson, *American Patriots.* Salt Lake City, Utah: A.G.E.S., 1982. Courtesy of Scott Thomas Genealogical Services, Inc., West Jordan, Utah.
3. The National First Ladies Library, 205 Market Avenue South, Canton, Ohio 44702.

Lucretia Garfield

1. Linda Carpenter Fry, Waunakee, Wisconsin.
2. Hans A.M. *Weebers-weebers@t-online.de* Website legacyfamilytree.com/uspresidents.
3. Ronald Vern Jackson and Altha Polson *American Patriots.* Salt Lake City, Utah: A.G.E.S., 1982. Courtesy of Scott Thomas Genealogical Services, Inc., West Jordan, Utah.
4. Robert Kline, Delta, British Columbia, Canada.
5. Larry Cheseboro, O'Fallon, Missouri.
6. Jeff Harper, San Diego, California.
7. Mark Willis Ballard, Chicago, Illinois.
8. Bill Williams, Ashtabula, Ohio. Used with permission © 2003.
9. The National First Ladies Library, 205 Market Avenue South, Canton, Ohio 44702.

Julia Grant

1. Dave Distler, Reminderville, Ohio.
2. Hans A.M. Weebers: E-Mail *weebers@t-online.de*, Website legacy-familytree.com/uspresidents.
3. Ronald Vern Jackson and Altha Polson *American Patriots.* Salt Lake City, Utah: A.G.E.S., 1982. Courtesy of Scott Thomas Genealogical Services, Inc., West Jordan, Utah.
4. Tom Buchanan, Roswell, Georgia.
5. Michael Hone, Taylorsville, North Carolina.
6. Steve Sims, Acwsorth, Georgia.
7. Kent McMahan, Louisville, Kentucky.
8. The National First Ladies Library, 205 Market Avenue South, Canton, Ohio 44702.

Florence Harding

1. Rod Davis, Hyde Park, New York.
2. Ronald Vern Jackson and Altha Polson *American Patriots.* Salt Lake City, Utah: A.G.E.S., 1982. Courtesy of Scott Thomas Genealogical Services, Inc., West Jordan, Utah.
3. Kristi Edington.
4. Jim Beecroft, Roy, Utah.
5. The National First Ladies Library, 205 Market Avenue South, Canton, Ohio 44702.

Anna Harrison

1. Hans. A.M. Weebers: E-Mail *weebers@t-online.de,* Website legacyfamilytree.com/uspresidents.
2. Brian Litteral, Broadview, Illinois.
3. Ronald Vern Jackson and Altha Polson *American Patriots.* Salt Lake City, Utah: A.G.E.S., 1982. Courtesy of Scott Thomas Genealogical Services, Inc., West Jordan, Utah.
4. Mitch Draper, Lexington, South Carolina.
5. John De Land, Cedar City, Utah.
6. Tanya Babcock, West Carthage, New York.
7. April Woolsey, Kennewick, Washington.
8. William Dunlap, Baton Rouge, Louisiana.
9. Christopher David Wade, Florissant, Missouri.
10. David B. Robinson, Davis, California.
11. Mark Tunnell, Berwyn, Pennsylvania.
12. The National First Ladies Library, 205 Market Avenue South, Canton, Ohio 44702.

Caroline Harrison

1. Linda Fry Carpenter, Waunakee, Wisconsin.
2. Ronald Vern Jackson and Altha Polson *American Patriots.* Salt Lake City, Utah: A.G.E.S., 1982. Courtesy of Scott Thomas Genealogical Services, Inc., West Jordan, Utah.
3. Pauline Davis, Mena, Arkansas.
4. The National First Ladies Library, 205 Market Avenue South, Canton, Ohio 44702.

Mary Harrison

1. Janice Lipsky-Pottsville, Pennsylvania.
2. Hans A.M. Weebers-E-Mail: weebers@t-online.de Website: legacyfamilytree.com/uspresidents.

Lucy Hayes

1. Carol Robertson White, Murfreesboro, Tennessee.
2. Hans A.M. Weebers: E-Mail *weebers@t-online.de,* Website legacyfamilytree.com/uspresidents.
3. Ronald Vern Jackson and Altha Polson *American Patriots.* Salt Lake City, Utah: A.G.E.S., 1982. Courtesy of Scott Thomas Genealogical Services, Inc., West Jordan, Utah.
4. Lori Ledsome, Parkersburg, West Virginia.
5. The National First Ladies Library, 205 Market Avenue South, Canton, Ohio 44702.

Lou Hoover

1. Michael Thompson: E-Mail mthompsoncm@netscape.net.
2. Susan Dennis Winters, West Palm Beach, Florida.
3. Ronald Vern Jackson and Altha Polson *American Patriots.* Salt Lake City, Utah: A.G.E.S., 1982. Courtesy of Scott Thomas Genealogical Services, Inc., West Jordan, Utah.
4. The Gloucester Historical Society, Woodbury, New Jersey.
5. Sue Yamtich, Munster, Indiana.
6. Ryan Pemble, Belen, New Mexico.
7. Barbara McCormick, Wilmington, North Carolina.
8. David B. Robinson, Davis, California.
9. The National First Ladies

Library, 205 Market Avenue South, Canton, Ohio 44702.

Rachel Jackson

1. Ronald Vern Jackson and Altha Polson *American Patriots*. Salt Lake City, Utah: A.G.E.S., 1982. Courtesy of Scott Thomas Genealogical Services, Inc., West Jordan, Utah.
2. Jean Rawlings Meaney, Hilton Head Beach, South Carolina.
3. The National First Ladies Library, 205 Market Avenue South, Canton, Ohio 44702.

Martha Jefferson

1. G.M. Perrin, E-Mail: irbyperrin@charter.net.
2. Hans A.M. Weebers: E-Mail *weebers@t-online.de,* Website legacyfamilytree.com/uspresidents.
3. Ronald Vern Jackson and Altha Polson *American Patriots*. Salt Lake City, Utah: A.G.E.S., 1982. Courtesy of Scott Thomas Genealogical Services, Inc., West Jordan, Utah.
4. Chris Olson, Yorkville, Illinois.
5. Helen J. Wilson, Rowlett, Texas.
6. Ryan Pemble, Belen, New Mexico.
7. Terry Frank, Tampa Bay, Florida.
8. Donna J. Baker, Wolcott, Vermont.
9. The National First Ladies Library, 205 Market Avenue South, Canton, Ohio 44702.
10. Thomas Jefferson Federation, P.O. Box 316, Charlottesville, Virginia 22902.

Claudia Alta (Lady Bird) Johnson

1. Lyndon B. Johnson Presidential Library, 2313 Red River Street, Austin, Texas 78705.
2. Hans A.M. Weebers: E-Mail *weebers@t-online.de,* Website legacyfamilytree.com/uspresidents.
3. Ronald Vern Jackson and Altha Polson *American Patriots*. Salt Lake City, Utah: A.G.E.S., 1982. Courtesy of Scott Thomas Genealogical Services, Inc., West Jordan, Utah.
4. John T. Pattillo, Winter Park, Florida.
5. Milly McGrane, Auckland, New Zealand.
6. Bill E. Newberry.
7. The National First Ladies Library, 205 Market Avenue South, Canton, Ohio 44702.

Eliza Johnson

1. Carmen Johnson, Lewiston, Idaho.
2. Hans A.M. Weebers: E-Mail *weebers@t-online.de,* Website legacyfamilytree.com/uspresidents.
3. Ronald Vern Jackson and Altha Polson *American Patriots*. Salt Lake City, Utah: A.G.E.S., 1982. Courtesy of Scott Thomas Genealogical Services, Inc., West Jordan, Utah.
4. Cory Stimpson.
5. The National First Ladies Library, 205 Market Avenue South, Canton, Ohio 44702.

Jacqueline Kennedy

1. June Ferguson: E-Mail *fergy@nemaine.com.*
2. Hans A.M. *Weebers-weebers@t-online.de* Website: legacyfamilytree.com/uspresidents.
3. Ronald Vern Jackson and Altha Polson *American Patriots*. Salt Lake City, Utah: A.G.E.S., 1982. Courtesy

of Scott Thomas Genealogical Services, Inc., West Jordan, Utah.

4. The National First Ladies Library, 205 Market Avenue South, Canton, Ohio 44702.

Mary Lincoln

1. Brian Litteral, Broadview, Illinois.
2. Hans A.M. Weebers: E-Mail *weebers@t-online.de,* Website legacyfamilytree.com/uspresidents.
3. Ronald Vern Jackson and Altha Polson *American Patriots.* Salt Lake City, Utah: A.G.E.S., 1982. Courtesy of Scott Thomas Genealogical Services, Inc., West Jordan, Utah.
4. Susan Rockford Bradley, Brundidge, Alabama.
5. Harnish MacLaren, Boulder, Colorado.
6. Marilyn Munoz, Redding, California.
7. Ryan Pemble, Belen, New Mexico.
8. Susan Selke, Michigan State University, East Lansing, Michigan.
9. Rev. Darrell and Sallyann Joiner, Lincoln, Maine.
10. Hal Bradley, Victorville, California.
11. Sheila Stratton-Peel, Niagara Falls, New York.
12. John De Land, Cedar City, Utah.
13. The National First Ladies Library, 205 Market Avenue South, Canton, Ohio 44702.

Dorothea (Dolley) Madison

1. Ronald Vern Jackson and Altha Polson *American Patriots.* Salt Lake City, Utah: A.G.E.S., 1982. Courtesy of Scott Thomas Genealogical Services, Inc., West Jordan, Utah.
2. M. Lynn Baugh, Americus, Georgia.
3. Shirley Crow Haskell, Chesapeake, Virginia.
4. Richard Hodgeson, West Sussex, England.
5. Bob Juch, Los Angeles, California.
6. Harnish MacLaren, Boulder, Colorado.
7. Verna Hudson, Homosassa, Florida.
8. Mark Willis Ballard, Chicago, Illinois.
9. Cathy Babbs, Charleston, Illinois.
10. Terry Lynn Marshall.
11. The National First Ladies Library, 205 Market Avenue South, Canton, Ohio 44702.

Ida McKinley

1. Hans A.M. Weebers: E-Mail weebers@t-online.de, Website legacyfamilytree.com/uspresidents.
2. Ronald Vern Jackson and Altha Polson *American Patriots.* Salt Lake City, Utah: A.G.E.S., 1982. Courtesy of Scott Thomas Genealogical Services, Inc., West Jordan, Utah.
3. Terry Frank, Tampa Bay, Florida.
4. Thomas C. Haydock, Village of Golf, Florida.
5. Rick Lewis, Harker Heights, Texas.
6. The National First Ladies Library, 205 Market Avenue South, Canton, Ohio 44702.

Elizabeth Monroe

1. Cathy Brooks, Chattanooga, Tennessee.
2. Hans A.M. Weebers: E-Mail *weebers@t-online.de,* Website legacyfamilytree.com/uspresidents.
3. Ronald Vern Jackson and Altha Polson *American Patriots.* Salt Lake City, Utah: A.G.E.S., 1982. Courtesy

of Scott Thomas Genealogical Services, Inc., West Jordan, Utah.

4. Robert Givens, Clovis, California.

5. Thomas Hadaway.

6. The National First Ladies Library, 205 Market Avenue South, Canton, Ohio 44702.

Thelma Catherine (Pat) Nixon

1. Thomas Haydock, Village of Golf, Florida.

2. Mark Tunnell, Berwyn, Pennsylvania.

3. Ronald Vern Jackson and Altha Polson *American Patriots*. Salt Lake City, Utah: A.G.E.S., 1982. Courtesy of Scott Thomas Genealogical Services, Inc., West Jordan, Utah.

4. The National First Ladies Library, 205 Market Avenue South, Canton, Ohio 44702.

Jane Pierce

1. Hans A.M. Weebers: E-Mail *weebers@t-online.de*, Website legacyfamilytree.com/uspresidents.

2. Ronald Vern Jackson and Altha Polson *American Patriots*. Salt Lake City, Utah: A.G.E.S., 1982. Courtesy of Scott Thomas Genealogical Services, Inc., West Jordan, Utah.

3. Herbert Davis, Salem, Utah.

4. Lary Moler, Houston, Texas.

5. Paul Neil Peterson, Tyler, Texas.

6. The National First Ladies Library, 205 Market Avenue South, Canton, Ohio 44702.

Sarah Polk

1. Ronald Vern Jackson and Altha Polson *American Patriots*. Salt Lake City, Utah: A.G.E.S., 1982. Courtesy of Scott Thomas Genealogical Services, Inc., West Jordan, Utah.

2. The National First Ladies Library, 205 Market Avenue South, Canton, Ohio 44702.

Jane Reagan (Wyman)

1. Ronald Reagan Presidential Library, 40 Presidential Drive, Simi Valley, California 93065.

2. Kevin Gibbs, Ottawa, Canada.

3. George Arthur Larson II-geolarson@juno.com.

4. Infoplease.com.

Nancy Reagan

1. Hans A.M. Weebers: E-Mail *weebers@t-online.de*, Websites legacyfamilytree.com/uspresidents.

2. Ronald Vern Jackson and Altha Polson *American Patriots*. Salt Lake City, Utah: A.G.E.S., 1982. Courtesy of Scott Thomas Genealogical Services, Inc., West Jordan, Utah.

3. Joe Weber, Bedford, Illinois.

4. Dave Distler, Remindersville, Ohio.

5. Rev. Darrell and Sallyann Joiner, Lincoln, Maine.

6. Clifford Ochletree.

7. Susan Embler, Dallas, Texas.

8. Marc Wheat, Arlington, Virginia.

9. Theresa and Gerald Affeldt, Madison, Illinois.

10. The National First Ladies Library, 205 Market Avenue South, Canton, Ohio 44702.

Alice Roosevelt

1. John De Land-Cedar City, Utah.

2. David Buchroder-Edgewood, British Columbia, Canada.
3. James Biggar-Cambridge, Massachusetts.

Edith Roosevelt

1. Irv Mitchell, Sun City, Arizona.
2. Hans A.M. Weebers: E-Mail *weebers@t-online.de,* Website legacyfamilytree.com/uspresidents.
3. Ronald Vern Jackson and Altha Polson *American Patriots.* Salt Lake City, Utah: A.G.E.S., 1982. Courtesy of Scott Thomas Genealogical Services, Inc., West Jordan, Utah.
4. Janice Lipsky, Pottsville, Pennsylvania.
5. Susan Shannon.
6. Cliff McCarthy, Belchertown, Massachusetts.
7. David B. Robinson, Davis, California.
8. Alla Henshaw, Pacific Palisades, California.
9. Irene Mast.
10. Roberta Bunn, Hyrum, Utah.
11. Jacquelyn Kyler, Mesa, Arizona.
12. The National First Ladies Library, 205 Market Avenue South, Canton, Ohio 44702.

Eleanor Roosevelt

1. The Franklin D. Roosevelt Presidential Library, 4079 Albany Post Road, Hyde Park, New York 12538.
2. Hans A.M. Weebers: E-Mail *weebers@t-online.de,* Website legacyfamilytree.com/uspresidents.
3. Ronald Vern Jackson and Altha Polson *American Patriots.* Salt Lake City, Utah: A.G.E.S., 1982. Courtesy of Scott Thomas Genealogical Services, Inc., West Jordan, Utah.
4. The National First Ladies Library, 205 Market Avenue South, Canton, Ohio 44702.

Helen Taft

1. Irv Mitchell, Sun City, Arizona.
2. Hans A.M. Weebers: E-Mail *weebers@t-online.de,* Website legacyfamilytree.com/uspresidents.
3. Ronald Vern Jackson and Altha Polson *American Patriots.* Salt Lake City, Utah: A.G.E.S., 1982. Courtesy of Scott Thomas Genealogical Services, Inc., West Jordan, Utah.
4. Cherlynn Wilson, Albuquerque, New Mexico.
5. James K. Stanley, Marietta, Georgia.
6. Deane Merrill, Shelburne Falls, Massachusetts.
7. John De Land, Cedar City, Utah.
8. Ryan Pemble, Belen, New Mexico.
9. Mark Willis Ballard, Chicago, Illinois.
10. The National First Ladies Library, 205 Market Avenue South, Canton, Ohio 44702.

Margaret Taylor

1. Irv Mitchell, Sun City, Arizona.
2. Hans A.M. Weebers: E-Mail *weebers@t-online.de,* Website legacyfamilytree.com/uspresidents.
3. Ronald Vern Jackson and Altha Polson *American Patriots.* Salt Lake City, Utah: A.G.E.S., 1982. Courtesy of Scott Thomas Genealogical Services, Inc., West Jordan, Utah.
4. Norvan Johnson, Tinley Park, Illinois.
5. C.C. Carpenter and Ray Jackson, Dahlonega, Georgia.
6. Patricia Whittaker, Simi Valley, California.

7. The National First Ladies Library, 205 Market Avenue South, Canton, Ohio 44702.

Elizabeth (Bess) Truman

1. Hans A.M. Weebers: E-Mail *weebers@t-online.de,* Website legacy-familytree.com/uspresidents.
2. Ronald Vern Jackson and Altha Polson *American Patriots.* Salt Lake City, Utah: A.G.E.S., 1982. Courtesy of Scott Thomas Genealogical Services, Inc., West Jordan, Utah.
3. Terry Frank, Tampa Bay, Florida.
4. Glen Scott Summitt, Beverly, Massachusetts.
5. John De Land, Cedar City, Utah.
6. Al Clovell.
7. James K. Stanley, Marietta, Georgia.
8. Ryan Pemble, Belen, New Mexico.
9. Darryl Boyd, Concord, California.
10. Rev. Darrell and Sallyann Joiner, Lincoln, Maine.
11. Mark Wheat, Arlington, Virginia.
12. The National First Ladies Library, 205 Market Avenue South, Canton, Ohio 44702.

Julia Tyler

1. Hans A.M. Weebers: E-Mail *weebers@t-online.de,* Website legacy-familytree.com/uspresidents.
2. Ronald Vern Jackson and Altha Polson *American Patriots.* Salt Lake City, Utah: A.G.E.S., 1982. Courtesy of Scott Thomas Genealogical Services, Inc., West Jordan, Utah.
3. Rev. David Gardiner.
4. Scot and Mary Cary, Buda, Texas.
5. The National First Ladies Library, 205 Market Avenue South, Canton, Ohio 44702.

Letitia Tyler

1. Hans A.M. Weebers: E-Mail *weebers@t-online.de,* Website legacy-familytree.com/uspresidents.
2. Ronald Vern Jackson and Altha Polson *American Patriots.* Salt Lake City, Utah: A.G.E.S., 1982. Courtesy of Scott Thomas Genealogical Services, Inc., West Jordan, Utah.
3. The Valentine-Coopers, Columbus, Ohio.
4. The National First Ladies Library, 205 Market Avenue South, Canton, Ohio 44702.

Hannah Van Buren

1. Irv Mitchell, Sun City, Arizona.
2. Hans A.M. Weebers, E-Mail: weebers@t-online.de. Website: legacy-familytree.com/uspresidents.
3. Ronald Vern Jackson, Ronald Vern Jackson and Altha Polson, "American Patriots," Published by A.G.E.S. Salt Lake City, Utah. Courtesy of Scott Thomas, Genealogical Services, Inc. West Jordan, Utah.
4. The National First Ladies Library, 205 Market Avenue South, Canton, Ohio 44702.

Martha Washington

1. Mark Willis Ballard, Chicago, IL.
2. Ronald Vern Jackson and Altha Polson *American Patriots.* Salt Lake City, Utah: A.G.E.S., 1982. Courtesy of Scott Thomas Genealogical Services, Inc., West Jordan, Utah.

3. Ryan Pemble, Belen, New Mexico.
4. The National First Ladies Library, 205 Market Avenue South, Canton, Ohio 44702.

Edith Wilson

1. Ronald Vern Jackson and Altha Polson *American Patriots.* Salt Lake City, Utah: A.G.E.S., 1982. Courtesy of Scott Thomas Genealogical Services, Inc., West Jordan, Utah.
2. Josie Bass, Cape Canaveral, Florida.
3. Verna Hudson, Homosassa, Florida.
4. The National First Ladies Library, 205 Market Avenue South, Canton, Ohio 44702.

Ellen Wilson

1. Irv Mitchell, Sun City, Arizona.
2. Hans A.M. Weebers: E-Mail *weebers@t-online.de*, Website legacyfamilytree.com/uspresidents.
3. Ronald Vern Jackson and Altha Polson *American Patriots.* Salt Lake City, Utah: A.G.E.S., 1982. Courtesy of Scott Thomas Genealogical Services, Inc., West Jordan, Utah.
4. David Reneer, St. Louis, Missouri.
5. Ken and Bev Matheson, West Valley City, Utah.
6. Rev. Darrell and Sallyann Joiner, Lincoln, Maine.
7. Edward Steele, St. Louis, Missouri.
8. Shirley Hornbeck.
9. Larry Moler, Houston, Texas.
10. The National First Ladies Library, 205 Market Avenue South, Canton, Ohio 44702.

INDEX